THE DOW JONES-IRWIN GUIDE TO
MUNICIPAL BONDS

THE DOW JONES-IRWIN GUIDE TO
MUNICIPAL BONDS

Sylvan G. Feldstein
Frank J. Fabozzi

DOW JONES-IRWIN
Homewood, Illinois 60430

SGF's CORNER
For my daughter, Hilary

FJF's CORNER
For my wife, Dessa

PREFACE

There are probably 25 different ways to approach the topic of investing in municipal bonds. Each has its own advantages, shortcomings, champions, and critics. Each serves the purposes of some participants in the municipal bond industry. We have chosen to write from the point of view of those who provide the capital and take the long-term risks: the bondholders. A book written from this perspective is particularly timely in light of the 1986 Tax Reform Act, which has significant consequences for the credit quality and investment attributes of both tax-exempt and taxable municipal bonds.

The purpose of this book is to provide descriptions of and conclusions about the critical points and questions regarding municipal bonds that investors should be aware of. Needless to say, the opinions expressed herein are those of the authors and not necessarily those of the organizations with which we are affiliated.

Sylvan G. Feldstein
Frank J. Fabozzi

CONTENTS

Investor. Zero-Coupon Bonds: *Credit Analysis of Zero-Coupon Bonds.* Bonds Backed by Repurchase Agreements, or "Repos": *What Is a Repo? Evaluating Repo Agreements.* FHA-Insured Mortgage Hospital Revenue Bonds: *What Is FHA Hospital Mortgage Insurance? What Is the Credit Risk? What Is the "Prudent Man" Evaluation Approach?* FSLIC-Backed Bonds: *Security for the Bonds. The Federal Savings and Loan Insurance Corporation. Evaluating the Bonds.* College Bonds Collateralized with Common Stocks and Taxable Bonds: *The New Volatility Factors. Volatility and Municipal Bonds. Indicators of Creditworthiness.* Municipal Bonds with Warrants: *Credit Considerations. Potential Financial Burden on the Issuer. Legality Concern.* Tax, Revenue, Grant, and Bond Anticipation Notes: *Two Major Purposes of Notes. Security behind Tax and Revenue Anticipation Notes. Information Needed before Buying Tax or Revenue Anticipation Notes. The Security behind Bond Anticipation Notes. Information Needed before Buying Bond Anticipation Notes. Security behind the General Obligation Pledge. Construction Loan Notes.*

Mac's "Second Resolution" Bonds: *The Security. The Flow of Funds. The Additional Bonds Test. The Capital Reserve Aid Fund. Credit Worthiness Strengths. Credit Weaknesses. Conclusion.* North Slope Borough, Alaska Sells Excessive Amounts of Bonds. Some Unusually Well-Secured San Francisco Bay Area Rapid Transit District (BART) Bonds: *Who Collects the Property Taxes? How Strong Is This Security? Did the 1978 Jarvis Tax-Reduction Law Weaken the Security?* Old New York City Housing Authority Bonds That Are Now Federally Backed: *Background. Conversion to the Federal Program. Conclusion.* New York City Bonds That Have Two Layers of Protection: *How the Security Structure Works. Bonds that Qualify. Drawbacks.* Texas "Guaranteed" School Bonds: *What Is the Texas Permanent School Fund? How the Bonds Qualify. How the Guaranteed Bond Procedure Would Work. Conclusion.* Texas State University "Constitutional Appropriation" Bonds: *What Are Constitutional Appropriation Bonds? How Does the Program Work? How Are the*

Funds Allocated? Conclusion. Pennsylvania School District "Act 150" Bonds: *State Aid to School Districts. Monitoring by The Department of Education. Act 150 Withholding Provisions. Act 150 Drawbacks.* Two Special Strengths of School Bonds in New York State: *School Districts in New York State. Why Is the Tax Collection Rate Always 100 Percent for Most School Districts? Additional Bond Security. How Important to the School District's Budget Are the State-Aid Payments? Section 99-b Drawbacks. Additional Case-Law Support.* New Jersey "Qualified" School and City Bonds: *Revenue Features. Bond Paying Procedures. Bond Strengths. Conclusion.* New Jersey's Own Insurance Program for Local School Bonds: *The New Jersey School Bond Reserve Act. Local General Obligation Bonds Covered by the School Bond Reserve. Allowed Investments of the Assets of the School Bond Reserve. Future Available Revenues from the State's Riparian Rights. Strengths and Weaknesses of the Security Structure.* "Qualified" School Bonds in Michigan. Texas Municipal Utility District (MUD) Bonds: *How Are the Bonds Secured? Questions to Ask Concerning the General Credit Risk. Conclusion.*

The Oklahoma Water Resources Board Tries to Sell Bonds That Are Unconstitutional. The Case of the City of Gahanna's Bond Anticipation Notes: *Did the Decision Affect Outstanding Limited Property Tax General Obligation Bonds?* Upgrading New York City's Credit Rating, 1970–1973: A Horror Story. *What Really Happened, and How?* How Feasible was the Feasibility Study for the Washington Public Power Supply System Bonds? What Really Went Wrong in Cleveland in 1978? *Restrictive Powers. Two-Year Term of Office. Limited Appointment and Removal Powers. Limited Taxing Powers. Limited Federal and State Support. Conclusion.* All That Glitters May Not be an Enforceable and Valid Obligation: The Case of the West Virginia State Building Commission Bonds: *Facts. The Lawsuit. Subsequent History. Conclusion.* The Problem Bonds of the Midlands Community Hospital, Sarpy County, Nebraska. Default of the Beaufort County, South Carolina, Hospital Facilities Gross Revenue and

First Mortgage Bonds (Hilton Head Hospital). The Urban Development Corporation Defaults on Its Notes: *Origins of UDC. The 1975 Bond Anticipation Note Default.* The 21-Year Default of the West Virginia Turnpike Commission Revenue Bonds. The Defaulted Chesapeake Bay Bridge and Tunnel District, Virginia, Series C, 5¾-Percent, Third-Pledge Revenue Bonds. The Muir Housing Project Struggles to Come Back from Default. The Bellevue Bridge Default. Chicago and Its Defaulted Calumet Skyway Revenue Bonds.

ance Company Demand. Commercial Bank Demand. The Reduced Supply of Tax-Exempt Bonds: *The New Definitions. Restrictions over Governmental versus Private Activity Bonds. The Volume Cap Restrictions. Arbitrage and Advance Refunding Restrictions. Other Restrictions and the 2 Percent Cost Rule.* Taxable Municipal Bonds: *Conclusion.* Data Sources.

1

The Nuts and Bolts of Municipal Bonds, and What This Book Is About

Municipal bonds are securities issued by state and local governments and their creations such as "authorities" and special districts. Most recent available information indicates that approximately 37,000 different states, counties, school districts, special districts, towns, and other public issuing bodies have issued municipal bonds.

Although some investors buy municipal bonds as a way of supporting public improvements such as schools, playgrounds, and parks, the vast majority buy them because interest income from most bonds is exempt from federal income taxes. Consequently, municipal bonds are purchased by those who are in high marginal tax brackets, because on an after-tax basis they offer a yield that is greater than comparable bonds that are taxable. For example, if an investor is in the 28 percent tax bracket, a municipal bond selling at par to yield 7.2 percent is equivalent to a taxable bond's before-tax yield of 10 percent. If otherwise comparable taxable bonds are offering a yield that is less than 10 percent, there is a yield advantage to purchasing municipal bonds; the higher the investor's tax bracket, the greater the advantage.

Municipal bonds come in a variety of types, with different redemption features, credit risks, and marketability. Consequently, the holder of municipal bonds is exposed to the same risks as the holder of corporate and Treasury bonds: interest-rate risk, reinvestment risk, and call risk. Moreover, the holder of a municipal bond, like the holder of a corporate bond, faces credit risk.

In this chapter we will discuss these various risks. Before we do so, we shall explain the features of municipal bonds, the types of

1

municipal obligations currently available, and the markets in which they trade.

FEATURES OF MUNICIPAL BONDS

In addition to the tax-exempt feature, there are other features of municipal bonds that an investor should be aware of.

Official Statement

When a corporation issues a new bond to the public, the Securities Act of 1933 requires that the issuer file a prospectus with the Securities and Exchange Commission. The contents of the prospectus must contain material information about the corporation and the particular issue. The prospectus is generally reviewed by the Securities and Exchange Commission prior to the issuance of the bonds. A prospectus must be furnished to prospective buyers of the issue.

The equivalent of the prospectus for a municipal offering is the *official statement.* The official statement is not subject to the review of the SEC or any other government agency. Instead, if the issuer prepares an official statement or a more abbreviated offering circular, a copy must be filed with the Municipal Securities Rulemaking Board,[1] and a copy must be distributed to investors.

Par Value

The par value is the amount paid to the bondholder when the bond matures. This is also known as the maturity value, redemption value, principal or face value.

Municipal bonds are generally issued in denominations of $5,000. The industry practice, however, is to call one $5,000 bond "five bonds," one for each $1,000 of par value. This convention was adopted because up until the 1960s most bonds were issued in $1,000 denominations. Most corporate bonds are still issued in $1,000 denominations. After issuance, the market price of a bond will differ from its par value as market interest rates change. A bond selling below its par value is said to be selling at a *discount.* When a bond sells above its par value it is said to be selling at a *premium.*

---

[1] The Municipal Securities Rulemaking Board is a self-regulating body with membership drawn primarily from the municipal bond industry but subject also to the jurisdiction of the Securities and Exchange Commission.

When participants in the bond markets refer to the price of a bond they do not refer to its actual cash value. Instead, they refer to the price of the bond as a percentage of its par value. For example, if a bond is selling for 100, this means it is selling for 100 percent of its par value. Hence, a bond with a par value of $5,000 selling for 100 is selling for $5,000. A bond selling at a discount will be selling for less than 100. For a $5,000 par value bond, a price of 80 means that the bond is selling for 80 percent of $5,000, or $4,000. When a bond is selling above 100 that means it is selling for a premium. For example, a $5,000 par value bond selling for 120¼ is selling for 120.25 percent of its par value or $6,012.50 ($5,000 × 1.2025).

Coupon Interest

The annual dollar interest that the issuer promises to pay to the bond-holder is called the *coupon interest.* The coupon is fixed throughout the life of the issue, except in the case of variable rate bonds. Coupon payments on municipal bonds are generally made semiannually. For example, a $250 annual interest payment would be divided into two $125 coupon payments.

The *coupon rate* is the annual interest expressed as a percentage of the par value. The coupon rate is also referred to as the face rate or the nominal rate. Consequently, if the par value of a municipal bond is $5,000 and the coupon interest is $250, the coupon rate is 5 percent.

For bonds not selling at par, the coupon rate does *not* reflect the yield that the investor may realize by owning the bonds.

Maturity Date

The maturity date is the date on which the issuer is obligated to pay the par value. Corporate issuers of debt generally schedule their bonds to mature in one or two different years in the future. Municipal issuers, on the other hand, frequently schedule their bonds to mature serially over many years. Such bonds are called *serial bonds.* It is common for a municipal issue to have 10 or more different maturities.

After the last of the serial maturities, some municipal issues these days lump together large sums of debt into one or two years—much the way corporate bonds are issued. These bonds, called *term bonds,* have become increasingly popular in the municipal market because active secondary markets for them can develop if the term is of sufficient size.

Call and Refunding Provisions

One important question in a new bond issue is whether the issuer shall have the right to redeem the entire amount of the bonds outstanding before maturity. Issuers generally want to have this right, and investors do not want them to have it. Both sides think that at some time in the future the general level of interest rates in the market may decline to a level well below the prevailing rate at the time the bonds are issued. If so, issuers may want to redeem all of the bonds outstanding and replace them with new bond issues at lower interest rates. But this is exactly what investors do not want. If bonds are redeemed when interest rates are low, investors have to take their money back and reinvest it at a lower rate.

The verb *to call* is commonly used with the same meaning as *to redeem,* and bonds are said to be *callable* or *noncallable.* When the right to call is denied for a specified period of time after issuance, the bond is said to have *call protection,* or a *deferred call.* The earliest possible call date is referred to as the *first call.*

Call provisions, which are usually described in the bond resolution and official statement of the issue, are of such significance to the investor that the Municipal Securities Rulemaking Board requires that brokers and dealers disclose the potential impact of the call provision on the investor's potential yield.

Most call provisions permit the issuer to retire the bonds only at a price above par value, thereby providing the investor with some call protection. Interest rates would have to drop by a greater amount to make it worthwhile for the issuer to refund the bond issue than if the bond could be called at par. A typical call provision allows the amount of the premium above par to decrease as the bond moves further from the first call. For example, if the first call is 10 years from the time of issuance, the call price to the first call may be 104. In the 11th year, the bond may be callable at 103½, for example, and in the 12th year at an even lower premium over par. Some issues offer no call premium at all; that is, the call price is equal to the par value.

Issuers often call only a small part of bond issues. Those bonds are chosen at random. Usually a set percentage of bonds is called from each term maturity of a bond issue. This is called a *strip call.* In recent years, however, some issuers have concentrated their call of bonds to a single term-maturity date from among several term maturities in the bond issue. The result is that more bonds of this maturity are likely to be called. These are called *super sinkers.*

By far the most common type of call provision is the *optional call,* in which the issuer has the choice of calling the bonds. But some bonds have a *mandatory call,* in which, if certain criteria are met, the issuer must redeem the bonds whether interest rates rise or decline. This type of call provision is most often used in housing revenue bond issues. The condition used to determine if these bonds will be called is the interest rate to be paid to the bond investors versus the interest rates on the money to be loaned to homeowners. If home mortgage interest rates rapidly decline after the bonds are sold but before the money is all loaned-out, the issuer may be forced to redeem some or all of the bonds with the unexpended bond proceeds. Such a condition is known as an "early redemption call." Another condition to determine is the mortgage prepayment rate—a reflection of homeowners paying off their mortgages when they sell their homes. Once a certain amount of mortgages is prepaid, the issuer, under the bond indenture, may have to use the prepayment monies to redeem bonds.

Mandatory call features differ in another respect from optional call provisions. The length of time before bonds can be called under mandatory call provisions is generally much shorter than under optional call features. Also there is usually no call premium in the call price with mandatory redemption.

Sinking Fund Provisions

With serial bonds, an issuer's repayments of debt are spread out over many years. To accomplish similar leveling out of debt repayment, term bonds may be paid off by operation of a *sinking fund.* A sinking fund means that money is applied periodically to redemption of the bonds before maturity.

The official statement and bond indenture specifies the portion of the term issue that must be retired each year. The sinking fund provision may be designed to retire all of a bond issue by the maturity date, or it may be designed to retire only a part of the total by the maturity date. In the latter case, the balance due at maturity is called the *final maturity.*

The issuer may satisfy the sinking fund requirement generally in one of two ways. A cash payment of the face amount of the bonds to be retired may be made by the issuer to the trustee. The latter then calls the bonds by lot for redemption. Bonds have serial numbers, and numbers may be randomly selected by lot for redemption. Owners of a bond called in this manner turn them in for redemption; *interest payments stop at the redemption date.* Alternatively, the issuer can deliver to the trustee bonds with a total face value equal to the amount that must be retired. The bonds are purchased by the issuer in the secondary market at current market yields. This option is elected by the issuer when the bonds are selling below par.

There are two advantages of a sinking fund requirement from the bondholder's perspective. First, the risk of default is reduced due to the orderly retirement of the issue before maturity. That is, the average life is reduced. Second, if bond prices decline as a result of an increase in interest rates, price support will be provided by the issuer or its fiscal agent, since it must enter the market on the buy side in order to satisfy the annual sinking fund requirements. However, the disadvantage is that the bonds may be called at the sinking fund call price at a time when interest rates are lower than rates prevailing at the time of issuance. In that case, the bonds could be selling in the market above par but may be retired by the issuer at the call price that may be equal to par value. Some traders and investors buy and sell these bonds without being fully aware of the par call feature.

Bearer Bonds, Registered Bonds, and Book-Entry

Municipal bonds used to be issued either as bearer bonds or in registered format. As their name implies, bearer bonds are negotiable by anyone who holds them. Attached to bearer bonds are coupons that investors clip and submit for payment. Issuers send coupon payments to whoever submits the coupon for payment.

With registered bonds, the holder's name is registered with the issuer. The issuer will only send registered bondholders principal and interest payments. There are no coupons attached to registered bonds— interest payments are sent directly to bondholders. Effective July 1, 1983, all new municipal bonds must be issued in registered form.

Additionally, some issuers do not issue any printed bond certificates. Instead, record of ownership is kept on computers by the representatives of the issuers. This is known as "book-entry" form, and is used to reduce the costs for the bond issuer of printing, mailing interest payments, agents, and transfer registrars.

Legal Opinion

Municipal bonds have legal opinions. There are two primary purposes of the legal opinion. First, bond counsel to the issuer must ascertain that the bonds are binding obligations of the issuer according to state and local statutes. Second, bond counsel must verify the tax-exempt status of the interest payments the bondholder will be receiving according to federal and local laws.

TYPES OF MUNICIPAL OBLIGATIONS

Bonds

In terms of municipal bond security structures, there are basically two different types. The first type is the general obligation bond, and the second is the revenue bond.

General obligation bonds are debt instruments issued by states, counties, special districts, cities, towns, and school districts. They are secured by the issuer's general taxing powers. Usually, a general obligation bond is secured by the issuer's unlimited taxing power. For smaller governmental jurisdictions such as school districts and towns, the only available unlimited taxing power is on property. For larger general obligation bond issuers such as states and big cities, the tax revenues are more diverse and may include corporate and individual income taxes, sales taxes, and property taxes. The security pledges for these larger issuers such as states are sometimes referred to as being *full faith and credit obligations.*

Additionally, certain general obligation bonds are secured not only by the issuer's general taxing powers to create monies accumulated in the general fund but also from certain identified fees, grants, and special charges, which provide additional revenues from outside the general fund. Such bonds are known as being *double barreled* in security because of the dual nature of the revenue sources.

Also, not all general obligation bonds are secured by unlimited taxing powers. Some have pledged taxes that are limited as to revenue sources and maximum property-tax millage amounts. Such bonds are known as *limited-tax general obligation bonds.*

The second basic type of security structure is found in a revenue bond. Such bonds are issued for either project or enterprise financings in which the bond issuers pledge to the bondholders the revenues generated by the operating projects financed. Below are examples of the specific types of revenue bonds that have been issued over the years.

Airport Revenue Bonds. The revenues securing airport revenue bonds usually come from either traffic-generated sources—such as landing fees, concession fees, and airline apron-use and fueling fees—

or lease revenues from one or more airlines for the use of a specific facility such as a terminal or hangar.

College and University Revenue Bonds. The revenues securing college and university revenue bonds usually include dormitory room rental fees, tuition payments, and sometimes the general assets of the college or university as well.

Hospital Revenue Bonds. The security for hospital revenue bonds is usually dependent on federal and state reimbursement programs (such as Medicaid and Medicare), third-party commercial payers (such as Blue Cross and private insurance), and individual patient payments.

Single-Family Mortgage Revenue Bonds. Single-family mortgage revenue bonds are usually secured by the mortgages and mortgage loan repayments on single-family homes. Security features vary but can include Federal Housing Administration (FHA), Federal Veterans Administration (VA), or private mortgage insurance.

Multifamily Revenue Bonds. These revenue bonds are usually issued for multifamily housing projects for senior citizens and low-income families. Some housing revenue bonds are usually secured by mortgages that are federally insured; others receive federal government operating subsidies, such as under section 8, or interest-cost subsidies, such as under section 236; and still others receive only local property tax reductions as subsidies.

Industrial Development and Pollution Control Revenue Bonds. Bonds have been issued for a variety of industrial and commercial activities that range from manufacturing plants to shopping centers. They are usually secured by payments to be made by the corporations or businesses that use the facilities.

Public Power Revenue Bonds. Public power revenue bonds are secured by revenues to be produced from electrical operating plants. Some bonds are for a single issuer, who constructs and operates power plants and then sells the electricity. Other public power revenue bonds are issued by groups of public and private investor-owned utilities for the joint financing of the construction of one or more power plants. This last arrangement is known as a *joint power* financing structure.

Resource Recovery Revenue Bonds. A resource recovery facility converts refuse (solid waste) into commercially salable energy, recoverable products, and a residue to be landfilled. The major revenues for a resource recovery revenue bond usually are (1) the "tipping fees" per ton paid by those who deliver the garbage to the facility for disposal; (2) revenues from steam, electricity, or refuse-derived fuel sold to either an electric power company or another energy user; and (3) revenues from the sale of recoverable materials such as aluminum and steel scrap.

Seaport Revenue Bonds. The security for seaport revenue bonds can include specific lease agreements with the benefiting companies or pledged marine terminal and cargo tonnage fees.

Sewer Revenue Bonds. Revenues for sewer revenue bonds come from hookup fees and user charges. For many older sewer bond issuers, substantial portions of their construction budgets have been financed with federal grants.

Sports Complex and Convention Center Revenue Bonds. Sports complex and convention center revenue bonds usually receive revenues from sporting or convention events held at the facilities and, in some instances, from earmarked outside revenues such as local motel and hotel room taxes.

Student Loan Revenue Bonds. Student loan repayments under student loan revenue bond programs are sometimes 100 percent guaranteed either directly by the federal government—under the Federal Insured Student Loan program (FISL) for 100 percent of bond principal and interest—or by a state guaranty agency under a more recent federal insurance program, the Federal Guaranteed Student Loan program (GSL). In addition to these two federally backed programs, student loan bonds are also sometimes secured by the general revenues of the specific colleges involved.

Toll Road and Gas Tax Revenue Bonds. There are generally two types of highway revenue bonds. The bond proceeds of the first type are used to build such specific revenue-producing facilities as toll roads, bridges, and tunnels. For these pure enterprise-type revenue bonds, the pledged revenues usually are the monies collected through the tolls. The second type of highway bond is one in which the bondholders are paid by earmarked revenues outside of toll collections, such as gasoline taxes, automobile registration payments, and driver's license fees.

Water Revenue Bonds. Water revenue bonds are issued to finance the construction of water treatment plants, pumping stations, collection facilities, and distribution systems. Revenues usually come from connection fees and charges paid by the users of the water systems.

Hybrid and Special Bond Securities

Though having certain characteristics of general obligation and revenue bonds, there are some municipal bonds that have more unique security structures as well. They include the following:

Federal Savings and Loan Insurance Corporation-Backed Bonds. In this security structure, the proceeds of a bond sale were deposited in a savings and loan association that, in turn, issued a Certificate of Deposit (CD). The CD was insured by the Federal Savings and Loan Insurance Corporation (FSLIC) up to a limit of $100,000 of combined principal and interest for each bondholder. The savings and loan association used the money to finance low- and moderate-income rental housing developments. While these bonds are no longer issued, there are billions of dollars of these bonds in the secondary market.

Insured Bonds. These are bonds that, in addition to being secured by the issuer's revenues, also are backed by insurance policies written by commercial insurance companies. The insurance, usually structured as an insurance contract, is supposed to provide prompt payment to the bondholders if a default should occur.

Lease-Backed Bonds. Lease-backed bonds are usually structured as revenue-type bonds with annual rent payments. In some instances the rental payments may only come from earmarked tax revenues, student tuition payments, or patient fees. In other instances the underlying lessee governmental unit is required to make annual appropriations from its general fund.

Letter of Credit-Backed Bonds. Some municipal bonds, in addition to being secured by the issuer's cash flow revenues, also are backed by commercial bank letters of credit. In some instances the letters of credit are irrevocable and, if necessary, can be used to pay the bondholders. In other instances the issuers are required to maintain investment quality worthiness before the letters of credit can be drawn upon.

Life Care Revenue Bonds. Life care bonds are issued to construct long-term residential facilities for older citizens. Revenues are usually derived from initial lump-sum payments made by the residents.

Moral Obligation Bonds. A moral obligation bond is a security structure for state-issued bonds that indicates that if revenues are needed for paying bondholders, the state legislature involved is legally authorized, though not required, to make an appropriation out of general state-tax revenues.

Municipal Utility District Revenue Bonds. These are bonds that are usually issued to finance the construction of water and sewer systems as well as roadways in undeveloped areas. The security is usually dependent on the commercial success of the specific development project involved, which can range from the sale of new homes to the renting of space in shopping centers and office buildings.

New Housing Authority Bonds. These bonds are secured by a contractual pledge of annual contributions from HUD. Monies from Washington are paid directly to the paying agent for the bonds, and the bondholders are given specific legal rights to enforce the pledge. These bonds can no longer be issued.

Tax Allocation Bonds. These bonds are usually issued to finance the construction of office buildings and other new buildings in formerly blighted areas. They are secured by property taxes collected on the improved real estate.

"Territorial" Bonds. These are bonds issued by United States territorial possessions such as Puerto Rico, the Virgin Islands, and Guam. The bonds are tax-exempt throughout most of the country. Also, the economies of these issuers are influenced by positive special features of the United States corporate tax codes that are not available to the states.

"Troubled City" Bailout Bonds. There are certain bonds that are structured to appear as pure revenue bonds but in essence are not. Revenues come from general purpose taxes and revenues that otherwise would have gone to a state's or city's general fund. Their bond structures were created to bail out underlying general obligation bond issuers from severe budget deficits. Examples are the New York State *Municipal Assistance Corporation for the City of New York Bonds (MAC)* and the state of Illinois *Chicago School Finance Authority Bonds.*

Refunded Bonds. These are bonds that originally may have been issued as general obligation or revenue bonds but are now secured by an "escrow fund" consisting of obligations that are sufficient for paying the bondholders. They are among the safest of all municipal bonds if the escrow is structured as a "pure escrow."

Notes

Tax-exempt debt issued for periods ranging not beyond three years is usually considered to be short term in nature. Below are descriptions of some of these debt instruments.

Tax, Revenue, Grant, and Bond Anticipation Notes: TANs, RANs, GANs, and BANs. These are temporary borrowings by states, local governments, and special jurisdictions. Usually, notes are issued for a period of 12 months, though it is not uncommon for notes to be issued for periods of as short as 3 months and for as long as three years. TANs and RANs (also known as TRANs) are issued in anticipation of the collection of taxes or other expected revenues. These are borrowings to even out the cash flows caused by the irregular flows of income into the treasuries of the states and local units of government. BANs are issued in anticipation of the sale of long-term bonds.

Construction Loan Notes: CLNs. CLNs are usually issued for periods up to three years to provide short-term construction financing for multifamily housing projects. The CLNs generally are repaid by the proceeds of long-term bonds, which are provided after the housing projects are completed.

Tax-Exempt Commercial Paper. This short-term borrowing instrument is issued for periods ranging from 30 to 270 days. Generally the tax-exempt commercial paper has backstop commercial bank agreements which can include an irrevocable letter of credit, a revolving credit agreement, or a line of credit.

In this book we shall refer to both municipal bonds and municipal notes as simply municipal bonds.

Newer Market-Sensitive Debt Instruments

Municipal bonds are usually issued with one of two debt retirement structures or a combination of both. Either a bond has a "serial" maturity structure (wherein a portion of the loan is retired each year), or a bond has a "term" maturity (wherein the loan is repaid on a final date). Usually term bonds have maturities ranging from 20 to 40 years and retirement schedules (which are known as sinking funds) that begin 5 to 10 years before the final term maturity.

Because of the sharply upward-sloping yield curve that has existed in the municipal bond market since 1979, many investment bankers have introduced innovative financing instruments priced at short or intermediate yield levels. These debt instruments are intended to raise money for long-term capital projects at reduced interest rates. Below are descriptions of some of these more innovative debt structures.

Put or Option Tender Bonds. A "put" or "option tender" bond is one in which the bondholder has the right to return the bond at a price of par to the bond trustee prior to its stated long-term maturity. The put period can be as short as one day and as long as 10 years. Usually, put bonds are backed by either commercial bank letters of credit in addition to the issuer's cash flow revenues or entirely by the cash flow revenues of the issuers.

Super Sinkers. A "super sinker" is a specifically identified maturity for a single-family housing revenue bond issue to which all funds from early mortgage prepayments are used to retire bonds. A super sinker has a long stated maturity but a shorter, albeit unknown, actual life. Because of this unique characteristic, investors have the opportunity to realize an attractive return when the municipal yield curve is upward sloping on a bond that is priced as if it had a maturity considerably longer than its anticipated life.

Variable-Rate Notes. Variable-rate notes have coupon rates that change. When a variable-rate note has a put feature it is called a *variable rate demand obligation* which may be puttable after one day, seven days, quarterly, semi-annually, annually or longer. The coupon rate is tied to one of various indices. Specific examples include percents of the prime rate, or the J. J. Kenney Municipal Index, or the Merrill Lynch Index or a percent of the 90-day Treasury bill rate. A bank letter of credit is usually required as liquidity backup for variable rate demand obligations.

A variation of variable rate obligations is one in which the investor in advance selects the interest rate and interest payment date from one up to 90 or 180 days. The security may have a nominal 30-year maturity. Such a bond has a put feature of a variable rate demand obligation and the maturity flexibility of tax-exempt commercial paper. One version of this new investment vehicle is called UPDATES (Unit Priced Demand Adjustable Tax-Exempt Securities).

Bonds with Warrants. Municipal bonds with warrants allow their holders to buy during a specified time period—usually two years—bonds from the issuer at par and at predetermined coupon rates.

Minicoupon and Zero-Coupon Bonds. At issuance, the coupon interest on a minicoupon bond is below the prevailing yield in the market. The bonds are sold at issuance at a substantial discount from par. If the bonds are held to maturity, the difference between the original-issue discount price and the par value is not taxable, since it represents tax-free income.

A zero-coupon bond is one in which no coupon interest payments are paid to the bondholder. Instead, the bond is purchased at a very deep discount and matures at par. The difference between the original-issue discount price and par represents a specified compounded annual yield. There are variants of zero-coupon bonds that we will discuss in Chapter 12.

PRIMARY AND SECONDARY MARKETS

In the municipal bond market, there is no institution comparable to either the New York Stock Exchange or the American Stock Exchange. All municipal bonds bought and sold in the country are traded over the phone among traders and bond brokers.

The market is broken down into the primary and the secondary markets. The primary market is all the new issues of municipal bonds being sold for the first time, and the secondary market is the buying and selling of older seasoned issues.

The Primary Market

A substantial number of municipal obligations are brought to market each week. A state or local government can market its new issue by offering them publicly to the investing community or by placing them privately with a small group of investors. When a public offering is selected, the issue is usually underwritten by investment bankers and municipal bond departments of commercial banks. Public offerings may be marketed by either competitive bidding or direct negotiations with underwriters. When an issue is marketed via competitive bidding, the issue is awarded to the bidder submitting the bid with the lowest interest cost for the issuer.

The Secondary Market

Although municipal bonds are not listed and traded in formal institutions such as are certain common stocks and corporate bonds on the New York and American stock exchanges, there are very strong and active billion-dollar secondary markets for municipals that are supported by municipal bond dealers across the country. Markets are maintained on local issues by regional brokerage firms and local banks. Some of the bigger national brokerage firms also maintain large regional trading desks around the country. General market names are supported by the larger brokerage firms and banks, many of whom have investment-banking relationships with the issuers. Buying and selling decisions are often made over the phone and through municipal bond brokers. For a small fee these brokers serve as intermediaries in the sale of large blocks of municipal bonds among dealers and large institutional investors. These brokers are primarily located in New York City and include Chapdelaine & Company, Drake & Company, the J. J. Kenny Company, and Titus & Donnelly, Inc., among others.

In addition to these brokers and the daily offerings sent out over *The Bond Buyer's* Munifacts teletype system, many dealers advertise their municipal bond offerings for the retail market in what is known as *The Blue List.* This is a 100+-page booklet that is published every weekday by the Standard & Poor's Corporation. In it are listed state municipal bond and note offerings and prices.

In the municipal bond market, an odd lot of bonds is $25,000 (five bonds) or less in par value for retail investors. For institutions, anything below $100,000 in par value is considered an odd lot. Dealer spreads—the difference between the dealer's bid and ask prices—depend on several factors. For the retail investor, the dealer's spread can range from as low as one quarter of one point ($12.50 per $5,000 of par value) on large blocks of actively traded bonds to four points ($200 per $5,000 of par value) for odd lot sales of an inactive issue. The average spread for retail investors seems to be around two points ($100 per $5,000 of par value). For institutional investors, the dealer's spread rarely exceeds one half of one point ($25 per $5,000 of par value) on the larger trades.

RISKS ASSOCIATED WITH INVESTING IN MUNICIPAL BONDS

The holder of a municipal bond is subject to five types of risk: (1) interest-rate risk (or market risk), (2) reinvestment risk, (3) inflation or purchasing-power risk, (4) call risk, and (5) credit risk.

Interest-Rate Risk

Municipal bond prices and interest rates move in the opposite direction. For example, if a 9-percent-coupon municipal bond with 20 years remaining to maturity is selling at par ($5,000) to yield 9 percent, the price of the bond will decrease to $4,571 if interest rates for comparable municipal bonds rise to 10 percent. Interest-rate risk (also known as *market risk*) is the risk that the price of the bond will decline because interest rates in the economy have increased. Not all municipal bonds have the same degree of interest-rate risk. We will discuss this further in Chapter 12.

Reinvestment Risk

A municipal bond investor may receive a return from three potential sources. Most obvious is the coupon interest. The second source is any capital appreciation that may be realized. Capital appreciation results when the investor receives more for the municipal bond than he paid for it. For example, if an investor purchased a bond for $3,800 and sold it for $4,400, he would realize capital appreciation of $600. Of course, an investor who purchases a municipal bond could sell it at a loss. This will reduce the return of the bondholder. The third source of return is the one most overlooked by investors: the interest that can be earned on the reinvestment of the coupon interest. This is commonly referred to as the *interest-on-interest* component of a bond's return.

A measure of a bond's potential total return that is frequently cited by brokers and the financial press is the "yield-to-maturity," or simply "yield." This measure of total return, however, is flawed because it assumes that (1) the investor will hold the bond until maturity, and (2) each time a coupon is received the investor will reinvest it at an interest rate that is equal to the yield-to-maturity.

To see the importance of the interest-on-interest component of a bond's total return, consider a municipal bond selling at its par value of $5,000, with a coupon rate of 12 percent and with seven years remaining to maturity. The yield-to-maturity for this bond is 12 percent. Let's suppose that the entire coupon interest can be reinvested for each of the seven years. However, suppose that the coupon interest can only be reinvested at 8-percent interest. Under these circumstances, it can be demonstrated that the holder of this municipal bond would realize a return of only 10.8 percent, not 12 percent! Thus, when an investor buys a municipal bond, there is the risk that the realized return will be less than the yield-to-maturity when the bond is purchased because of the problem of reinvesting the coupon payments at rates below the prevailing yield-to-maturity. This is known as *reinvestment risk*. In Chapter 12 we will explain how to mitigate or even eliminate reinvestment risk.

Inflation or Purchasing-Power Risk

Inflation or purchasing-power risk is the risk that the return realized will not be sufficient to offset the loss in purchasing power due to inflation. For example, if a municipal bond with a coupon rate of 8 percent selling for $5,000 to yield 8 percent is held for one year and interest rates do not change, the value of the investment will be $5,400 ($5,000 of market value plus $400 in coupon interest). Suppose that over the same period, inflation was 10 percent. The purchasing-power value of the investment would be $4,910. As a result, even though in nominal dollars the value of the investment has increased by $400 (from $5,000 to $5,400), in real dollars (i.e., purchasing-power dollars), the value of the investment has declined by $90 from $5,000 to $4,910.

Call Risk

Call risk is the risk that an issuer will call the bonds and force the investor to reinvest the proceeds at a rate that is lower than the yield when the bonds were purchased. Call risk is therefore tied to reinvestment risk. Another risk associated with call risk is that any capital-appreciation potential will be truncated. For example, suppose that a 12-percent-coupon municipal bond with seven years to maturity is selling for $5,000 and is callable at $5,400. The yield for this bond is 12 percent. Suppose that interest rates decline to 7 percent. The bond's price would ordinarly rise to $6,365. However, because the bond is callable at $5,400, and it may be beneficial for the issuer to call the bond because rates have declined dramatically, the bond's price may not rise to $6,365. The reason is that if the bond is called, the investor will only receive $5,400.

Credit Risk

Credit risk, also known as default risk, is the risk that the issuer will default on the contractual payment of interest and/or principal. The obligations of the U.S. government are considered to be free of credit risk. For other issuers, the risk of default has been commonly measured by ratings provided by commercial rating companies such as Standard & Poor's and Moody's. Appendix B summarizes the ratings assigned by these two commercial rating companies.

A major focus of this book is on evaluating credit risk since the track record of the commercial rating agencies while fairly reliable in many instances, has been far from perfect. In the section below we shall discuss why investors are now more concerned about credit risk than ever before.

WHY INVESTORS ARE NOW MORE CONCERNED ABOUT CREDIT RISK THAN EVER BEFORE

While in the past investing in municipal bonds had been considered second in safety only to that of U.S. government debt obligations, there has now developed among many investors ongoing concerns about the credit risks of municipal bonds. This is true regardless of whether or not the bonds are given high investment-grade credit ratings by the commercial rating companies.

Defaults and the Federal Bankruptcy Law

The first reason for this concern results primarily from the New York City billion-dollar financial crisis in 1975. The financial crisis sent a loud and clear warning to municipal bond investors in general. That warning was that regardless of the supposedly ironclad protections for the bondholder, when issuers such as large cities have severe budget-balancing difficulties, the political hues, cries, and financial stakes of public-employee unions, vendors, and community groups may be dominant forces in the budgetary process.

This reality was further reinforced by the new federal bankruptcy law, which took effect on October 1, 1979, and which makes it easier for municipal bond issuers to seek protection from bondholders by filing for bankruptcy. Of course, the investor should always avoid bonds of issuers that may go into bankruptcy. The judicial process usually involves years of numerous court hearings and litigation that no bond investor should want to be a party to regardless of whether or not he may eventually win.

Innovative Financing Techniques and Legally Untested Security Structures

The second reason for increased interest in credit risk analysis results from the proliferation in the municipal bond market of innovative financing techniques to secure new bond issues. In addition to the more traditional general obligation bonds and toll road, bridge, and tunnel revenue bonds, there are now more nonvoter-approved, innovative, and legally untested security mechanisms. These innovative financing mechanisms include "moral obligation" housing bonds, "take or pay" electric utility bonds with "step-up" provisions requiring the participants to increase payments to make up for those that may default, "lease rental" bonds, medicare- and medicaid-dependent hospital bonds, commercial bank-backed letter of credit bonds, "put" bonds, and tax-exempt commercial paper. What distinguishes these newer bonds from the more traditional general obligation and revenue bonds is that there is no history of court decisions and other case law that firmly establishes the rights of the bondholders and the obligations of the issuers. For the newer financing mechanisms, it is not possible to determine the probable legal outcome if the bond securities were challenged in court. Therefore, credit analysis has become important in order to identify those bonds that—because of strong finances and other characteristics—are not likely to result in serious litigation.

Of course, the need for the independent review of the credit worthiness of bonds secured by legally untested structures is perhaps most recently shown in the troubled bonds of the Washington Public Power Supply System (WPPSS). Both of the major commercial rating companies gave their highest ratings to these bonds in the early 1980s. One of them, Moody's, had given the WPPSS Projects 1, 2, and 3 bonds its very highest credit rating of Aaa and the Projects 4 and 5 bonds its rating of A–1. This latter investment-grade rating is defined as having the strongest investment attributes within the upper-medium grade of creditworthiness. The other major commercial company, Standard & Poor's, also had given the WPPSS Projects 1, 2, and 3 bonds its highest rating of AAA and the Projects 4 and 5 bonds its rating of A+, which is comparable to Moody's A-1 rating. While these high-quality ratings were in effect, WPPSS sold over $8 billion in long-term bonds. By 1986 Moody's had no ratings on any of the bonds. Standard & Poor's only rated the defaulted Projects 4 and 5 bonds. Its rating was D.

Cutbacks in Programs

The third reason, and one that began with the first electoral victory of President Reagan in 1980, is the impact that the scaling down of federal grants and aid programs will have on the credit worthiness of both general obligation and revenue bonds. As an example of the change in federal funding policies, the president in December 1981 signed into law an extension of the Clean Water Act of 1970. Among other changes, the new amendments reduce the total federal contribution to local waste-treatment programs from $90 billion projected under the old law to $36 billion. Additionally, after October 1, 1984, the federal matching contribution to local sewerage-construction projects declined from 75 percent to 55 percent of the costs. Over the previous 20 years, many state and local governments had grown dependent on this and other federal grant programs as direct subsidies to their own capital construction and operating budgets. These federal grants had provided indirect subsidies to their local economies as well.

The fiscally conservative federalism can be expected to continue through the 1980s. The Reagan election victories in 1980 and 1984 can be seen as an electoral message from the American people that they want a major change in federal-state financial relationships. The passage of the 1982 Tax Equity and Fiscal Responsibility Act, with its reduction in hospital aid, is but an example of these changes. With the continued support from a broad-based, fiscally conservative national political constituency, we can expect the scaling-down process of federal aid to state and local governments to continue. The increased population growth in the more conservative Sun Belt regions of the country would indicate a further strengthening of this electoral base for fiscal conservatism. What this means for credit analysis is that many general obligation and revenue bond issuers may undergo serious financial stresses as the federal grant and aid reductions are implemented over the coming years. This is discussed further in the Appendix.

Secular Declines Within the American Economy

The fourth reason for investor concern is that the American economy is undergoing a fundamental change, which is resulting in a decline of various sectors of the economy. This decline has widespread implications for whole regions of the country. Many general obligation and revenue bond issuers can be expected to undergo significant economic deterioration that could negatively impact their tax collections and wealth indicators such as personal income, bank deposits, retail sales, and real property valuations. An example of this would be in the mid-west, where the basic structure of employment is shifting away from higher-paying manufacturing jobs to lower-paying trade and service jobs. Another example of change is in the energy states some of whom are experiencing significant economic deteriorations.

The Strong Public Demand for Municipal Bonds

The fifth reason for the increased interest in municipal bond credit risk analysis is derived from the changing nature of the municipal bond market. For most of the 1970s the municipal bond market was characterized by strong buying patterns among both private investors and institutions. This was caused in part by high federal, state, and local income tax rates. Additionally, inflation, or "bracket creep," pushed many investors into higher and higher income tax brackets. Tax-exempt bonds increasingly became an important and convenient way for sheltering income. One corollary of the strong buyer's demand for tax exemption was an erosion of the traditional security provisions and bondholder safeguards that had grown out of the default experiences of the 1930s. General obligation bond issuers with high tax and debt burdens, declining local economies, and chronic budget-balancing problems had little difficulty finding willing buyers. Also, revenue bonds increasingly were brought to market with legally untested security provisions, modest rate covenants, reduced debt reserves, and weak additional bonds tests.

In regard to the rate convenant, while it is desirable that the rates charged should provide cover to the extent necessary to pay for debt service, operations, and prudent reserves, more and more rate covenants were structured to provide cover only to the extent necessary to pay debt service, operations, and *required* improvements. Excess monies were credited against the succeeding year's revenue requirements. Such an arrangement is known as *Chinese coverage.* This form of coverage has become more of a norm in the industry than the exception it has been in the past. Because of the widespread weakening of security provisions, it has become more important than ever before that the prudent investor carefully evaluate the credit worthiness of a municipal bond before making a purchase.

"Buy and Hold" versus "Buy and Trade" Investment Strategies

The last reason for the increased interest in credit risk analysis results from a fundamental philosophical change that is developing among large institutional investors such as fire and casualty insurance companies, commercial banks, and tax-exempt bond funds. More and more municipal bond buyers no longer "buy and hold" their municipal bonds to maturity—which had been the traditional investment approach. Instead, they try to "buy and trade." This trading interest has grown out of two developments. First, because of the market volatility since 1978, many "buy and hold" investors have seen the paper value of their assets decline at times by as much as 30 percent. Second, because of the great volatility in the market that now exists (where swings of up to 200 basis points have occurred in a single day), some investors see the opportunity for substantial capital gains through active trading. This could occur if they buy in a sector of the municipal bond market that has become underpriced or "cheap" and sell when the sector becomes overpriced or "rich." Of course, knowing which bonds are likely credit-rating downgrades or upgrades can be very valuable to such an investor.

WHY IS IT IMPORTANT TO KNOW THE CREDIT RISK BEFORE BUYING A MUNICIPAL BOND?

While the purpose of a common stock analysis is for the analyst to predict the future earnings and profitability of individual corporations and product sectors, the role of municipal bond credit analysis, while less dramatic, is nevertheless very important. It should be noted, furthermore, that there are several different approaches to municipal bond credit analysis. There are no universally accepted theories of municipal credit analysis, as there are in the fields of common stock and corporate bond analysis.

As an example of the diversity of municipal bond analysis, one can look at the relationship of intergovernmental aid programs to general obligation bond security. There is one viewpoint held in the investment community that the bonds of any local government such as a city, town, county, or school district that is heavily dependent on outside revenue sources are less attractive as an investment than bonds for a community that has a strong taxable economic base. However, the financial and budgetary operations of the bond issuer may be significantly strengthened by the outside support. For instance, the school district of Hoboken, New Jersey, issues its own general obligation bonds and maintains its own budgetary accounts. In the late 1970s the school district has received approximately 75 percent of its revenues from the state, and an annually declining amount from local property taxpayers. In this instance it is a New Jersey state-constitutional provision and a resulting statute which provide that if a community's property tax base declines, the state correspondingly makes up the difference with increased payments of state aid to education. Did this feature make the general obligation school bonds of Hoboken stronger or weaker credit risks?

While the field of municipal bond credit analysis is not characterized by standardized and universally accepted analytical techniques, there is general acceptance of the three basic purposes of a bond analysis. Additionally, it should be noted that while the municipal bond investor will not make a "killing" on the basis of a competent credit worthiness analysis, he or she should be aware of risk factors in three respects, discussed below. By knowing the degree of credit worthiness, he can better protect and utilize his investment funds.

The Potential for Default

First, the municipal bond credit risk analysis should determine whether the bond issuer is likely, under a reasonable economic and financial scenario, to ever default either permanently or temporarily in making bond and interest payments when due. That is, the first purpose of a municipal bond credit analysis is to determine if the bond is going to have serious problems in which the investor could lose his capital. Furthermore, it should be noted that over the past 25 years there have been some municipal bonds and notes that have indeed defaulted.[2]

---

[2] These are discussed in Chapter 11.

There have been a few that have had to go to the federal bankruptcy courts. The Advisory Commission on Intergovernmental Relations reported in a 1985 study that, between 1972 and 1983 alone, there were recorded defaults by at least 113 issuers. Of these, ten were general obligation debts, six were for water supply systems and sewers, five each were for housing and hospitals, three were for utilities other than water and sewers, and 82 were for bonds issued to finance private-purpose commercial and industrial facilities. Clearly, such bonds and notes were ones that the prudent investor should have avoided.

Degrees of Safety

Second, besides identifying the likely default candidates, a related purpose of the risk analysis is to identify among the nondefault candidates those that are financially and legally stronger than others as well as those that are the most strongly secured bonds. Terms such as *gilt-edged* are usually reserved for describing municipal bonds with very little credit risk and very remote default possibilities, whereas bonds identified as either not being for "widows and orphans" or as being "businessmen's risks" would be at the lower end of the investment-risk spectrum.

It should be noted, furthermore, that while the rating companies give ratings that show degrees of safety, a shortcoming of relying on their ratings exclusively is that they tend to review a credit only when it comes to the new-issue market. With credit deterioration possible over a very short period of time, the investor must look beyond the assigned credit rating.

Short-Term versus Long-Term Opportunities

The third and final purpose of the credit risk analysis is to provide the investor with an indication of what direction the credit worthiness of a particular municipal bond is headed. Is the bond becoming stronger, deteriorating in quality, or remaining the same? Knowing the direction in which the bond is headed can provide tremendous short-term trading opportunities for the sophisticated investor who buys or sells on the basis of potential credit upgrades or downgrades. Additionally, the credit-risk analysis of a bond may uncover certain attractive features of the bond security that are not generally recognized in the marketplace, are not adequately reflected in the credit ratings, but eventually may be. Such bonds provide short-term investment opportunities as well.

As an example, certain bonds issued by the New York City Housing Authority were originally secured only by authority revenues and the guarantee of the city of New York. In the late 1970s they were converted to a federal program whereby the debt service began to be paid directly by the federal government to the paying agent for the bonds.[3] For some years, however, the bonds continued to be rated only B by Moody's. Some investors, aware of this new security feature, bought the bonds when they were priced as B-rated credits. After the Authority applied for the credit upgrade, Moody's assigned Aaa ratings to the bonds. Once this became known in the marketplace, the value of the bonds increased by 200–250 basis points.

A final point in determining the credit direction of a bond is for the investor to be aware that because demographic, economic, and financial changes can take place very rapidly, the time horizon of this credit-risk analysis should not be expected to cover a longer period than a few years.

PURPOSE OF THIS BOOK

The primary purpose of this book therefore is to explain the basic analytical tools that an investor can use to assess the credit worthiness of a municipal bond. Previous defaults going back to the 19th century as well as more contemporary ones are discussed. These demonstrate that most, but not all, municipal bonds are second only to U.S. government debt obligations in terms of safety. While the analysis of municipal bonds—and particularly general obligation bonds—is more an art than a science, we have tried to set forth the basic analytical questions and answers that should always be addressed. Once this is done, we go on in Chapter 12 to discuss investment strategies which have evolved using municipal bonds.

---

[3] For additional information about this program, see Chapter 10.

2

Municipal Bonds Do Default, but Most Don't: Our Colorful History

Over the past 150 years there have been difficult economic and social periods when relatively large amounts of municipal bonds and notes defaulted.[1] For example, during the economic panic and depression of the 1837–43 period, it has been estimated that the total indebtedness of the default issuers represented more than 50 percent of the municipal bonds then outstanding. During the period after the Civil War, in the 1870s approximately 25 percent of state and local indebtedness was in default. During the economic depression of the middle 1890s, 10 percent of all municipal bonds were estimated to be in default. During the Great Depression of the 1930s, it has been estimated that the actual amount of principal and interest past due in any one year was less than 2 percent of the municipal debt outstanding. However, overall, during the Great Depression 10 percent of all municipals had been affected by defaults. Actual accumulated past-due interest and principal peaked in 1933 when it was estimated to be 16 percent of annual debt service due on all outstanding municipal bonds and notes.

While this looks severe, when compared to all municipal bond

---

[1] For additional information about these defaults, see Advisory Commission on Intergovernmental Relations, *Understanding the Market for State and Local Debt* (Washington, D.C., 1976), pp. 23–27; *Ibid., Bankruptcies, Defaults, and Other Local Government Financial Emergencies* (Washington, D.C., 1985), pp. 19–27; A. M. Hillhouse, *Municipal Bonds* (New York: Prentice-Hall, 1936); George H. Hempel, *The Postwar Quality of State and Local Debt* (New York: National Bureau of Economic Research, 1971), pp. 101–124; William A. Scott, *The Repudiation of State Debts* (New York: Thomas Y. Crowell and Co., 1893); and selected back issues of the *Bond Buyer* and *Banknote Reporter*.

issuers or other types of issuers, defaults so far have not been so numerous or so acute as to significantly weaken long-term investor confidence in municipal credits. As examples, while only 1.8 percent of all municipal bonds were in default in 1932, 3.5 percent of railroad bonds, 5.4 percent of public utility bonds, 7.2 percent of industrial bonds, and 19.4 percent of all foreign bonds were.

History shows us that states, counties, and municipalities have all at one time or other been to the default "party." Like many party-goers, some of them came early and stayed late. Between 1839 and 1985 there have been over six thousand recorded defaults, with some communities having defaulted two or three times. In recent times we have had defaults—some of them well publicized and of significant size. For example, in 1975 the notes of the New York State Urban Development Corporation and the general obligation notes of New York City, and in 1978 the general obligation notes of Cleveland, Ohio, were in default.

One conclusion that can be made at the outset is that we have a long and rich history of municipal bond defaults.

EARLY DEFAULTS

A brief discussion of these early municipal bond defaults may help put in perspective the issue of default today (see Exhibit 1 for a full page of examples of defaulted notes). The first major wave of defaults occurred during the depression years of 1837–45. In fact, the earliest municipal default in the United States was that of Mobile in 1839. Because of the panic of 1837, two major fires in 1839, and a resulting yellow fever epidemic, the city could not pay its debts, and, instead, began negotiations with the bondholders on its outstanding debt of $513,000. Though Mobile tried to sell public land to pay the bondhold-ers, the sales brought very little, and the bondholders agreed in 1843 to a partial settlement. In the 1870s Mobile again defaulted. This time it was caused by the financing of railroad construction, the eco-nomic decline of Mobile after the Civil War, and questionable budget-ary operations brought about by the "carpetbagger" governments. By 1880 the bondholders and the city had finally agreed to a refunding bond issue.

Another early default occurred in Detroit in the 1840s. In the 1830s, public support developed for the city to purchase the privately owned waterworks. Although the improvement could have been bought for $25,000, the city instead borrowed $50,000, which it used to buy the waterworks and extend the system as well. By the late

1830s, Detroit began experiencing business stagnation and faced bankruptcy. By 1841, the city had stopped paying debt service along with many of its day-to-day expenses. While other creditors promptly took the city to court and even attached Detroit's fire engines, the bondholders, who included John Jacob Astor and Cornelius Van Schaak Roosevelt (grandfather of Theodore Roosevelt) for some unknown reason were more patient. By 1843, when unpaid coupons had mounted to a substantial sum, the city, with the consent of these bondholders, refunded the issue with 10-year bonds.

Other defaults occurred in Philadelphia and Chicago during the panic of 1857. Philadelphia's problems stemmed from its earlier municipal consolidation. After the state legislature in 1854 authorized the city to incorporate the entire county into the new municipality, the old jurisdictions, with their enterprising politicians, immediately voted for excessive public improvements and subscriptions to railroad stock, and issued debt that was shifted to the new corporate body. The new city found itself burdened with a debt of more than $17 million, one fourth of which had been issued within 30 days prior to the consolidation. With local bank failures, high unemployment, and a high debt burden, Philadelphia was in default by 1857. The following year, with an improved economy, however, debt-service payments were resumed.

Chicago's default in 1857 resulted from a combination of a high debt burden, caused in part by inflated borrowing costs, and a recession. As an example of the former, in 1852 the city had issued $400,000 of 6 percent bonds for a new water and sewer system, maturing over a period of 25 years. After deducting issuing "expenses," the city received only $361,280 from the bond sale. In 1857 the city went into default. The booming real estate valuations, however, made the default short-lived.

Early defaults were not just limited to eastern, midwestern, and southern communities. San Francisco was in default as early as 1851 as the result of excessive and questionable real estate purchases. Also, running from the 1880s on into the 1900s, the city was in default on bonds issued in the 1870s for special assessment purposes (i.e., the "Dupont Street" and "Montgomery Avenue" Bonds).

The Civil War Defaults

Many southern states and cities issued municipal bonds during the Civil War, most of which were never paid. As an example, in March of 1862 the city of New Orleans issued general obligation bonds. A month later, however, the federal general, Benjamin Butler, who is

EXHIBIT 1 Defaulted Interest Bearing State and Local Government Notes

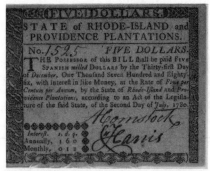

State of Rhode Island, Five Dollar Note, July 2, 1780.

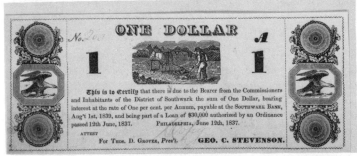

District of Southwark, Philadelphia, One Dollar Note, June 12, 1837.

State of Mississippi Union Bank, One Hundred Dollar Note, April 1, 1839.

EXHIBIT 1 *(continued)*

City of Omaha, Nebraska, Five Dollar Note, October 1, 1857.

State of Virginia, Twenty Dollar Note, July 1, 1861.

State of Missouri, Five Dollar Note, January 1, 1862.

EXHIBIT 1 *(concluded)*

State of Arkansas, Ten Dollar Note, April 11, 1862.

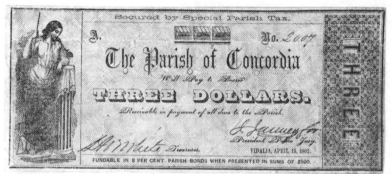

Parish of Concordia, Louisiana, Three Dollar Note, April 15, 1862.

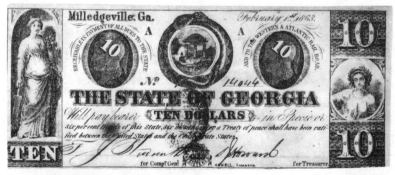

State of Georgia, Ten Dollar Note, February 1, 1863.

known in some southern circles as "Beast" or "Spoons" Butler, captured the city. Not only did he prevent the city from paying its bondholders and took half the specie left in the South from the banks, but it is also believed that he took as much silverware as he could from private homes throughout New Orleans. He got his nickname "Beast" Butler from his proclamation threatening to treat "as a woman of the town plying her profession" any secessionist female who insulted any Federal soldier. The defaulted New Orleans bonds (see Exhibit 2) are now known either as the "Beast" or "Spoons" Butler bonds.

Ironically, during the Civil War, investors throughout the South and in Europe preferred to buy state and local municipal bonds instead of Confederate bonds. Their thinking was that even if the South lost the war, the state and local governments would still pay their debts.

Unfortunately, this belief proved to be incorrect. Section 4 of the 14th Amendment to the United States Constitution specifically stated that:

> Neither the United States, nor any state shall assume or pay any debts or obligations incurred in aid of insurrection or rebellion against the United States, or any claim for the loss or emancipation of any slave; but all such debts or obligations shall be held illegal and void.

Many of these bonds now are quite popular at flea markets and coin shows.

STATE REPUDIATIONS, "WHOREHOUSES," AND VACATIONING TREASURERS

Besides municipalities and counties, many states were also at the default party. Their unique feature is that many, particularly before and after the Civil War, repudiated their debts entirely.[2] In fact, in the 19th century over $300 million in general obligation bonds were repudiated by the states.

The first known to repudiate its debt in the 19th century was Mississippi, which as early as the 1840s refused to pay debt service on $4 million in outstanding bonds that it had issued to buy stock in a bank, the Union Bank, that later failed and subsequently disap-

---

[2] Information in this section is also from: Francis Butler Simkins and Robert Hilliard Woody, *South Carolina During Reconstruction* (Chapel Hill: University of North Carolina Press, 1932), pp. 113–14; *The Clinton Collection* (New York: NASCA, 1985); and informant interviews in 1984–85 with Clarence Rareshide and Douglas B. Ball, numismatic collectors.

EXHIBIT 2 "Spoons Butler" Bond

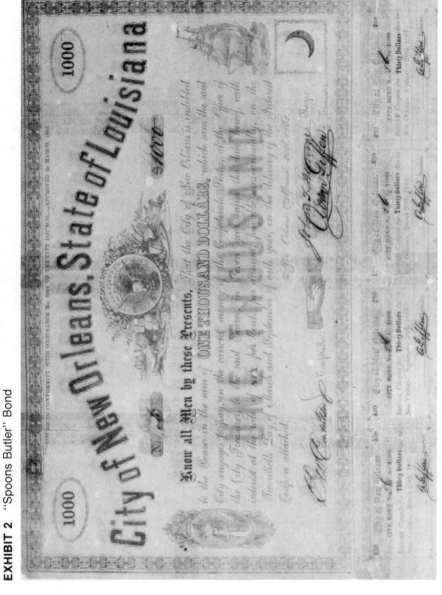

City of New Orleans, One Thousand Dollar Bond With Coupons, March 20, 1862.

peared. Since the bonds and notes had various legal deficiencies and since the local farmers were not eager to tax themselves, all the bonds were repudiated. In 1850, Jefferson Davis, future President of the Confederate states, ran for governor on the pledge to repay the debt. He was defeated largely because of this position. Later, in the State Constitution of 1875, the people ratified an amendment denying any obligation to pay the debt holders. (An interest bearing note of the Union Bank is in Exhibit 1).

South Carolina is also worthy of special mention. As the story goes, the governor of the state in the early 1870s, Robert K. Scott, had a strong desire for women and drink. Every night he would go to a local house of ill repute and the *"employees"* there would assist him in signing state general obligation bonds. On at least one occasion the star of the local burlesque stage was given a percentage commission to induce the drunken governor to sign the bonds. To make a long story short, an investigation was eventually undertaken and it was discovered that while the state was supposed to issue only $1.2 million in the bonds, the governor instead had issued over $22 million. Some of these bonds were refunded at 50 percent of face value and the others repudiated. These bonds are now known among municipal bond history buffs as the "whorehouse" bonds (see Exhibit 3).

Louisiana is also interesting for its history of defaults. During the period immediately following the Civil War, Louisiana was governed by a federally appointed governor and legislature. In the North this period was known as the *Reconstruction era* (*Carpetbagger era* in the South). During this period the governor and legislature, known locally as *carpetbaggers,* sold $100 million in state bonds, the proceeds of which were misappropriated by them. After the Reconstruction era ended, the bonds were repudiated on the basis that since proceeds had been stolen by these officials, the state had received no benefit from the bonds and therefore had no obligation to pay them. The state did authorize and sell some $2 million worth of bonds in $5 denominations to refund by exchange the bonds sold in the Reconstruction era, with the exchange being only for pennies on the dollar of par value of the bonds surrendered.

The $2 million of bonds issued subsequent to the Reconstruction era, having a picture of a small girl on the front, were called *Baby Bonds* (see Exhibit 4) . The plates used for the original Baby Bond issue were held in the custody of the state treasurer. While he was "vacationing" in Europe during the 1880s it was discovered that the plates had been used to reprint the bonds with identical numbers at least three times. The treasurer had allegedly taken $420,000 of the

EXHIBIT 3 "Whorehouse" Bond

State of South Carolina, One Thousand Pound Bond With Coupons, April 1, 1871.

34

EXHIBIT 4 Louisiana "Baby Bond"

State of Louisiana, Five Dollar Bond With Coupons, 1873.

Baby Bonds with him, and another $300,000 was purportedly found in his safety deposit box. He had also taken cash from the state treasury, for which it was said he had substituted additional Baby Bonds to keep all funds and accounts in proper balance. Since the treasurer extended his vacation permanently, he was not available to make full disclosure concerning his transactions. The state subsequently used surplus revenues in the general fund to buy up some of the irregularly issued Baby Bonds, the purchase price being 50 cents for each of the $5-denomination bonds.[3]

Other states that also repudiated general obligation debt in the 19th century included Florida, Alabama, North Carolina, Georgia, Arkansas, Tennessee, Minnesota, Michigan, and Virginia. Today, many of these states are considered to be of the highest credit worthiness.

---

[3] This aspect of Louisiana history was discussed in an Official Statement for a sale of state of Louisiana General Obligation Bonds, dated June 13, 1978.

DEFAULTS BECAUSE OF ECONOMIC DEVELOPMENT PROJECTS THAT WENT SOUR

Other defaults and repudiations also occurred after the Civil War. Many of these were caused by real estate speculation, railroad financing, and economic adversity. In fact, of the 300 municipalities in Illinois that had issued railroad aid bonds (for an example of a state of North Carolina railroad bond, see Exhibit 5), over one third repudiated them.

An interesting default occurred in Duluth, Minnesota, in 1877, where a population of only 3,000 people had piled up a debt of $400,000. When the town defaulted, the state legislature tried to negate the creditors' rights by creating a new municipal corporation to replace the former debt-ridden one. Eventually the courts held the new unit responsible for the old town's debt, and the bondholders had to be paid.

Another community, Dallas County, Missouri, was in default on its bonds from 1868 until 1919 when a federal court arbitrated the dispute. Of the $235,000 original issue, by 1919 the debt had increased to $2 million. Even federal court orders in some instances were not sufficient to retire the debt as tax collectors and elected public officials preferred to go to jail rather than increase property taxes.

THE DEFAULTS OF THE GREAT DEPRESSION

Of course, the Depression of the 1930s resulted in additional defaults. As examples, general obligation issuers in Florida defaulted because of real estate speculations, and note issuers defaulted in New Jersey— Asbury Park, Brigantine, and Fort Lee—because of excessive note issues. Big cities defaulted—Detroit, Cleveland, Miami, Toledo, New York City, and Chicago—because of the general economic decline, and "dust bowl" issuers not only defaulted but also physically disappeared.

Florida occupied a prominent role in these defaults. Approximately 21 percent of all defaulting taxing units were in Florida, and by the end of the crisis in 1940, 85 percent of the municipal debt outstanding in Florida had been in default.[4]

In fact, Florida's problems began three years before the Great Depression and were caused by widespread real estate speculation

---

[4] For additional information about Florida municipal bond defaults, see David M. Currie, "Municipal Debt Adjustments in Florida, 1926–1940," *Municipal Finance Journal* 4(Summer 1983), pp. 199–229.

EXHIBIT 5 North Carolina Railroad Bond

State of North Carolina, One Thousand Dollar Bond With Coupons, April 1, 1869.

and over-issuance of bonds. In 1925 alone, Florida new bond issues represented more than a third of all new issues in that year.

By early 1926, Florida was hit by a variety of events that led to the collapse of land prices. First, the Florida East Coast Railway, in order to modernize its rail system to Miami, in effect closed the railroad to the southeast coast, the focus of much of the speculation in real estate prices. Second, a ship sank in the narrow channel to Miami. While it was finally removed, construction materials had been prevented from reaching Miami by sea and rail, and the building industry collapse had begun. Third, later in the year a hurricane devastated much of the more valuable property in Miami. Last, the state's major agricultural crop, citrus fruit, was destroyed by the Mediterranean fruit fly.

The first important default was the city of Lake Worth in 1927, and by 1933 more than 80 percent of Florida issuers were in default. It was not uncommon for the debts of the defaulting Florida issuers to be greater than their assessed valuations. As an example, in 1938 the debt of Lake Worth was $4,822,435 though the assessed valuation was only $2,950,000.

While by the Depression many municipal bonds had been given credit risk ratings by Moody's, this proved to be of little help. In fact, of the rated bonds that plunged into default, 78 percent of the defaulting issues had been rated Aaa or Aa in 1929, and even a year prior to default 44 percent were still rated Aaa or Aa by Moody's.[5]

---

[5] Hempel, *The Postwar Quality of State and Local Debt,* pp. 108, 112.

3

The New Theoretical Framework for Municipal Bond Analysis

The economic deterioration of some regions of the country, the proliferation in the marketplace of innovative bond security structures, and the federal government's pullback of grant monies for local governments force the municipal bond investor today to apply an eclectic research methodology for determining credit worthiness. Because the research procedures of the past do not always provide the structure for analyzing many of the risks that now face investors, the investor must tailor the methodology to match each particular type of bond security. Yet, there are certain basic features of the analysis that are more important now than ever before. This chapter outlines the elements of an unconventional, or "left-handed," perspective for assessing credit risk that may help to identify a few investment dangers as well as opportunities. While this approach is applicable to revenue bonds and the innovative financial-deficiency-makeup structures, it may be relevant to general obligation bonds as well.

FIRST: LOOK AT INVESTMENT AGREEMENTS VERY CLOSELY

One mistake the investor can make is not to fully investigate with whom the issuer is temporarily investing its money. The insolvency of ESM Government Securities Inc. of Ft. Lauderdale, Florida in 1985 again heightened awareness concerning the potential problems associated with repurchase agreements, or "repos" as they are known in the capital markets and municipal finance industry.[1] In the case of ESM, several municipalities invested cash from operating, capital, and debt service funds and failed to take possession of the collateralized securities or have them held by a third party in an account in their name. When business operations ceased, the municipalities were unable to prove that they had a "perfected lien" in the securities.

These problems related to "repos," however, are not new. In August of 1982 a New York City based firm, Lombard-Wall, Inc., filed for reorganization relief under Chapter 11 of the Federal Bankruptcy Code. At the time of the bankruptcy Lombard-Wall had repos outstanding with over 50 municipal bond and note issuers or their designated bank trustees across the country. While the issuers faced significant potential losses, an upsurge in the bond market ultimately saved Lombard-Wall. In May 1984, two more small securities dealers, Lion Capital Group and RTD Securities, declared voluntary bankruptcy. Many municipalities and school districts, mainly in New York State, held repos with these firms which they believed to have been fully collateralized. However, the collateral was not held in an account of the municipal corporation and was subsequently claimed by more than one party as collateral for loans which had been made.

The investor should distinguish between investment agreements made with established investment-banking firms, government bond dealers, and banking institutions on the one hand, and those entered into with under-capitalized government securities arbitrage and trading firms. Large financial institutions have certain public-image sensitivities which, particularly in stable economic times, can be viewed by the investor as a credit strength.

SECOND: LOOK CLOSELY AT THE TRUSTEE

With the development of innovative and highly complicated cash-flow structured municipal financings, there has developed the need for the bond and note trustees to really become more involved with and knowledgeable about the specific construction project's overall status. Historically, however, trustees have seen their primary responsibilities as acting as paying agents on the debt, receiving the due monies, and receiving interest income on the various investments made under the indentures. While the trustee is not a participant in the project transaction, he does represent the bond and noteholder and many believe

---

[1] For additional information on the guidelines for evaluating Repurchase or "Repo" agreements, see Chapter 9.

he should vigorously monitor the construction project, particularly one that has a more complicated financing structure. For example, this was particularly important in the case of construction loan notes that required the timely completion and certification of the project for FHA insurance. This had rarely been the case as most trustees have not attempted to anticipate problems and thus avoid them. In general, bond security structures that appear to require vigorous monitoring by the trustee should not be assumed to be a credit strength.

THIRD: IS WHAT YOU SEE, WHAT YOU GET?

Another mistake an investor can make is to treat unaudited financial statements as if they were audited. A case in point is the bonds issued by Tampa General Hospital in 1982.[2] At the time of the original bond sale, the hospital issued unaudited financial information that showed only a modest loss from operations of $436,000 on revenues of $73,053,000.[3] Later, the audited report for this Florida hospital showed an actual operating loss of $3,592,000 as well as deepening financial problems. It turned out that the hospital faced stiff competition from neighboring hospitals and health-care facilities, and had an uncertain financial future resulting in part from federal medicare cutbacks. These bonds are in the speculative category of credit worthiness.

Another pitfall for the investor is that construction schedules and revenue collections may not be met as projected. Of course, the commercial rating companies sometimes use "interim" ratings on new 20–30-year bonds secured by the revenues to be generated by the completed projects and additions. Examples include electric generating plants and hospitals. For such projects the ratings assigned by the rating companies assume that the construction schedules and revenues projected in the feasibility studies are accurate. Yet, there always is a risk when project financing is involved, no matter how well reasoned the feasibility study may appear to be. Remember, feasibility studies are commissioned by the issuer and not by the investor or the analyst. As an example of this risk, in 1981 the Sebring Utilities Commission in Florida sold $92,750,000 in 30-year revenue bonds to construct a

---

[2] For a detailed review of the problems of this hospital, see Merrill Lynch's Municipal Research Department's Perspective Report on Tampa General Hospital, dated November 7, 1983, and written by Richard A. Radoccia.

[3] When issued these bonds were rated conditional Baa–1 by Moody's, and provisional A– by Standard & Poor's.

power plant. The feasibility study had concluded that surplus power could be sold to others on the spot market. The sale of this power was a necessary ingredient for the economic success of the project. However, after the plant was completed and had become operational, it could not sell the generated power. As a result the bonds had become very speculative. When they were issued they had been given a conditional A by Moody's. Later, they were rated Caa.

Still another example is the $5,070,000 in bonds issued by Northwest General Hospital in 1980 to finance the construction of additions and renovations to a hospital in Detroit. Of course, some events could not have been anticipated in a feasibility study. However, the issue came to market based on utilization trends contained in a feasibility study, and the bond issue correspondingly was considered by some to be of above-average investment quality. Within a few years the hospital was experiencing severe financial problems. Anticipated rental income did not materialize; the hospital's only surgeon resigned and was not replaced; project construction was significantly delayed; and the occupancy rate was 10 to 15 percent below the original feasibility-study projections. Additionally, the hospital's administrator had died and all the members of the Board of Trustees had resigned. Clearly, investors who believed in the infallibility of the feasibility study for these bonds did not have their hopes materialize.[4]

LAST: DO INNOVATIVE SECURITY STRUCTURES ALWAYS POSE EQUAL CREDIT RISKS FOR THE INVESTOR?

In light of the Washington State Supreme Court decision on June 15, 1983, concerning the Washington Public Power Supply System (WPPSS) Projects 4 and 5 bonds, the investor must now question whether the security structure of an issue is innovative and to what extent the legal structure is untested. In recent years, more and more municipal bonds have come to market with legal structures that are conceptually innovative, believed by very responsible attorneys to be legal, but that are also unproven as to their validity in relevant courts of law. Specifically, these structures are financial-deficiency-makeup concepts that in worst-case scenarios require communitywide financial support. Because of possibly strong surrounding economies and approving legal opinions, many investors have felt comfortable in purchasing these bonds even when the yields reflected an assumed high

---

[4] These bonds originally had been rated conditional Baa–1 by Moody's. As of August 1986, they were rated Ba.

level of safety. Yet, in difficult economic scenarios one can assume that the structures more than likely will be legally tested if local governmental revenue-raising powers are pledged and have to be used. While such bonds may still have a place in an investor's portfolio, the yields should be high enough to compensate for the real risks involved. Many times they are not.

The ultimate assessment of risk for any financial-deficiency-makeup structure such as take-or-pay bonds (and even for lease rentals) now has to be derived from three factors in addition to the fact that there is an approving legal opinion. The factors are:

1. Does the project to be financed by the bond proceeds have wide community support and serve a generally accepted, noncontroversial public purpose? Sports stadiums, large construction projects with complicated construction procedures, and private-purpose endeavors may fall outside this category.

2. Is the project well reasoned, tightly managed by proven construction managers, and designed to be self-supporting within reasonable economic parameters? In other words, the smaller the degree of construction risk and the greater the financial viability of the completed project, the stronger the credit should be. The analysis, of course, is improved by periodic visits to the construction site and by an ongoing assessment of the quality of management. Historically the chances appear to be better that the courts will force debt-service payments, if a project has been completed.

3. Is there a strong history of political and financial support by the relevant state and local governments for bond structures that have similar financial-deficiency-makeup provisions?

As implied above, legally untested take-or-pay and lease-rental bonds may well have some features that might be legally questionable and that are not nailed down by the courts. Yet some may be perfectly good investments with nominal risk if they include other basic security features such as the above three elements. Even within the state of Washington, examples include the bonds of the Grant County P.U.D. #2 (for Wanapum hydro and Priest Rapids hydro), the Douglas County P.U.D. #1 (Wells hydro), and the Chelan County P.U.D. #1 (Columbia River–Rock Island hydro, Lake Chelan hydro, and Rocky Reach hydro). Because of the legal cloud over the enforceability of the take-or-pays resulting from the WPPSS court decision, these bonds may now be viewed by some as being of weaker credit quality. Yet all of these projects meet the above criteria and are still very sound credits from a fundamental standpoint. They are bond issues that were sold years ago to finance hydroelectric generating facilities that are now on-line. Additionally, they provide power at very low cost to investor-owned utilities that are financially weak but that clearly support the projects. While the current purchasers of the power may or may not legally have to take the power, it is available and its cost is so low that it is in their economic self-interest to do so for a very long time.

In conclusion, it should be noted that in this chapter we have attempted to identify certain features of bond and note security structures that the investor should consider while looking for credit strengths and weaknesses. We have labeled them collectively the "left-handed approach." We hope that they might provide some insights into the subtleties of the world of municipal credit risk analysis and give some ideas for future thought as well.

4

Why the "Legal Opinion" for a Municipal Bond Is So Important

The popular notion is that much of the legal work done in a bond issue is boiler plate in nature, but from the bondholder's point of view the legal opinions and document reviews should be the ultimate security provisions. This is because if all else fails, the bondholder may have to go to court to enforce his or her security rights. Therefore, the integrity and competency of the lawyers who review the documents and write the legal opinions that usually are summarized and stated in the official statements are very important.[1]

The relationship of the legal opinion to the safety of municipal bonds for both general obligation and revenue bonds is threefold. First, the lawyer should check to determine if the issuer is indeed legally able to issue the bonds. Second, the lawyer is to see that the issuer has properly prepared for the bond sale by having enacted the various required ordinances, resolutions, and trust indentures and without violating any other laws and regulations. This preparation is particularly important in the highly technical areas of determining whether the bond issue is qualified for tax exemption under federal law and whether the issue has not been structured in such a way as to violate federal arbitrage regulations. Third, the lawyer is to certify that the security safeguards and remedies provided for the bondholders and pledged either by the bond issuer or by third parties, such as banks with letter-of-credit agreements, are actually supported by federal, state, and local government laws and regulations.

---

[1] For specific studies on recent problems with legal opinions, see Chapter 11 on contemporary defaults and related problems.

General Obligation Bonds

General obligation bonds are debt instruments issued by states, counties, towns, cities, and school districts. They are secured by the issuers' general taxing powers. The investor should review the legal documents and opinion as summarized in the official statement to determine what specific *unlimited* taxing powers, such as those on real estate and personal property, corporate and individual income taxes, and sales taxes, are legally available to the issuer, if necessary, to pay the bondholders. Usually for smaller governmental jurisdictions, such as school districts and towns, the only available unlimited taxing power is on property. If there are statutory or constitutional taxing-power limitations, the legal documents and opinion should clearly describe what impact they have on the security for the bonds.

For larger general obligation bond issuers, such as states and big cities that have diverse revenue and tax sources, the legal opinion should indicate the claim of the general obligation bondholder on the issuer's general fund. Does the bondholder have a legal claim, if necessary, to the first revenues coming into the general fund? This is the case with bondholders of state of New York general obligation bonds. Does the bondholder stand second in line? This is the case with bondholders of state of California general obligation bonds. Or are the laws silent on the question altogether? This is the case for most other state and local governments.

Additionally, certain general obligation bonds, such as those for water and sewer purposes, are secured in the first instance by user charges and then by the general obligation pledge. (Such bonds are popularly known as being *double barreled.*) If so, the legal documents and opinion should state how the bonds are secured by revenues and funds outside the issuer's general taxing powers and general fund.

Revenue Bonds

Revenue bonds are issued for enterprise financings that are secured by the revenues generated by the completed projects themselves, or for general public-purpose financings in which the issuers pledge to the bondholders tax and revenue resources that were previously part of the general fund. This latter type of revenue bond is usually created to allow issuers to raise debt outside general obligation debt limits and without voter approvals. The trust indenture and legal opinion for both types of revenue bonds should provide the investor with legal comfort in six bond-security areas.

1. The limits of the basic security.
2. The flow-of-funds structure.
3. The rate, or user-charge, covenant.
4. The priority-of-revenue claims.
5. The additional-bonds test.
6. Other relevant covenants.

Limits of the Basic Security. The trust indenture and legal opinion should explain what are the revenues for the bonds and how they realistically may be limited by federal, state, and local laws and procedures. The importance of this is that although most revenue bonds are structured and appear to be supported by identifiable revenue streams, those revenues sometimes can be negatively impacted directly by other levels of government. As an example, the Mineral Royalties Revenue Bonds that the state of Wyoming sold in December 1981 have most of the attributes of revenue bonds. The bonds have a first lien on the pledged revenues, and additional bonds could only be issued if a coverage test of 125 percent is met. Yet the basic revenues themselves were monies received by the state from the federal government as royalty payments for mineral production on federal lands. The U.S. Congress was under no legal obligation to continue this aid program. Therefore the legal opinion as summarized in the official statement must clearly delineate this shortcoming of the bond security.

Flow-of-Funds Structure. The trust indenture and legal opinion should explain what the bond issuer has promised to do concerning the revenues received. What is the order of the revenue flows through the various accounting funds of the issuer to pay for the operating expenses of the facility, to provide for payments to the bondholders, to provide for maintenance and special capital improvements, and to provide for debt-service reserves. Additionally, the trust indenture and legal opinion should indicate what happens to excess revenues if they exceed the various annual-fund requirements.

The flow of funds of most revenue bonds is structured as *net revenue* (i.e., debt service is paid to the bondholders immediately after revenues are paid to the basic operating and maintenance funds, but before paying all other expenses). A *gross revenue* flow-of-funds structure is one in which the bondholders are to be paid even before the operating expenses of the facility are paid. Examples of gross revenue bonds are those issued by the New York Metropolitan Transportation Authority. However, although it is true that these bonds legally have a claim to the fare-box revenues before all other claimants, it is doubtful that the system could function if the operational expenses, such as wages and electricity bills, were not paid first.

Rate, or User-Charge, Covenants. The trust indenture and legal opinion should indicate what the issuer has legally committed itself to do to safeguard the bondholders. Do the rates charged only have to be sufficient to meet expenses, including debt service, or do they have to be set and maintained at higher levels so as to provide for reserves? In regard to the rate covenant, the investor should determine if the rates charged are to provide cover only to the extent necessary to pay for debt service, operations, and required improvements with excess monies being credited against the succeeding year's revenue requirements. Such an arrangement is known as *Chinese* or *revolving coverage,* and it is not a strong credit feature. The legal opinion should also indicate whether or not the issuer has the legal power to increase rates or charges on users without having to obtain prior approvals by other governmental units.

Priority-of-Revenue Claims. The legal opinion as summarized in the official statement should clearly indicate whether or not others can legally tap the revenues of the issuer even before they start passing through the issuer's flow-of-funds structure. An example would be the Highway Revenue Bonds issued by the Puerto Rico Highway Authority. These bonds are secured by the revenues from the Commonwealth of Puerto Rico gasoline tax. However, under the Commonwealth's constitution, the revenues are first subject to being applied to the commonwealth government's own general obligation bonds if no other funds are available for them.

Additional-Bonds Test. The trust indenture and legal opinion should indicate under what circumstances the issuer can issue additional bonds that share equal claims to the issuer's revenues. Usually, the legal requirement is that the maximum annual debt service on the new bonds as well as on the old bonds be covered by the projected net revenues by a specified minimum amount. This can be as low as one times coverage. Some revenue bonds have stronger additional-bonds tests to protect the bondholders. As an example, the state of Florida Orlando–Orange County Expressway Bonds have an additional-bonds test that is twofold. First, under the Florida constitution the previous year's *pledged historical revenues* must equal at least 1.33 times maximum annual debt service on the outstanding and to-be-issued bonds. Second, under the original trust indenture *projected revenues* must provide at least 1.50 times estimated maximum annual debt service on the outstanding and to-be-issued bonds.

Other Relevant Covenants. Lastly, the trust indenture and legal opinion should indicate whether there are other relevant covenants for the bondholder's protection. These usually include pledges by the issuer of the bonds to have insurance on the project (if it is a project-financing revenue bond), to have the accounting records of the issuer annually audited by an outside certified public accountant, to have outside engineers annually review the condition of the capital plant, and to keep the facility operating for the life of the bonds.

In addition to the above aspects of the specific revenue structures of general obligation and revenue bonds, two other developments over the recent past make it more important than ever that the legal documents and opinions summarized in the official statements be carefully reviewed by the investor. The first development involves the mushrooming of new financing techniques that rest on legally untested security structures. The second development is the increased use of legal opinions provided by local attorneys who may have little prior municipal bond experience. (Legal opinions have traditionally been written by recognized municipal bond attorneys.)

Legally Untested Security Structures and New Financing Techniques

In addition to the more traditional general obligation bonds and toll road, bridge, and tunnel revenue bonds, as noted earlier there are now more nonvoter-approved, innovative, and legally untested security mechanisms. These innovative financing mechanisms include lease-rental bonds, moral obligation bonds, take-or-pay power bonds with step-up provisions requiring the participants to increase payments to make up for those that may default, and commercial bank-backed letter of credit "put" bonds. What distinguishes these newer bonds from the more traditional general obligation and revenue bonds is that they have no history of court decisions and other case law to firmly protect the rights of the bondholders. For the newer financing mechanisms, the legal opinion should include an assessment of the probable outcome if the bond security were challenged in court. It should be noted, however, that in most official statements this is not provided to investors because they have not demanded it.

The Need for Reliable Legal Opinions

For many years before the 1970s, concern over the reliability of the legal opinion was not as important as it is now. As the result of the numerous bond defaults and related shoddy legal opinions in the 19th century, the investment community demanded that legal documents and opinions be written by recognized municipal bond attorneys. As a consequence, over the years a small group of primarily Wall Street–based law firms and certain recognized firms in other financial centers dominated the industry and developed high standards of professionalism.

In the 1970s, however, more and more issuers began to have their legal work done by local law firms, some of whom had little experience in municipal bond work. This development, along with the introduction of more innovative and legally untested financing mechanisms, has created a greater need for reliable legal opinions. An example of a specific concern involves the documents the issuers' lawyers must complete so as to avoid arbitrage problems with the Internal Revenue Service. Legal opinions written entirely by unknown law firms and local lawyers raise serious credibility questions for the investor. On negotiated bond issues, one remedy has been for the underwriters to have their own counsels review the documents and to provide separate legal opinions. If the bond has come to market through a competitive sale and there is a question about a local attorney performing the functions traditionally performed by recognized bond attorneys, then the prudent investor may wish to avoid the bond altogether.

5

What Are "Refunded" Bonds and Why Are They So Safe?

While originally issued as either general obligation or revenue bonds, municipals are sometimes "refunded." A refunding usually occurs when the original bonds are escrowed or collateralized by either direct or indirect obligations or by those guaranteed by the U.S. government. The maturity schedules of the securities in the escrow fund are such so as to pay when due bond, coupon, and premium payments (if any) on the refunded bonds. Once this cash flow match is in place, the refunded bonds are no longer secured as either general obligation or revenue bonds. They now have a new security: the escrow fund. Such bonds, if escrowed with U.S. government securities, have little if any credit risk. They are the safest municipal bond investments available.

In this chapter refunded bonds are discussed in terms of (1) the general structure of an escrow fund, (2) the reasons why bond issuers refund their bonds, (3) the two major types of refunded bonds, and (4) how the analyst or investor should determine the degree of insulation from adversity of an escrow fund—and thereby, the credit worthiness of the refunded bonds.

Pure versus Mixed Escrow Funds

An escrow fund is an irrevocable trust established by the original bond issuer with a commercial bank. Government securities are deposited in an escrow fund that will be used to pay debt service on the refunded bonds. A pure escrow fund is one in which the deposited securities are solely direct or guaranteed obligations of the U.S. govern-

51

ment, whereas a mixed escrow fund is one in which the deposited securities are not 100 percent direct or guaranteed U.S. government securities. Other securities that could be placed in mixed escrow funds include federal agency bonds, certificates of deposit from banks, other municipal bonds, and even annuity policies from insurance companies.

REASONS FOR REFUNDINGS

Removing Restrictive-Bond Covenants

Many refunded municipal bonds were originally issued as revenue bonds. Revenue bonds are usually secured by the fees and charges generated by the completed projects, such as toll roads, water and sewer systems, hospitals, airports, and power generating plants. The specific security provisions are promised by the bond issuer in the bond trust indenture before the bonds are sold. The trust indenture describes the flow-of-funds structure, the rate or user-charge covenant, the additional-bonds test requirements, and other covenants. Many refundings occur because an issuer wants to eliminate restrictive bond covenants such as rate-charge covenants, additional-bonds tests, or mandatory program expenditures. A refunding eliminates, or defeases, the earlier covenants since the bonds are deemed to have been paid once they are refunded and cease to exist on the books of the issuing jurisdiction.

Changing the Debt Maturity Schedule

Some bonds are refunded in order to change the issuer's debt maturity schedule—either to make the yearly debt service payments more level or to stretch out the maturity schedule.

Saving Money for the Bond Issuer

Still another reason for issuers to refund municipal bonds is to reduce their interest payment expenses. Typically, substantial interest cost savings can occur when interest rates decline approximately 200 to 300 basis points from the levels when the bonds were originally issued. By refunding the outstanding bonds with a new issue, the bond issuer in effect is refinancing the loan at a lower interest rate. Additionally, based upon certain interpretations of Internal Revenue Service arbitrage procedures, some refundings that save money for the issuer can even take place in an interest-rate environment that has not dramatically declined.

TWO TYPES OF REFUNDED BONDS

The escrow fund for a refunded municipal bond can be structured so that the refunded bonds are to be called at the first possible date established in the original bond indenture. The call price usually includes a premium of from 1 to 3 percent above par. This type of structuring usually is used for those refundings that either reduce the issuer's interest payment expenses or change the debt maturity schedule.

While many refunded bonds are to be retired at the first callable date, some escrow funds are structured differently. In these refundings, the maturity schedules of the escrowed funds match the regular debt-service requirements on the refunded bonds as originally stated in the bond indenture. This type of structure usually is used when the objective is to defease any restrictive bond covenants.

Refunded bonds can be called by the issuer before the first call date and prior to the stated maturity of the bond if there is a mandatory sinking fund provision in the original bond indenture. As an example, in 1977 the state of Massachusetts refunded an issue of 9-percent general obligation bonds that had been issued in 1976 and were to mature on June 1, 2001. Under the refunding, the bonds—now fully secured by U.S. government securities—are to be called on June 1, 1987, at 104 percent. However, under the original sinking fund provisions, each June 1 from 1978 to 1987 the state of Massachusetts must call at par a preset portion of the outstanding 9-percent bonds.

DETERMINING THE SAFETY OF THE REFUNDED BONDS

Refunded municipal bonds are generally the safest investments because they are the most insulated from adversity, provided that the escrow funds have only direct U.S. government securities, or those backed by the U.S. government (i.e., *that they are pure escrows*). Specific questions to ask are:

1. Have sufficient monies been deposited in an irrevocable escrow fund at a commercial bank or a state treasurer's office to pay the bondholder?

2. Has the bond issuer signed an escrow agreement naming the bank or state treasurer as the irrevocable trustee for the escrow fund?

3. Have certified public accountants reviewed the contents of the escrow fund to determine if it consists of either direct U.S. government obligations (U.S. Treasury notes, state and local government series) or obligations unconditionally guaranteed by the U.S. government? Examples of the latter would include: obligations of the Government National Mortgage Association (Ginnie Mae), obligations that have a Ginnie Mae guarantee, Farmers Home Administration (FmHA) Insured Notes, and Export-Import Bank obligations, among others.

4. Have the certified public accountants also certified that the cash flow from the escrow fund will provide sufficient revenue to pay the debt service as required in the refunding?

5. Has a qualified, nationally recognized attorney reviewed the complete transaction and given an opinion that no federal, state, or local laws have been violated, including arbitrage limitations in Section 103 of the Internal Revenue Code of 1954, as amended?

6. What size commercial bank is involved? Preferably a large bank that is well capitalized should be used so as to minimize the impact if an embezzlement of funds or other irregularity should ever occur.

6

Municipal Bonds Insured by Commercial Insurers*

Insurance on a municipal bond or note is an agreement by an insurance company to pay debt service that is not paid by the bond or note issuer. Municipal bond insurance contracts are relatively new types of contracts that insure the payment of debt service on a municipal bond to the bondholder. That is, the insurance company promises to pay the issuer's obligation to the bondholder if the issuer does not do so.

The insurance usually is for the life of the issue. If the trustee or investor has not had his bond or note paid by the issuer on its due date, he notifies the insurer, giving it the defaulted bond and coupon. Under the terms of the insurance contract, the insurer is generally obligated to pay sufficient monies to cover the value of the defaulted insured principal and coupon interest.

WHO ARE THE INSURERS?

There are two major groups of municipal bond insurers. The first are the monoline companies that primarily are in the business of insur-

---

* Data sources for this chapter include: interviews with personnel of the New York State Insurance Department; Annual Reports, publications, and correspondence (including informant interviews) with MBIA and AMBAC; interviews with the Merrill Lynch municipal bond traders for insured bonds; interviews with a Merrill Lynch insurance-industry analyst; *The Wall Street Journal,* May 2, 1986, "Ratings on 30 Issues Insured by TICOR Unit Withdrawn by S&P," p. 20; *Moody's Municipal Credit Report,* March 12, 1986, "Single Family Housing Mortgage Revenue Bonds with TICOR Insured Loan Portfolios"; and various issues of Standard and Poor's *Creditweek.*

ing municipal bonds. The second group of municipal bond insurers are the multiline property and casualty companies which usually have a wide base of business including insurance for fires, collisions, hurricanes, and health problems. Identified below are the major insurers of municipal bonds.

The Monoline Companies

There are three major monoline companies that are currently issuing municipal bond insurance contracts.

AMBAC. AMBAC has been insuring municipal bonds since 1971. On June 28, 1985, 80 percent of AMBAC was acquired by Citibank with the remainder owned by AMBAC's management, the Xerox Corporation, and Stephens, Inc. (of Little Rock, Arkansas). AMBAC had been owned by the MGIC Investment Corporation which in turn was owned by the Baldwin-United Corporation.

Financial Guaranty Insurance Company (FGIC). This company was created in late 1983. It is owned by a group of equity investors: J. P. Morgan & Company, Inc., General Electric Credit Corporation, General Re Corporation, Kemper Group's Lumbermans Mutual Casualty Co., Merrill Lynch, Pierce, Fenner & Smith, Inc., Shearson Lehman/American Express Company, and FGIC's president.

Bond Investors Guaranty Insurance Company (BIG). This company is owned by a group of equity investors consisting of the American International Group, Phibro-Salomon Inc., Xerox Credit Corporation, Bankers Trust, and the Government Employees Insurance Company.

The Multiline Companies

Below are the major property and casualty insurance companies that insure municipal bonds.

Municipal Bond Insurance Association (MBIA). MBIA represents a pool of insurers and has been insuring municipal bonds since 1974. The pool of insurers now includes five property and casualty insurance companies that participate in predetermined percentages. MBIA policies of the participating insurers are "several and not joint." The individual insurance company's liability is generally limited to a previously agreed upon percentage of the debt-service risk of each bond issue. If an insurance company decides to withdraw from MBIA, its existing liabilities remain in force unless assumed by a remaining company or by a new one. The MBIA participants, under the MBIA constitution, could create a "joint and several" obligation. This authority, however, is permissive and not mandatory.

Below are the five members of the MBIA pool of insurers, and their respective percentages of MBIA liability as of 1986:

Company	Percentage of Participation
The Aetna Casualty and Surety Company	33%
Fireman's Fund Insurance Company	30
The Travelers Indemnity Company	15
Aetna Insurance Company (an affiliate of Cigna)	12
The Continental Insurance Company	10
	100%

It should be noted that in February, 1986 CIGNA's 12% participation in MBIA was reinsured by the other members.

Other Multiline Municipal Bond Insurance Issuers.

- Continental Casualty Company (CNA).
- Fireman's Fund Insurance Company.
- Industrial Development Bond Insurance (Continental Insurance Company).
- Industrial Indemnity Company (Crum & Forster).
- National Union Fire Insurance Company of Pittsburgh, Pa.
- Old Republic Insurance Company.
- The Travelers Indemnity Company.
- TICOR Mortgage Insurance Company (TMIC)
- USF&G Financial Security Company.

It should be noted that TICOR by 1986 was insolvent and under the conservatorship of the state of California Insurance Commissioner.

WHY ARE BONDS INSURED?

The overriding reason for municipal bond insurance is that it increases the marketability of some municipal bonds. This improvement in the marketability is so great in some instances that it provides a net interest cost savings to the issuer or provides access to the market that more than justifies the costs of the insurance premiums. This can be particularly important for large bond issuers of less than high quality who need to raise money in very weak market environments.

Both the bond issuer and the bond investor could be helped in the following ways.

Reduce Borrowing Costs for the Issuer. A major reason why issuers obtain municipal bond insurance is that with the insurance, the commercial rating companies generally rate them in the highest categories of safety. With the high ratings, the issuer's interest costs can be significantly reduced. In fact, average gross interest savings for the bond issuer over the life of the municipal bond issue can amount to three or more times the cost of the original insurance premium.

It should be noted, however, that since yield differentials between the credit quality rating categories are important to cost savings, and since such differentials vary with the level of interest rates, there may be periods when interest rates in general are too low for an issuer to use bond insurance. That is, the credit-rating spreads may be too narrow to provide the issuer with real dollar savings.

Still another concern that may prevent an issuer from insuring its bonds is the potential limitation that the insured bonds place on the issuer. That is, once a bond has been insured, the financial advantage to the issuer of calling the issue for early redemption or refunding is therefore reduced. This is because the present value savings needed to offset the cost of the insurance must occur over a period of years. If the insured bonds are called before the accumulation of the savings, then the issuer could experience a net interest cost loss. Therefore, the issuer must carefully weigh the reduced call or refunding option against the reduced interest rate on the insured bond issue.

Reduce Risk for the Investor. Because municipal bond insurance reduces the investment risk for the investor, the marketability of certain municipal bonds can be greatly expanded. Municipal bonds that benefit most from the insurance would include lower-quality bonds, bonds issued by smaller governmental units not widely known in the financial community, bonds that have a sound though complex and difficult-to-understand security structure, and bonds issued by infrequent local-government borrowers who do not have a general market following among investors.

Of course, a major factor for an issuer to obtain bond insurance is that its credit worthiness without the insurance is substantially lower than what it would be with the insurance. That is, the interest cost savings are only of sufficient magnitude to offset the cost of the insurance premium when the underlying credit worthiness of the issuer is lower. Clearly, issuers most likely to use the insurance are those with more credit risks.

THE RATINGS OF THE COMMERCIAL RATING COMPANIES

Until very recently, Standard & Poor's was the only commercial rating company to give ratings on insured municipal bonds. As of 1984, Moody's also began to rate insured bonds. Two insurance programs, MBIA and FGIC, are rated triple A by both rating agencies. By mid-1986 the following insurance programs were rated triple A by only Standard and Poor's: AMBAC; BIG; Fireman's Fund Insurance Company; Industrial Development Bond Insurance (Continental Insurance Company); National Union Fire Insurance Company of Pittsburgh, Pa.; and The Travelers Indemnity Company.

By mid-1986 five other insurance programs, CNA; Old Republic Insurance Company; Industrial Indemnity Company (Crum & Forster); CIGNA; and USF&G Financial Security Company were rated double A by Standard and Poor's. The last three insurers had previously been rated triple A.

By mid-1986 the bonds with TICOR insurance that had been rated by Moody's as high as double A were without ratings or as low as "B1." While originally rated double A by Standard and Poor's, most ratings were either withdrawn or substantially lowered.

In regard to MBIA's rating by Standard & Poor's, it should be noted that it is based on the respective AAA ratings on the underlying insurance companies. In response to a question at a Public Securities Association seminar entitled "What Are the Guidelines for the Credit Analysis of Municipal Bond Insurance," held on June 7, 1984, in New York City, a Standard & Poor's rating spokesman indicated that the AAA rating would be jeopardized if the S&P rating of AAA on any one of the underlying insurance companies were to change.

The other major rating company, Moody's, has not indicated the specific circumstances under which a rating would be lowered.

DO INSURED BONDS SELL AND TRADE LIKE Aaa/AAA CREDITS?

In general, while insured municipal bonds sell at yields lower than they would without the insurance, they tend to have yields higher than other Aaa/AAA-rated bonds such as deep-discount refunded bonds. Of course, supply-and-demand forces and in-state taxation factors can distort market trading patterns from time to time. Insured bonds as a generic group may not be viewed as having the same superior degree of safety as either refunded bonds secured with escrowed U.S. Treasuries or those general obligation bonds of states that have robust and growing economies, fiscally conservative budgetary operations, and very low debt burdens.

7

Municipal Bonds Backed by Commercial Banks

Over the past five years, municipal bonds and short-term notes have increasingly been supported by various types of credit facilities provided by commercial banks. In general, it should be noted that the first level of analysis for the investor should be the credit worthiness of the bond or note issuer. Credit facilities provided by commercial banks should not be viewed as substitutes for the credit quality of the underlying debt, but only as enhancements. For strongly secured municipals, such credit facilities can improve their marketability.

There are four basic types of bank support. Each type of credit facility is described below.

LETTER OF CREDIT

Under the traditional letter-of-credit agreement (LOC), the commercial bank is required to advance funds to the trustee even if a default has occurred under any of the documents governing the bond issue. The LOC is the strongest type of support available from a commercial bank.

LOC agreements vary from bond issue to bond issue. The strongest ones should provide that:

1. The bank is required to pay the bondholders all payments when due that either are required through an acceleration of debt service caused by a default or regular debt service.
2. Should the bond issuer be required to provide additional interest payments, if at a future date there is a determination of

61

taxability, then the LOC should cover the additional monies required also.

3. In order to avoid "preference" payment problems caused by an issuer's bankruptcy, payments by the bank must be made at least 91 days before they are to be paid to the bondholders.

Generally, the credit worthiness of the bond issue is determined by looking at the underlying credit of the bank issuing the LOC along with the credit worthiness of the bond or note issuer. Of course, it should be noted that not all LOC-backed municipals cover debt service on defaulted municipal bonds. A careful reading of the LOC agreement, along with a legal opinion from a nationally recognized, experienced bond attorney is required for determining the exact obligations of the bank providing the LOC.

"IRREVOCABLE" LINE OF CREDIT

An "irrevocable" line of credit is not a guarantee of the bond issue though it does provide a level of security. It is a conditional commitment, and the investor should determine the credit worthiness of the underlying credit of the bank as well as of the bond issuer.

REVOLVING LINE OF CREDIT

This is a liquidity-type credit facility that provides a source of liquidity for payment of maturing debt in the event no other funds of the issuer are currently available. Because a bank can cancel a revolving line of credit without notice if the issuer fails to meet certain covenants, bond security depends entirely on the credit worthiness of the bond issuer.

BOND PURCHASE AGREEMENT

This is an agreement by the bank which can be unconditional or conditional. As an example of a conditional bond purchase agreement and in regard to put bonds, often the agreement only backs the put option. If the actual underlying bonds default, the bank providing the bond purchase agreement may not be legally obligated to pay the bondholders.

8

How Moral Are the "Moral Obligation" Bonds?*

In several states, state agencies have issued revenue-type bonds that carry a potential state liability for making up deficiencies in their one-year reserve funds, should any occur. In most cases if a drawdown of the reserve occurs, the state agency must report the amount used to the governor and state budget director. The state legislature, in turn, may appropriate the requested amount, although there is no legally enforceable obligation to do so. Bonds with this makeup provision are the so-called moral obligation bonds.

The Moral Obligation Pledge

Below is an example of the legal language that explains this procedure and that is usually enacted into law by the particular state legislature involved:

> In order to further assure the maintenance of each such debt reserve fund, there shall be annually apportioned and paid to the agency for deposit in each debt reserve fund such sum, if any, as shall be certified by the chairman of the agency to the governor and director of the budget as necessary to restore such reserve fund to an amount equal to the debt reserve fund requirement. The chairman of the agency shall annually, on or before December first, make and deliver to the governor and director of the budget his certificate stating the sum or sums, if any, required to restore each such debt reserve fund to the amount aforesaid, and

---

* This chapter was coauthored with Walter D. Carroll.

the sum so certified, if any, shall be apportioned and paid to the agency during the then current state fiscal year.

Since 1960 over 20 states have issued bonds with this unique revenue-deficiency makeup feature. The first state was New York State with its housing finance agency (HFA) moral obligation bonds. This feature was developed by a well-known bond attorney, John Mitchell, who had extensive experience and knowledge of state constitutions and laws.

In the history of moral obligation financing, most of this debt has been self-supporting. However, in most of the instances where the moral pledge was called upon, the respective state legislatures responded by appropriating the necessary amounts of monies. This occurred in Pennsylvania with the bonds of the Pennsylvania HFA, in New Jersey with the bonds of the South Jersey Port Authority, and in New York State with the bonds of the UDC and with housing bonds of the HFA.

Determining the Value of the Moral Obligation

In terms of bond quality, while the moral obligation is not legally enforceable by the bondholders, it does indicate legislative support. Of course, while the general obligation pledge provides the highest degree of legal comfort to the bondholder, a moral obligation does provide some comfort as well—though certainly not on the same level and not legally enforceable.

The evaluation of the moral obligation pledge varies widely. To those who place a high degree of emphasis on legal protections, the moral-obligation pledge is given no weight whatsoever in the evaluation of the bond since it involves no legally binding obligation upon the governmental unit to replenish the reserve fund; that is, the bond is rated solely on the evaluation of the initial source of payment. To those investors who place a high degree of emphasis on ability and willingness to pay, rather than legal protections, the moral- obligation pledge is viewed as almost equal to the general obligation pledge.

Despite the nomenclature of the financial mechanism, the bondholder is not relying on the morality of future legislatures but rather on their practicality. The governmental unit may be expected to replenish the debt reserve fund because the cost of doing so is viewed as less severe than the increase costs associated with the bond market penalizing the governmental unit for not replenishing the fund. Increased costs could arise from higher interest rates that the governmental unit making the moral obligation pledge (and even related units of government) would have to pay on future issues of its own debt.

There are certain factors that the investor should investigate when evaluating a particular moral obligation bond.

The Purpose. What is the purpose for which the moral obligation bond is being issued? A future legislature is more likely to make the necessary appropriation to replenish a debt reserve fund if the issue was sold to finance a governmental building or low-income housing than if it was sold to finance a sports stadium. In the latter case, the legislature being asked to make the appropriation to replenish the reserve fund might seriously question the appropriateness of the actions taken by the legislature that made the moral obligation pledge.

Feasibility of Project. Is the project one that has a strong probability of being self-supporting from its planned source of payment? Even if the project should not attain full self-supporting status, the smaller the amount of the shortfall, the less controversy should result over an appropriation to replenish a reserve-fund shortfall. The debate about the appropriation could be much more heated if such support is so sizable and continuous as to raise concern that the project should never have been undertaken.

History of Moral Obligation Support. Clearly, the bondholder can take more comfort in the moral obligation pledge if the particular state has a demonstrated track record of replenishing a debt reserve fund when necessary, as is the case in New York, New Jersey, and Pennsylvania.

Amount of Moral Obligation Debt. Even the moral obligation believer would prefer a general obligation bond in a worst-case economic and financial scenario. Thus, careful consideration should be given to the budgetary resources and debt burden of the governmental body making the moral obligation pledge, including both its direct debt and the amount of moral obligation debt.

9

Questions to Ask before Buying

The credit analysis of many types of municipal bonds and notes is more of an art than a science. Nonetheless, most municipal bond analysts would agree that for each particular type of security structure there are elemental questions that must be asked and answered before an extensive credit risk analysis can be completed.

When Arthur Buck and Luther Gulick wrote their classic book on municipal research in 1926, there were no types of municipal securities other than the general obligation and public utility-secured bonds and notes.[1] In this chapter, over 20 different types of security structures are identified. Many of these structures are innovative and reflect the increased broadening of the use of municipal securities for various public and private purposes that has occurred since the Buck and Gulick book was written. Some of these innovative structures, such as zero-coupon and put bonds, also have been used by issuers to enhance the marketing of their bonds in a municipal bond market that over the past seven years has become increasingly more volatile. In any event, this chapter discusses the basic questions that should be asked to determine the relative credit worthiness of these bonds and notes.

GENERAL OBLIGATION BONDS

For general obligation bonds, one must ask questions and obtain answers in four specific areas: debt burden, budget soundness, tax burden, and the overall economy.

---

[1] A. E. Buck, ed., in collaboration with other staff members of the National Institute of Public Administration and the New York Bureau of Municipal Research *Municipal Finance* (New York: Macmillan, 1926).

Debt Burden. Concerning the debt burden of the general obligation bond issuer, some of the more important concerns include the determination of the total amount of debt outstanding and to be issued that is supported by the general taxing powers of the issuer as well as by earmarked revenues. Those general obligation bonds that are additionally secured by earmarked revenues outside the issuer's general fund, such as charges on users and aid payments, are known as being double-barreled in security.

For example, general obligation bonds issued by school districts in New York State and certain general obligation bonds issued by the city of New York are general obligations of the issuer and are also secured by state-aid-to-education payments due the issuer. If the issuer defaults, the bondholder can go to the state comptroller and be made whole from the next state-aid payment due the local issuer. An example of another double-barreled general obligation bond is the state of Illinois General Obligation Transportation, Series A Bond. Besides being state general obligations, debt service is secured by gasoline taxes in the state's transportation fund as well.

The debt of the general obligation bond issuer includes, in addition to the general obligation bonds outstanding, leases and "moral obligation" commitments, among others. Additionally, the amount of the unfunded pension liabilities should be determined. Key debt ratios that reveal the burden on local taxpayers include determining the per capita amount of general obligation debt as well as the per capita debt of the overlapping or underlying general obligation bond issuers. Other key measures of debt burden include determining the amounts and percentages of the outstanding general obligation bonds of the overlapping or underlying jurisdictions to real estate valuations. These numbers and percentages can be compared to the history of the issuer to determine whether the debt burden is increasing, declining, or remaining relatively stable.

Budgetary Soundness. Concerning the budgetary operations and budgetary soundness of the general obligation bond issuer, some of the more important questions include: How well over (at least) the previous five years has the issuer been able to maintain balanced budgets and fund reserves? How dependent is the issuer on short-term debt to finance annual budgetary operations? How have increased demands by residents for costly social services been handled? That is, how frugal is the issuer? How well have the public-employee unions been handled? They usually lobby for higher salaries, liberal pensions, and other costly fringe benefits. Clearly, it is undesirable for the pattern of dealing with the constituent demands and public-employee unions to result in raising taxes and drawing down nonrecurring budget reserves. Finally, another general concern in the budgetary area is the reliability of the budget and accounting records of the issuer. Are interfund borrowings reported? And who audits the books?

Tax Burden. Concerning the tax burden, it is important to learn two things initially. First, what are the primary sources of revenue in the issuer's general fund? Second, how dependent is the issuer on any one revenue source? If the general obligation bond issuer relies increasingly on either a property tax, wage and income taxes, or a sales tax to provide the major share of financing for annually increasing budget appropriations, taxes could quickly become so high as to drive businesses and people away. Many larger northern states and cities with relatively high income, sales, and property taxes in the 1970s experienced this phenomenon. Still another concern is the degree of dependency of the issuer on intergovernmental revenues, such as federal or state revenue sharing and grants-in-aid to finance its annual budget appropriations. Political coalitions on the state and federal levels that support these financial transfer programs are not permanent and could undergo dramatic change very quickly. Therefore, a general obligation bond issuer that currently has a relatively low tax burden but receives substantial amounts of intergovernmental monies should be carefully reviewed by the investor. If it should occur that the aid monies are reduced, as has been occurring under many of President Reagan's legislative programs, certain issuers may primarily increase their taxes, instead of reducing their expenditures to conform to the reduced federal grants-in-aid.

Overall Economy. The fourth and last area of general obligation bond analysis concerns the issuer's overall economy. For local governments, such as counties, cities, towns, and school districts, key items include learning the annual rate of growth of the full value of all taxable real estate for the previous 10 years and identifying the 10 largest taxable properties. What kinds of business or activity occur on the respective properties? What percentage of the total property tax base do the 10 largest properties represent? What is the building permit trend for at least the previous five years? What percentage of all real estate is tax-exempt, and what is the distribution of the taxable ones by purpose such as residential, commercial, industrial, railroad, and public utility? Last, who are the five largest employers? Concerning the final item, those communities that have one large employer are more susceptible to rapid adverse economic change than communities that have more diversified employment and real estate bases. Additional information that reveals either economic health or decline includes determining whether the population of the community over the previous 10 years has been increasing or declining by age, income, and ethnicity, and how the monthly and yearly unemployment rates compare with the comparable national averages as well as to the previous history of the community.

For state governments that issue general obligation bonds, the economic analysis should include many of the same questions applied to local governments. In addition, the investor should determine the annual rates of growth on the state level for the previous five years of personal income and retail sales, and how much the state has had to borrow from the Federal Unemployment Trust Fund to pay unemployment benefits. This last item is particularly significant for the long-term economic attractiveness of the state, since under current federal law, employers in those states with large federal loans in arrears are required to pay increased unemployment taxes to the federal government.

Red Flags for the General Obligation Bond Investor

In addition to the areas of analysis described above, certain red flags, or negative trends, suggest increased credit risks for general obligation bonds. The signals that indicate a decline in the ability of a state, county, town, city, or school district to function within fiscally sound parameters include the following:

1. Declining property values and increasing delinquent taxpayers.
2. An annually increasing tax burden relative to other regions.
3. An increasing property tax rate in conjunction with a declining population.
4. Declines in the number and value of issued permits for new building construction.
5. Actual general fund revenues consistently falling below budgeted amounts.
6. Increasing end-of-year general fund deficits.
7. Budget expenditures increasing annually in excess of the inflation rate.
8. Increasing unfunded pension liabilities.
9. General obligation debt increasing while property values are stagnant.
10. Declining economy as measured by increased unemployment and declining personal income.

AIRPORT REVENUE BONDS

For airport revenue bonds, the questions vary according to the type of bond security involved. There are two basic security structures.

The first type of airport revenue bond is one based on traffic-generated revenues that result from the competitiveness and passenger demand for the airport. The financial data on the operations of the airport should come from independently audited financial statements going back at least three years. If a new facility is planned, a feasibility study prepared by a recognized consultant should be reviewed. The feasibility study should have two components: (1) a market and demand analysis to define the service area and examine demographic and airport utilization trends and (2) a financial analysis to examine project operating costs and revenues.

Revenues at an airport may come from landing fees paid by the airlines for their flights, concession fees paid by restaurants, shops, newsstands, and parking facilities, and from airline apron and fueling fees.

Also, in determining the long-term economic viability of an airport, the investor should determine whether or not the wealth trends of the service area are upward; whether or not the airport is either dependent on tourism or serves as a vital transfer point; whether or not passenger enplanements and air cargo handled over the previous five years have been growing; whether or not increased costs of jet fuel would make such other transportation as trains and automobiles more attractive in that particular region; and whether or not the airport is a major domestic hub for an airline, which could make the airport particularly vulnerable to route changes caused by schedule revisions and changes in airline corporate management.

The second type of airport revenue bond is secured by a lease with one or more airlines for the use of a specific facility such as a terminal or hangar. The lease usually obligates them to make annual payments sufficient to pay the expenses and debt service for the facility. For many of these bonds, the analysis of the airline lease is based on the credit quality of the lessee airline. Whether or not the lease should extend as long as the bonds are outstanding depends on the specific airport and facility involved. For major hub airports it may be better not to have long-term leases, since without leases, fees and revenues can be increased as the traffic grows, regardless of which airline uses the specific facility. Of course, for regional or startup airports, long-term leases with trunk (i.e., major airline) carriers are preferred.

HIGHWAY REVENUE BONDS

There are generally two types of highway revenue bonds. The bond proceeds of the first type are used to build specific revenue-producing facilities such as toll roads, bridges, and tunnels. For these pure enterprise revenue bonds, the bondholders have claims to the revenues collected through the tolls. The financial soundness of the bonds depends on the ability of the specific projects to be self-supporting. Proceeds from the second type of highway revenue bond generally are used for public highway improvements, and the bondholders are paid by earmarked revenues such as gasoline taxes, automobile registration payments, and driver's license fees.

Concerning the economic viability of a toll road, bridge, or tunnel revenue bond, the investor should ask a number of questions.

1. What is the traffic history, and how inelastic is the demand? Toll roads, bridges, and tunnels that provide vital transportation links are clearly preferred to those that face competition from interstate highways, toll-free bridges, or mass transit.

2. How well is the facility maintained? Has the issuer established a maintenance reserve fund at a reasonable level to use for such repair work as road resurfacing and bridge painting?

3. Does the issuer have the ability to raise tolls to meet covenant and debt-reserve requirements without seeking approvals from other governmental actors such as state legislatures and governors? In those few cases where such approvals are necessary, one should ask how sympathetic these other power centers have been in the past in approving toll-increase requests.

4. What is the debt-to-equity ratio? Some toll road, bridge, and tunnel authorities have received substantial nonreimbursable federal grants that have helped to subsidize their costs of construction. This, of course, reduces the amount of debt that has to be issued.

5. What is the history of labor-management relations, and can public-employee strikes substantially reduce toll collections?

6. When was the facility constructed? Generally, toll roads financed and constructed in the 1950s and 1960s tend now to be in good financial condition. This is because the cost of financing was much less than it is today. Many of these older revenue bond issuers have been retiring their bonds ahead of schedule by buying them at deep discounts to par in the secondary market.

7. If the facility is a bridge that could be damaged by a ship and made inoperable, does the issuer have adequate "use and occupancy" insurance?

Those few toll road and bridge revenue bonds that have defaulted have done so because of either unexpected competition from toll-free highways and bridges, poor traffic projections, or substantially higher than projected construction costs. An example of one of the few defaulted bonds is the West Virginia Turnpike Commission's Turnpike Revenue Bonds issued in 1952 and 1954 to finance the construction of an 88-mile expressway from Charleston to Princeton, West Virginia. The initial traffic-engineering estimates were overly optimistic, and the construction costs came in approximately $37 million higher than the original budgeted amount of $96 million. Because of insufficient traffic and toll collections, between 1956 and 1979 the bonds were in default. By the late 1970s with the completion of various connecting cross-country highways, the turnpike became a major link for interstate traffic. Since 1979 the bonds have become self-supporting in terms of making interest coupon payments.

Concerning the economics of highway revenue bonds that are not pure enterprise type but instead are secured by earmarked revenues such as gasoline taxes, automobile registration payments, and driver's license fees, the investor should ask the following questions.

1. Are the earmarked tax revenues based on either state constitutional mandates, such as the state of Ohio's Highway Improvement Bonds, or are they derived from laws enacted by state legislatures, such as the state of Washington's Chapters 56, 121, and 167 Motor Vehicle Fuel Tax Bonds? A constitutional pledge is usually more permanent and reliable.

2. What has been the coverage trend of the available revenues to debt service over the previous 10 years? Has the coverage been increasing, stable, or declining?

3. If the earmarked revenue is a gasoline tax, is it based either on a specific amount of cents per gallon of gasoline sold, or on a percentage of the price? With greater conservation and more efficient cars, the latter tax structure is sometimes preferred because it is not as susceptible to declining sales of gasoline and in an inflationary environment it benefits directly from any increased gasoline prices.

HOSPITAL REVENUE BONDS

Two unique features of hospitals make the analysis of their debt particularly complex and uncertain. The first concerns their sources of revenue, and the second concerns the basic structure of the institutions themselves.

During the past 20 years, major sources of revenue for most hospitals have been (1) payments from the federal (Medicare) and combined federal-state (Medicaid) hospital reimbursement programs and (2) appropriations made by local governments through their taxing powers. It is not uncommon for hospitals to receive at least two thirds of their annual revenues from these sources.

While hospital bonds from a technical point of view are structured as revenue bonds, their major revenues come from payment formulas established through the annual political-legislative conflicts and compromises on the federal, state and local levels of government. Therefore, the analysis of hospital revenue bonds should start on the political-legislative levels and then move to the specific hospitals involved. How well the hospital management markets its service to attract more private-pay patients, how aggressive it is in its third-party collections, such as from Blue Cross, and how conservatively it budgets for the governmental reimbursement payments are key elements for distinguishing weak from strong hospital bonds.

Particularly for community-based hospitals (as opposed to teaching hospitals affiliated with medical schools), a unique feature of their financial structure is that their major financial beneficiaries, physicians, have no legal or financial liabilities if the institutions do not remain financially viable over the long term. An example of the problems that can be caused by this lack of liability is found in the story of the Sarpy County, Nebraska, Midlands Community Hospital Revenue Bonds. These bonds were issued to finance the construction of a hospital three miles south of Omaha, Nebraska that would replace an older one located in the downtown area. Physician questionnaires prepared for the feasibility study prior to the construction of the hospital indicated strong support for the replacement facility. Many doctors had used the older hospital in downtown Omaha as a backup facility for a larger nearby hospital. Unfortunately, once the new Sarpy hospital opened in 1976, many physicians found that the new hospital could not serve as a backup because it was 12 miles further away from the major hospital than the old hospital had been. With these physicians not referring their patients to the new Sarpy hospital, it was soon unable to make bond principal payments and was put under the jurisdiction of a court receiver.

The above factors raise long-term uncertainties about many community-based hospitals, but certain key areas of analysis and trends reveal the relative economic health of hospitals that have revenue bonds outstanding. The first area is the liquidity of the hospital as measured by the ratio of dollars held in current assets to current liabilities. A five-year trend of high values for the ratio is usually desirable because it implies an ability by the hospital to pay short-term obligations and thereby avoid budgetary problems. The second indicator is the ratio of long-term debt to equity, as measured in the unrestricted end-of-year fund balance. In general, a lower long-term debt to equity ratio indicates a stronger hospital, financially. The third indicator is the actual debt-service coverage of the previous five years as well as the projected coverage. The annual bed-occupancy rates for the previous five years is a fourth indicator. The fifth is the percentage of physicians at the hospital who are professionally approved (board certified), their respective ages, and how many of them use the hospital as their primary institution.

For new or expanded hospitals, much of the above data are provided to the investor in the feasibility study. One item in particular that should be covered for a new hospital is whether or not the physicians who plan to use the hospital actually live in the area to be served by the hospital. Because of its importance in providing answers to these questions, the national reputation and experience of the people who prepare the feasibility study are of critical concern to the investor.

HOUSING REVENUE BONDS

For housing revenue bonds the questions vary according to the type of bond security involved. There are two basic types of housing revenue bonds—each with a different type of security structure. One is the housing revenue bond secured by *single-family* mortgages, and the other is the housing revenue bond secured by mortgages on *multifamily* housing projects.

Concerning single-family housing revenue bonds, the strongly secured bonds usually have four characteristics.

1. The single-family home loans are insured by the Federal Housing Administration (FHA), Federal Veterans Administration (VA), or an acceptable private mortgage insurer. If the individual home loans are not insured, then they should have a loan-to-value ratio of 80 percent or less.

2. If the conventional home loans have less than 100% primary mortgage insurance coverage, an additional 5–10 percent mortgage-pool insurance policy would be required. The private mortgage insurer should be of high quality in terms of company capitalization and in terms of having conservative underwriting standards and limits.

3. In addition to a debt reserve that has an amount of monies equal at least to six-months interest on the single-family housing reve-

nue bonds, there is a mortgage reserve fund that has an amount equal at least to 1 percent of the bond issue outstanding.

4. The issuer of the single-family housing revenue bonds is in a region of the country that has either stable or strong economic growth as indicated by increased real estate valuations, personal income, and retail sales, as well as low unemployment rates and relatively low state and local government overall tax burdens.

In the 1970s state agency issuers of single-family housing revenue bonds assumed certain prepayment levels in structuring the bond maturities. In recent years most issuers have abandoned this practice but investors should review the retirement schedule for the single-family mortgage revenue bonds to determine whether or not the issuer has assumed large, lump-sum mortgage prepayments in the early year cash flow projections. If so, how conservative are the prepayment assumptions, and how dependent is the issuer on the prepayments to meet the annual debt-service requirements?

It should be noted that single-family housing revenue bonds issued by local governments, such as towns, cities, and counties, usually have conservative bond-retirement schedules that have not included any home-mortgage prepayment assumptions. Single-family housing revenue bonds issued by states did use prepayment assumptions. This positive feature of local government-issued bonds is balanced somewhat by the facts that the state-issued bonds generally no longer include prepayment assumptions and usually are secured by home mortgages covering wider geographic areas. Additionally, the state issuing agencies usually have professional in-house staffs that closely monitor the home-mortgage portfolios, whereas the local issuers do not. Finally, state issuing agencies have accumulated substantial surplus funds over the years that can be viewed as an additional source of security for the bonds.

For multifamily housing revenue bonds, there are four specific, though overlapping, security structures. The first type of multifamily housing revenue bond is one in which the bonds are secured by mortgages that are federally insured. Usually the federal insurance covers all but the difference between the outstanding bond principal and collectible mortgage amount (usually 1 percent), and all but the *nonasset* bonds (i.e., bonds issued to cover issuance costs and capitalized interest). The attractiveness of the federal insurance is that it protects the investor against bond default within the limitations outlined. The insurance protects the bondholders regardless of whether or not the projects are fully occupied and are generating rental payments.

The second type of multifamily housing revenue bond is one in which the federal government subsidizes under the federal Section 8 program all annual costs, including debt service, of the project not covered by tenant rental payments. Under Section 8 the eligible low-income and elderly tenants pay only 15 to 30 percent of their incomes for rent. Since the ultimate security comes from the Section 8 subsidies, which escalate annually with the increased cost of living in that particular geographic region, the bondholder's primary risks concern the developer's ability to complete the project, find tenants eligible under the federal guidelines to live in the project, and then maintain high occupancy rates for the life of the bonds. The investor should carefully review the location and construction standards used in building the project, as well as the competency of the project manager in selecting tenants who will take care of the building and pay their rents. In this regard, state agencies that issue Section 8 bonds usually have stronger in-house management experience and resources for dealing with problems than do the local development corporations that have issued Section 8 bonds. It should be noted that the federal government has eliminated new appropriations for the Section 8 program and there is little new issuance of tax exempt debt supported by this subsidy program.

The third type of multifamily housing revenue bond is one in which the ultimate security for the bondholder is the ability of the project to generate sufficient monthly rental payments from the tenants themselves to meet the operating and debt-service expenses. Some of these projects may receive governmental subsidies (such as interest cost reductions under the federal Section 236 program and property tax abatements from local governments), but the ultimate security is the economic viability of the project. Key information includes the location of the project, its occupancy rate, whether large families or the elderly will primarily live in the project, if the rents necessary to keep the project financially sound are competitive with others in the surrounding community, and whether or not the project manager has a proven record of maintaining good services and establishing careful tenant-selection standards.

A fourth type of multifamily housing revenue bond is one that includes some type of private credit enhancement to the underlying real estate. These credit enhancements can include guarantees by an insurance company, the Federal National Mortgage Association (FNMA), or a bank letter of credit.

Other financial features desirable in all multifamily housing bonds include a debt-service reserve fund, which should contain an amount of money equal to the maximum annual debt service on the bonds, a mortgage reserve fund, and a capital repair and maintenance fund.

Still another feature of many multifamily housing revenue bonds, and particularly of those issued by state housing agencies, is the state moral obligation pledge. Several state agencies have issued housing revenue bonds that carry a potential state liability for making up deficiencies in their one-year debt-service reserve funds, should any occur. In most cases if a drawdown of the debt reserve occurs, the state agency must report the amount used to its governor and state budget director. The state legislature, in turn, may appropriate the requested amount, though there is no legally enforceable obligation to do so.

In 1975, because the New York State Urban Development Corporation's General Purpose Bonds (UDC) were on the brink of default, and in fact UDC was in default on its notes for several months, the state and its local units of government experienced severe difficulties in selling their own general obligation bonds and notes. Responding to these market pressures the state legislature and the governor provided an appropriation of several hundred million dollars to keep UDC's housing bonds solvent. This experience in New York State has been cited by many on Wall Street who argue now that every state legislature would honor the moral obligation pledge to their respective state housing agencies out of fear of losing market access for their own bonds. For the investor, it is far from certain that this would always be the response.

The moral obligation only provides a state legislature with permissive authority—*not mandatory authority*—to make an appropriation to the troubled state housing agency. Therefore the analysis should determine (1) whether the state has the budgetary surpluses for subsidizing the housing agency's revenue bonds and (2) whether or not there is a consensus within the executive and legislative branches of that particular state's government to use state general-fund revenues for subsidizing multifamily housing projects.

INDUSTRIAL REVENUE BONDS

Generally, industrial revenue bonds are issued by state and local governments on behalf of individual corporations and businesses. The security for the bonds usually depends on the economic soundness of the particular corporation or business involved. If the bond issue is for a subsidiary of a larger corporation, one question to ask is whether or not the parent guarantees the bonds. Is it only obligated through a lease, or does it not have any obligation whatsoever for paying the bondholders? If the answer is that the parent corporation has no responsibility for the bonds, then the investor must look very closely at the operations of the subsidiary in addition to those of the parent corporation. Here the investor must determine also whether the bond is guaranteed by the company or is a lease obligation.

For companies that have issued common stock that is publicly traded, economic data are readily available either in the annual reports or in the 10-K reports that must be filed annually with the Securities and Exchange Commission. For privately held companies, financial data are more difficult to obtain.

In assessing the economic risk of investing in an industrial revenue bond, another question to ask is whether the bondholder or the trustee holds the mortgage on the property. Although holding the mortgage is not an important economic factor in assessing either hospital or low-income, multifamily housing bonds where the properties have very limited commercial value, it can be an important strength for the holder of industrial development revenue bonds. If the bond is secured by a mortgage on a property of either a fast-food retailer, such as McDonalds, or an industrial facility, such as a warehouse, the property location and resale value of the real estate may provide some protection to the bondholder, regardless of what happens to the company that issued the bonds. Of course, the investor should always avoid possible bankruptcy situations regardless of the economic attractiveness of the particular piece of real estate involved.

LEASE–RENTAL BONDS

Lease-rental bonds are usually structured as revenue bonds, and annual rent payments, paid by a state or local government, cover all costs including operations, maintenance, and debt service. The public purposes financed by these bond issues include the construction of public office buildings, fire houses, police stations, university buildings, mental health facilities, and highways, as well as the purchase of office equipment and computers. In some instances the rental payments may only come from student tuition, patient fees, and earmarked tax revenues, and the state or local government is not legally obligated to make lease-rental payments beyond the amount of available earmarked revenues. However, for many lease-rental bonds the underlying lessee state, county, or city is required to make annual appropriations from its general fund. For example, the Albany County, New York, Lease Rental South Mall Bonds were issued to finance the construction of state office buildings. Although the bonds are technically general obligations of Albany County, the real security comes from the annual lease payments made by the state of New York. These payments are annually appropriated. For such bonds, the basic economic and financial analysis should follow the same guidelines as for general obligation bonds.

PUBLIC POWER REVENUE BONDS

Public power revenue bonds are issued to finance the construction of electrical generating plants. An issuer of the bonds may construct and operate one power plant, buy electrical power from a "wholesaler" and sell it "retail," construct and operate several power plants, or join with other public and private utilities in jointly financing the construction of one or more power plants. This last arrangement is known as a joint-power financing structure. Although there are revenue bonds that can claim the revenues of a federal agency (for example, the Washington Public Power Supply System's Nuclear Project No. 2 Revenue Bonds, which if necessary can claim the revenues of the Bonneville Power Administration) and many others that can require the participating underlying municipal electric systems to pay the bondholders whether or not the plants are completed and operating (for example, the North Carolina Municipal Power Agency Number 1 Catawba Electric Revenue Bonds), the focus here is how the investor determines which power projects will be financially self-supporting without these backup security features.

There are at least five major questions to ask when evaluating the investment soundness of a public power revenue bond.

1. Does the bond issuer have the authority to raise its electric rates in a timely fashion without going to any regulatory agencies? This is particularly important if substantial rate increases are necessary to pay for either new construction or plant improvements.

2. How diversified is the customer base among residential, commercial, and industrial users?

3. Is the service area growing in terms of population, personal income, and commercial/industrial activity so as to warrant the electrical power generated by the existing or new facilities?

4. What are the projected and actual costs of power generated by the system, and how competitive are they with other regions of the country? Power rates are particularly important for determining

the long-term economic attractiveness of the region for those industries that are large energy users.

5. How diversified is the fuel mix? Is the issuer dependent on one energy source, such as hydro dams, oil, natural gas, coal, or nuclear fuel?

Concerning electrical generating plants fueled by nuclear power, the aftermath of the Three Mile Island nuclear accident in 1979 has resulted in greater construction and maintenance reviews and costly safety requirements prompted by the Federal Nuclear Regulatory Commission (NRC). The NRC oversees this industry. In the past, although nuclear power plants were expected to cost far more to build than other types of power plants, it was also believed that once the generating plants became operational, the relatively low fuel and maintenance costs would more than offset the initial capital outlays. However, with the increased concern about public safety brought about by the Three Mile Island accident, repairs and design modifications are now expected to be made even after plants begin to operate. This of course increases the ongoing costs of generating electricity and reduces the attractiveness of nuclear power as an alternative to the oil, gas, and coal fuels. For ongoing nuclear-plant construction projects, the investor should review the feasibility study to see that it was prepared by experienced and recognized consulting engineers and that it has realistic construction, design-schedule, and cost estimates.

RESOURCE RECOVERY REVENUE BONDS

A resource recovery facility converts refuse (solid waste) into commercially salable energy, recoverable products, and a residue to be landfilled. The major revenues for a resource recovery bond usually are the "tipping fees" per ton paid monthly by those who deliver the garbage to the facility for disposal; revenues from steam, electricity, or refuse-derived fuel sold to either an electric power company or another energy user; and revenues from the sale of recoverable materials, such as aluminum and steel scrap.

Resource recovery bonds are secured in one of two ways or a combination thereof. The first security structure is one in which the cost of running the resource recovery plant and paying the bondholders comes from the sale of the energy produced (steam, electricity, or refuse-derived fuel) as well as from fees paid by the haulers, both municipal and private, who bring the garbage to the facility. In this financing structure the resource recovery plant usually has to be operational and self-supporting for the bondholders to be paid. The second security structure involves an agreement with a state or local government, such as a county or municipality, that contractually obligates the government to haul or to have hauled a certain amount of garbage to the facility each year for the life of the facility and to pay a tipping fee (service fee) sufficient to operate the facility. The tipping fee should include amounts sufficient to pay bondholders regardless of whether or not the resource recovery plant has become fully operational.

When deciding to invest in a resource recovery revenue bond, one should ask the following questions:

1. How proven is the system technology to be used in the plant? *Mass burning* is the simplest method, and it has years of proven experience, primarily in Europe. In mass burning the refuse is burned with very little processing. Prepared fuels and shredding, the next most proven method, requires the refuse to be prepared by separation or shredding so as to produce a higher-quality fuel for burning. More innovative and eclectic approaches require the most detailed engineering evaluations by qualified specialists.

2. How experienced and reliable are the construction contractors and facility operators (vendors)?

3. Are there adequate safeguards and financial incentives for the contractor/vendor to complete and then maintain the facility?

4. What are the estimated tipping fees that will have to be charged, and how do they compare with those at any available nearby landfills? One way for a state resource recovery revenue bond issuer to deal with the latter concern occurred with the Delaware Solid Waste Authority's Resource Recovery Revenue Bonds, Series 1979. The state of Delaware enacted a law requiring that all residential garbage within a specified geographic region be hauled to its plant.

5. Is the bondholder protected during the construction stage by reserves and by fixed-price construction contracts?

6. Are the prices charged for the generated energy fixed, or instead are they tied to the changing costs of the fuel sources, such as oil and gas, in that particular market place?

Because of the uniqueness of the resource recovery technology, there are additional questions that should be asked. First, even if the plant-system technology is a proven one, is the plant either the same size as others already in operation, or is it a larger-scale model that would require careful investor review? Second, if the system technology used is innovative and eclectic, is there sufficient redundancy, or low-utilization assumptions, in the plant design to absorb any unforeseen problems once the plant begins production? Last, in addition to the more routine reserves and covenants—such as debt, maintenance, and special capital-improvement reserves along with covenants that commercial insurance be placed on the facility and that the contractor (or vendor) pledge to maintain the plant for the life of the bonds—yearly plant reviews by independent consulting engineers should also be required. The vendor should be required to make the necessary repairs so that the facility will be operational for the life of the bonds.

For resource-recovery revenue bonds that have a security structure involving an agreement with a local government, additional questions for the investor to ask are the following: Is the contractual obligation at a fixed rate, or is the tipping fee elastic enough to cover all the increasing costs of operations, maintenance, and debt service? Would strikes or other *force majeure* events prevent the contract either from being enforceable or preclude the availability of an adequate supply of garbage? Last, the investor should determine the soundness of the budgetary operations and general-fund reserves of the local government that is to pay the tipping or service fee. For these bonds, the basic economic analysis should follow the same guidelines as for general obligation bonds.

STUDENT LOAN REVENUE BONDS

Student loan revenue bonds are usually issued by statewide agencies and are used for purchasing either new guaranteed student loans for higher education or existing guaranteed student loans from local banks.

The student loans are 100-percent guaranteed. They are either guaranteed directly by the federal government—under the Federal Insured Student Loan (FISL) program for 100 percent of principal and interest—or by a state guaranty agency—under a more recent federal insurance program, the Federal Guaranteed Student Loan (GSL) program. This latter program provides federal reimbursement for a state guaranty agency on an annual basis for 100 percent of the payment on defaulted loans up to approximately 5 percent of the amount of loans being repaid, 90 percent for claims in excess of 5 percent but less than 9 percent, and 80 percent for claims exceeding 9 percent. The federal commitments are not dependent on future congressional approvals. Loans made under the FISL and GSL programs are contractual obligations of the federal government.

Although most student loans have federal government support, the financial soundness of the bond program that issues the student loan revenue bonds and monitors the loan portfolio is of critical importance to the investor. This is because of the unique financial structure of a student loan portfolio. Although loan repayments from the student or, in the event of student default, repayments from the guaranty agency are contractually assured, it is difficult to precisely project the actual loan-repayment cash flows, because the student does not begin repaying the loan until he or she leaves college or graduate school and all other deferments, such as military service, have ended. Before the student begins the loan repayments, the federal government pays the interest on the loans under prescribed formulas. Therefore the first general concern of the investor should be to determine the strength of the cash flow protection.

The second general concern is the adequacy of the loan guaranty. Under all economic scenarios short of a depression (in which the student loan default rate could be 20 percent or greater), the GSL sliding federal reinsurance scale of 100–90–80 should provide adequate cash flow and bond default protection as long as the student loan revenue bond issuer effectively services the student loan repayments, has established and adequately funded loan-guaranty and debt-reserve funds, employs conservative loan-repayment assumptions in the original bond-maturity schedule, and is required to call the bonds at par if the student loan repayments are accelerated. This final factor prevents a reinvestment risk for the bondholder.

There are eight specific questions for the investor to ask.

1. What percentage of the student loans are FISL and GSL backed, respectively?

2. Has a loan-guarantee fund been established and funded? Usually a fund that is required to have an amount at least equal to 2 percent of the loan principal outstanding is desirable.

3. Is the issuer required to maintain a debt-reserve fund? Usually, for notes a fund with at least six-months interest, and for bonds a fund with a one-year maximum annual debt-service amount are desirable.

4. If the bond issuer has purchased portfolios of student loans from local banks, are the local lenders required to repurchase any loans if there are either defaults or improperly originated loans?

5. What in-house capability does the issuer have for monitoring and servicing the loan repayments?

6. What is the historic loan-default rate?

7. How are the operating expenses of the agency met? If federal operating subsidies are received under the "Special Allowance Payment Rate" program, what are the rate assumptions used? In this program the issuer receives a supplemental subsidy, which fluctuates with the 91-day U.S. Treasury bill rate.

8. If a state agency is the issuer, is it dependent on appropriations for covering operating expenses and reserve requirements?

Also, beginning in mid-1982, student loan bonds have been issued that also are secured by the general obligation pledge of the particular private college or university involved, but without any substantial federal support. An example would be the Dartmouth College-Series 1 Bonds issued by the New Hampshire Higher Educational and Health Facilities Authority. Questions for the investor to ask include: Are college endowment funds available if necessary, and if so, are they substantial and sufficiently liquid? How prominent is the school in terms of admission standards and enrollment history? What are the general financial resources of the school? And lastly, is there a debt-service reserve fund available with an amount of monies that are at least equal to maximum annual debt service?

WATER AND SEWER REVENUE BONDS

Water and sewer revenue bonds are issued to provide for a local community's basic needs and as such are not usually subject to general economic changes. Because of the vital utility services performed, their respective financial structures are usually designed to have the lowest possible user changes and still remain financially viable. Generally, rate covenants requiring that user charges cover operations, maintenance, and approximately 1.2 times annual debt-service and reserve requirements are most desirable. On the one hand, a lower rate covenant provides a smaller margin for either unanticipated slow collections or increased operating and plant maintenance costs caused by inflation. On the other hand, rates that generate revenues in excess of 1.2 times could cause unnecessary financial burdens on the users of the water and sewer systems. A useful indication of the soundness of an issuer's operations is to compare the water or sewer utility's average quarterly customer billings to those of other water or sewer systems. Assuming that good customer service is given, the water or sewer system that has a relatively low customer billing charge generally indicates an efficient operation, and therefore strong bond-payment prospects.

Key questions for the investor to ask include the following:

1. Has the bond issuer, through local ordinances, required mandatory water or sewer connections? Local board of health directives against well-water contaminations and septic tank usage can often accomplish the same objective as the mandatory hookups.

2. In regard to sewer revenue bonds in particular, how dependent is the issuer on federal grants either to complete ongoing construction projects or to supplement the cost of future expansions of the sewer system? The level of dependence is particularly important in light of

efforts in Congress to reduce the multibillion-dollar federal sewage-treatment grant program for states and local governments.

3. What is the physical condition of the facilities in terms of plant, lines, and meters, and what capital improvements are necessary for maintaining the utilities as well as for providing for anticipated community growth?

4. For water systems in particular, it is important to determine whether the system has water supplies in excess of current peak and projected demands. An operating system at less than full utilization is able to serve future customers and bring in revenues without having to issue additional bonds to enlarge its facilities.

5. What is the operating record of the water or sewer utility for the previous five years?

6. If the bond issuer does not have its own distribution system, but instead charges other participating local governments that do, are the charges or fees either based upon the actual water flow drawn (for water revenue bonds) and sewage treated (for sewer revenue bonds), or upon gallonage entitlements?

7. For water revenue bonds issued for agricultural regions, what kind of produce is grown? An acre of oranges or cherries in California will provide the grower with more income than will an acre of corn or wheat in Iowa.

8. For expanding water and sewer systems, does the issuer have a record over the previous two years of achieving net income equal to or exceeding the rate covenants, and will the facilities to be constructed add to the issuer's net revenues?

9. Has the issuer established and funded debt and maintenance reserves to deal with either unexpected cash flow problems or system repairs?

10. Does the bond issuer have the power to place tax liens against the real estate of those who have not paid their water or sewer bills? Although the investor would not want to own a bond for which court actions of this nature would be necessary before the investor could be paid, the legal existence of this power usually provides an economic incentive for water and sewer bills to be paid promptly by the users.

Additional bonds should be issued only if the need, cost, and construction schedule of the facility have been certified by an independent consulting engineer and if the past and projected revenues are sufficient to pay operating expenses and debt service. Of course, for a new system that does not have an operating history, the quality of the consulting engineer's report is of the uppermost importance.

RED FLAGS FOR THE REVENUE BOND INVESTOR

For the revenue bonds discussed above there are general signals that indicate a decline in credit quality. The signals are:

1. Annually decreasing coverage of debt service by net revenues.
2. Regular use of debt reserve and other reserves by the issuer.
3. Growing financial dependence of the issuer on unpredictable federal and state-aid appropriations for meeting operating budget expenses.
4. Chronic lateness in supplying investors with annual audited financials.
5. Unanticipated cost overruns and schedule delays on capital construction projects.
6. Frequent or significant rate increases.
7. Deferring capital plant maintenance and improvements.
8. Excessive management turnovers.
9. Shrinking customer base.
10. New and unanticipated competition.

ZERO-COUPON BONDS

A zero-coupon bond is one in which no interest coupons are paid to the bondholder. Instead, the bond is usually purchased at a very deep discount and matures at par. The difference between the original issue discount price and par represents a specified compounded annual interest rate on the bond. As explained in Chapter 12, there is no reinvestment risk as with regular coupon bonds, since the compound annual interest is virtually assured provided the bondholder keeps the bond to maturity and the issuer is financially able to make the payment at the time of the issue's maturity. Variations of the zero-coupon, compound-interest concept are municipal bonds marketed and sold as municipal multipliers, capital accumulators, capital-appreciation bonds, or compound-interest bonds.

The advantage to the investor of purchasing zero-coupon bonds is that reinvestment risk is eliminated. Because of this, the investor should be willing to purchase the issue at a somewhat lower yield than comparable issues with regular coupon payments. The lower interest cost should also be attractive to the issuer. Additionally, since there are no semiannual interest payments to be paid, the issuer does not have to pay cash until the bond matures. It should also be noted that, since the zero-coupon bonds do not bear interest on a semiannual basis, the administrative costs should be reduced for the issuer as well.

The risk for the issuer is primarily an increased interest cost risk. Unlike full-coupon municipal bonds where the issuer only pays annual interest, the zero-coupon bond issuer eventually has to pay the bond-holder compounded annual interest. While the issuer may enjoy a yield give-up for providing the investor with this compounded annual interest rate, if interest rates substantially decline by the time the zero-coupon bonds come due, the issuer may have been better off having paid annual (noncompounded) interest.

Credit Analysis of Zero-Coupon Bonds

Zero-coupon bonds present a unique credit risk for the investor. On the one hand, if interest rates substantially decline during the time horizon when the zero is outstanding and the zero matures in a relatively low interest-rate environment, the buyer of such a bond will have made a good decision—from an interest-rate perspective—to have bought the zero. On the other hand, if interest rates do substantially decline, it may not have been a very prudent decision for the issuer to have sold the compound interest bonds. A lower interest-rate environment could present financial problems—particularly for weaker revenue bond issuers—in generating sufficient monies to pay the zero-coupon bondholders as well as annual operating and routine maintenance expenses.

In determining the relative credit worthiness of specific zero-coupon bonds, there are at least three areas of concern. They are:

1. If the zero-coupon bond is issued as part of a revenue bond issue, the zero-coupon portion should not be a balloon maturity. That is, the issuer's financial plan for its funded debt should be characterized by level debt service.

2. If the interest-rate environment does substantially decline after the zero-coupon bonds are issued, the indenture should provide the issuer with the flexibility to call the bonds prior to maturity at a price substantially below par; that is, as a percentage of the bond's compound accreted value. While weak protection from an early call is not an attractive feature to the investor, from the analyst's point of view zero-coupon bonds with early call provisions do provide the issuer with greater financial flexibility. Of course, if a 30-year zero-coupon bond is callable after 10 years, the investor should review the bond for investment in terms of its compound annual yield to the first call date and not to its maturity date.

3. Since the time horizon for the maturity of some zero-coupon bonds ranges up to 30 years, the bond issuers could be expected to undergo various economic cycles that could negatively affect their

ability to make the final debt payments. Clearly, the more insulated the issuer is from financial adversity at the time when the zero-coupon bond is issued, the stronger it should be—to cushion adverse economic stresses. Therefore, the most attractive zeros are those of the highest credit worthiness when issued, whether they are state general obligation bonds, or well-secured revenue and hybrid bonds.

BONDS BACKED BY REPURCHASE AGREEMENTS, OR "REPOS"

As noted in Chapter 3, investors should fully investigate with whom the bond or note issuer is temporarily investing its money. A popular way to do this is with repos. Here, we provide the guidelines for evaluating such instruments.

What Is a Repo?

A repo is a contractual agreement between a municipal issuer (or its bank trustee) and a commercial bank, investment banking firm, or other government bond dealer. In the transaction, the repo issuer (such as a government bond dealer) receives cash and, in turn, usually provides interest-bearing U.S. government securities to a municipal issuer as collateral for the cash with the contractual commitment to repurchase the securities at pre-determined dates and prices. Often, long-term bond proceeds, construction loan note proceeds, and even cash flow revenues are invested through repos until the money is needed to pay either debt service or construction expenses associated with the specific projects. Over the years, investment bankers and municipal issuers have found repos to be attractive short-term investment vehicles since they can match the maturity of the repo to their specific cash flow needs.

Evaluating Repo Agreements

If repos are used in financial transactions, the investor or analyst should consider the following factors:

1. Are construction funds, any other bond proceeds, or project enterprise revenues invested through repos? If so, to what extent is the bond or note issuer dependent on the repo monies? Clearly, construction loan note proceeds, debt reserve funds, mortgage loan repayments, and grant receipts invested in repos are of greater concern to the analyst than are idle funds.

2. Are the repos with well-capitalized, established, investment-banking firms, government bond dealers, or banking institutions? Repos should not be with under-capitalized government securities arbitrage and trading firms. Inclusion on an approved trading list of the Federal Reserve Bank is not sufficient evidence of credit worthiness.

3. Are the repos fully secured with collateral which is in negotiable form and in the possession and control of the municipality or trustee? Title to the collateral should at all times be with the trustee.

4. The collateral should only include *(a)* direct general obligations of, or obligations for which the payment of principal and interest are unconditionally guaranteed by, the United States of America; *(b)* bonds, debentures, or notes issued by any of the following federal agencies: Federal Home Loan Banks, Federal Land Banks, Bank for Cooperatives, Federal Financing Bank, or Federal Home Loan Mortgage Corporation (including participation certificates); and, *(c)* public housing bonds, temporary notes, or preliminary loan notes fully secured by contracts with the United States of America.

5. Because the vagaries of the bond markets impose the risk that the fair market value of the collateral may substantially decline at any time, the collateral should be valued at least monthly. The "fair market value" of the securities, as stated in the repo agreements, should mean the bid prices as they appear in the "Composite Closing Quotations for Government Securities," published by the Federal Reserve Bank of New York.

6. If the value of the collateral decreases below the levels agreed upon under the repurchase agreements and are not replenished immediately upon notification, then the bond or note trustees should have the right to sell the respective securities. Similarly, if the repo issuer defaults in an interest payment after one business day's notice, the bank trustee should have the option to declare the repo agreement terminated.

7. The repo agreements should state that third parties are not owners of any of the collateral, and that the collateral is free of all liens.

Repos may perform necessary timing functions in many financial transactions. For bond and note issuers their use is widespread and beneficial in keeping financing costs as low as possible. While repos can play an important role in an investment program of a municipality, the investor or analyst must look carefully at the structure of the repos, using the guidelines detailed above.

FHA–INSURED MORTGAGE HOSPITAL REVENUE BONDS

Administered by the U.S. Department of Housing and Urban Development and the Department of Health and Human Services, the Federal Housing Administration (FHA) hospital mortgage insurance program began in 1968 under Section 242 of the National Housing Act, as amended. Since the program began about 200 hospitals have participated; however, only a few issued tax-exempt bonds. The Atlantic City Medical Center bonds of the New Jersey Health Care Facilities Financing Authority and the Buffalo General Hospital bonds of the New York State Medical Care Facilities Finance Agency are examples of tax-exempt hospital revenue bonds that are secured in part by FHA-insured mortgages. By 1986 only three hospitals, all involving special nonoperating reasons, have received insurance benefits.

This section describes the security features provided by this program and outlines the questions the investor should ask when determining the credit worthiness of hospital bonds with FHA-insured mortgages. It should be noted that these security structures are very complex and this brief discussion identifies only the general areas to be addressed by the investor or analyst.

What Is FHA Hospital Mortgage Insurance?

Under the FHA hospital mortgage insurance program, once a hospital defaults on its mortgage payment, the bonding authority or the trustee files a claim for the FHA mortgage insurance. The claim can be paid in debentures in an amount equal to 99 percent of the outstanding mortgage balance. The debentures would be due 20 years from the date of the mortgage default, but could be redeemable at par by the U.S. government on any debenture interest rate. The payment dates are January 1 and July 1 of each year. After the trustee files a claim, FHA issues a debenture, though the timing of its doing so is at its discretion. It is reasonable to assume that debenture issuance may take no longer than 12 months, but no time period is guaranteed.

What Is the Credit Risk?

Several features of the FHA hospital mortgage insurance program could present impediments to the timely payment of debt service if there is a mortgage payment default by the particular hospital involved. These potential problems result because of the following provisions:

1. The FHA insurance covers only 99 percent of the outstanding mortgage balance when the mortgage payment default occurs.

2. The claim is almost certainly to be paid in 20-year, interest-bearing debentures, not cash.

3. The U.S. government is not required to issue the debentures within a specific time period, and debt service on the bonds could become due before the debentures are issued. It should be noted, however, that FHA should be able to process the claim and issue debentures within 12 months.

4. Thirty days' interest on the bonds is not covered by the FHA insurance. This occurs because insurance claims bear interest from the date of default (nonpayment) and a missed payment would include interest for the month prior to the payment date.

Of course, these credit features are in addition to the traditional security features of a hospital revenue bond. In the first instance, it is expected that debt service will be paid from hospital revenues. Briefly, the factors to consider include determining the range and quality of health care provided, (i.e., primary, secondary, and tertiary), whether the hospital is a start-up or ongoing facility, the historical and projected annual hospital occupancy rates, the degree of dependency of patient day revenues derived from medicare and medicaid, and the hospital's operating ratio among other ratios and financial-health indicators.

It should be noted however, that a hospital using the FHA insurance program usually is of far lower credit quality than other hospitals, or it would not go to FHA. Even so, the analyst or investor should still determine if the hospital is of at least "bare bones" investment quality; that is, it has the basic financial viability and cash flow to pay debt service.

What Is the "Prudent Man" Evaluation Approach?

While the FHA hospital mortgage insurance does not, by itself, provide complete backup security to the bondholders, it does (when properly supplemented by special debt and reserve-fund structures) provide a high degree of safety. For any particular hospital revenue bond that has FHA mortgage insurance, the investor or analyst should be concerned about the following:

1. Is there a reserve fund (which is often called a mortgage reserve fund or collateral account) that contains an amount at least equal to the sum of the 30 days of bond interest that is not covered by the FHA insurance, as well as the difference between the principal amount of the bonds outstanding and 99 percent of the mortgage balance? If this reserve is backed by a letter of credit, it must be irrevocable and from a well-capitalized commercial bank.

2. Is there a debt-service reserve fund containing an amount at least equal to maximum annual interest? If repurchases (repos) are used, they must be overcollateralized with direct or indirect U.S. government-guaranteed securities; evaluated periodically with prompt makeup provisions and remedies given to the trustees; and provided by well-capitalized credit worthy financial institutions.

3. The structure of the bond issue is very important because the debentures that would be issued by the U.S. government mature 20 years after the date of the mortgage default, and because the hospital bonds generally have maturities of much longer periods. Should a mortgage default occur when less than 20 years remain for ultimate bond maturity, or any intermediate maturity, the debenture interest received should be sufficient to provide for all bond principal and interest payments. Should a mortgage default occur when more than 20 years remain for ultimate bond maturity, the semiannual debenture interest and maturing principal (due 20 years after the date of the default) should be able to provide for bond principal and interest requirements. This is usually accomplished if the bonds are amortized at a more rapid rate than is the mortgage—that is, in general the mortgage and debenture interest rates should be fixed at higher rates than the interest rates of the municipal bond. Consequently, over time as the amount of bonds is reduced the FHA insurance—which covers 99 percent of the outstanding mortgage—covers more and more bonds outstanding. This structure, along with the mortgage reserve fund and the debt-service reserve fund, should provide strong security to the issue.

4. Since HUD could redeem the debentures in cash prior to their stated 20-year maturities, the projected cash flows, if available in the official statement, must demonstrate the ability to retire the outstanding bonds in case of early debenture redemptions.

5. Because of the possible need to draw upon them, the investments in the mortgage reserve and debt-service reserve funds must be of high quality and be liquid. Additionally, the investments must be controlled by the trustee.

It should also be noted that since the FHA hospital mortgage insurance is a remedy for a mortgage default, obviously the stronger the hospital is on its own merits, the more attractive the overall credit worthiness of the bond issue.

FSLIC–BACKED BONDS

This section discusses the analytical factors that should be considered in determining the credit worthiness of municipal bonds that are secured by Federal Savings and Loan Insurance Corporation-insured certificates of deposit. This was a financing structure that had been introduced to investors in the early 1980's and secured well-over a billion dollars of long-term bonds.

Security for the Bonds

In this security structure, the proceeds of a bond sale are deposited in a savings and loan association that, in turn, issues a certificate of deposit (CD). The CD is insured by the Federal Savings and Loan Insurance Corporation up to a limit of $100,000 of combined principal and interest for each bondholder. The savings and loan association uses the money to finance low- and moderate-income rental housing developments.

The Federal Savings and Loan Insurance Corporation

The Federal Savings and Loan Insurance Corporation (FSLIC) was created under the National Housing Act of 1934, as amended, and is supervised by the Federal Home Loan Bank Board. The Federal Savings and Loan Insurance Corporation insures individual accounts in FSLIC-insured savings and loan associations up to a maximum of $100,000, inclusive of principal and interest.

It should also be noted that while the FSLIC's obligations are not legally backed by the full faith and credit of the United States, on March 16, 1982, the House of Representatives with the Senate concurring passed a nonbinding concurrent resolution (H. Con. Res. 290) stating that "deposits up to the statutorily prescribed amount in federally insured depository institutions are backed by the full faith and credit of the United States."[2] It should also be noted that FSLIC is authorized to borrow up to $750 million from the U.S. Treasury for insurance purposes.

Evaluating the Bonds

In determining the degree of credit worthiness of an FSLIC-backed bond, the analyst or investor should consider the following eight factors:

1. The final maturity date of the certificate of deposit with the savings and loan association should be concurrent with the principal maturity of the bonds.

---

[2] This is reported in the official statement for the $42.2 million Panhandle Regional Housing Finance Corporation, Texas bond issue (dated November 1, 1982), p. 11.

2. There should be a reserve fund that can pay debt service on the bonds if a default occurs on the certificate of deposit. The amount of money in the fund should equal at least 60 days of interest on the bonds. Since interest on the certificate of deposit is not insured by FSLIC after the date of default, this fund can be used to pay up to 30 days of accrued but unpaid interest on the CD prior to the default. It also can be used to pay up to 30-days interest on the bonds from the time a default on the CD occurs to the date on which FSLIC pays the insurance claim. While FSLIC is not under any legal obligation to pay its claims within any specified time period, one default by an insured association was covered by payment of 90 percent of all insured claims within 12 business days.[3] Of course, future experience may require a longer period to be covered in the reserve fund.

3. The reserve-fund monies should be under the control of the trustee and governed by an investment agreement that provides for high liquidity. If repurchase agreements are used, they should conform to the guidelines discussed in the section above.

4. Because the holder of the CD does not have a security interest in the specific assets financed by the bond proceeds, and FSLIC has no taxing power and its obligations are not backed by the full faith and credit of the U.S. government, the analyst should determine if the particular savings and loan association involved is well established, in an economically stable region of the country, and has retained earnings well above the amount required by the Federal Savings and Loan Insurance Corporation.

5. The bond trustee must have established procedures for determining the aggregate principal amount of bonds owned in excess of $100,000 by any one bondholder. The trustee should accept for registration only bonds owned by the following entities, and should be provided all of the following information: *(a)* an individual (including joint ownership): with name, address, and social security number for each owner; *(b)* a corporation: with name, address, and tax identification number; *(c)* a partnership: with name, address, and tax identification number; and *(d)* a trust: with trustee's name and address, name of

---

[3] As reported in the Federal Home Loan Bank Board 1981 Annual Report, on May 18, 1981, the Economy Savings and Loan Association of Chicago, Illinois, was placed in receivership. This action was requested by the state of Illinois, and required payment by FSLIC of the insured deposits. The Economy Savings and Loan Association had over 8,000 accounts and $74 million in deposits. FSLIC reopened the savings and loan association five days following the default date and began paying the insured depositors. Within 12 days following the default, over 90 percent of all insured savers had been paid.

the settlor of the trust, the trust's tax identification number, and, if known, the settlor's social security or tax identification number. Also, the trustee should be required to notify the transferee and transferor if the transfer causes a bondholder to own bonds in an amount in excess of FSLIC insurance limits.

6. The bond trustee must also have procedures for promptly applying for FSLIC insurance on behalf of the specific bondholders should a CD default occur. Failure to promptly apply could cause the loss of FSLIC insurance coverage for the bondholders.

7. Under current federal tax law, 20 percent (15 percent for housing projects located in targeted areas) of the housing rental units financed by the bond proceeds must be occupied by low- or moderate-income tenants. If rental units are not available for occupancy on a continuing basis for low- and moderate-income tenants, the bonds can lose their tax-exempt status as of the date of issuance of the bonds. This could occur 60 days after the noncompliance is first discovered. Because of this possibility, the developer should be required through formal documentation to comply with these requirements at all times. Sometimes a special warranty deed can be filed in the real-property records of the county where the project is located; it can be a restrictive covenant binding upon and running with the title to the project.

8. There should be a legal opinion by a nationally recognized bond attorney that FSLIC insurance is applicable for the specific bonds involved.

While the FSLIC insurance security concept initially appears clear-cut, the above eight concerns indicate the high degree of investigation that must be undertaken in the analysis. While these bonds do have the potential of being high-quality investments, they also require careful analysis.

COLLEGE BONDS COLLATERALIZED WITH COMMON STOCKS AND TAXABLE BONDS

A new municipal bond credit risk has developed over the last few years as the result of the changing nature of the equity and taxable-bond markets. Specifically, the unprecedented volatility in these capital markets has required the analyst to view the stability of stored wealth—which common stocks and fixed-income debt are supposed to be—much more cautiously than in the past. This is particularly so when they are used as collateral to provide security to municipal bondholders.

The New Volatility Factors

As examples of the volatility of the equity markets, the Dow Jones Industrial Average dropped from 918 to 730 between February and March 1980. This represented a loss in value of 20 percent over a two-month period. Also, in 1981, the Dow dropped from a high of 1,031 in April to a low of 807 in September, for a drop of almost 22 percent.

Volatility has racked the fixed-income capital markets as well. In the U.S. Treasury bond market, long-bond yields jumped from a low of 9.75 percent in June 1980 to a high of 12.35 percent the following December. If the "govies" had been bought at par at the 9.75-percent yield rate, they would have declined in market value by almost 20 percent in less than six months. Similar volatility has occurred in the corporate bond market. Between September 1979 and March 1980, for example, yields on long high-grade corporate bonds jumped from approximately 9.70 percent to 13.50 percent. That is, collateral that had been priced at par in September was worth one fourth less if it had to be liquidated six months later in March 1980.

Volatility and Municipal Bonds

Increased volatility in the capital markets has required the analyst to further refine the credit risk criteria as related to collateralized debt. The volatility factor has weakened the degree of insulation from adversity of those municipal bonds collateralized by portfolios of stocks and bonds—primarily those issued for private colleges and universities and secured in part with separately collateralized securities funds. Under this financing arrangement, which first became popular in the 1970s, investment securities of a college were deposited in a collateral or debt-service reserve fund held by the bond trustee, to be used, if necessary, to pay debt service on the bonds. Private colleges and universities with ample, unrestricted endowment funds found this security structure an attractive way of reducing their interest costs through the improved credit worthiness of collateralized bonds.

In determining the degree of insulation from adversity, or margin of protection, of these bonds, analysts previously looked for the securities used as collateral to be limited only to being readily marketable. If the basic criterion is met, and if the college or university has the financial ability to replenish the collateral in the event of any deficiency and is itself of good credit quality, generally one could feel very comfortable with the security structure.

Indicators of Credit Worthiness

Indicators of good credit quality for a private institution of higher education usually include the following:

1. High levels of endowment. Generally, an endowment of at least $10,000 to $15,000 per student in 1986 dollars is desirable.
2. A trend, over at least the last three years, of favorable operating-fund end-of-year balances—that is, no operating deficits and strong financial controls.
3. Stable student enrollments.
4. Selective admission standards.

In a volatile market such as existed in the late 1970s and early 1980s, however, the standard of readily marketable securities was too broad even for colleges of good credit quality. Under this standard, eligible collateral funds could include primarily lower-quality or very volatile securities.

A fundamental consideration is the composition and level of the collateral: eligible investments should only include U.S. governments, corporate bonds, preferred stock, and common stock of corporations whose bonds are of high credit worthiness. The required collateral amount usually should vary from 100 percent to about 120 percent of the par value of the bonds outstanding. If the collateral is not all of high quality, additional coverage such as 150 percent of total debt service may be desirable. Another security feature would be for the annual cash flow from the collateral to cover debt service at least 1.5 times.

In addition, the frequency of evaluation is important. The trustee should be required at least quarterly, if not on a more regular basis, to evaluate the collateral to determine that its market value equals the amount required in the indenture. While the norm for evaluating the collateral has varied from a monthly to a quarterly requirement, the former time frame is preferred.

There should also be provisions for replenishment by the institution if necessary. An institution must be required by a covenant to replenish the fund within a specified time horizon. For some of the older outstanding issues, this time period has ranged up to six months, whereas a two-week deadline is most desirable.

Of course, the strongest secured collaterized bonds would be those in which the collateralized securities are limited to prime quality; that is, only in direct obligations of the U.S. government, such as treasury bonds, and those in which the maturing principal and coupon payments roughly match the debt service schedule on the outstanding municipal bonds. An example is the collateralized issue of the Minnesota Higher Education Facilities Authority on behalf of Carleton College: Revenue Bonds, Series Two–E. It should be noted that other issues of Carleton College—Revenue Bonds, Series O (1975) and Revenue Bonds, Series T (1977)—are of weaker credit quality for two reasons. First, the cash flow structure of the collateralized securities and the debt service on the municipal bonds do not match. Second, the permitted collateral can be of less than prime quality. While the credit characteristics of the college are strong, the pledged collateral provides limited credit strength.

In addition to an evaluation of the institution's credit quality, careful attention also should be given to the quality of collateral and the coverage and replenishment provisions.

MUNICIPAL BONDS WITH WARRANTS

This section indicates the concerns that the investor should have when determining the credit quality of "warrants."[4] Warrants allow their holders to buy bonds from the issuer at par and at predetermined coupon rates during a specified time period—usually two years.

The first time a municipal bond with a warrant was issued was in 1981 when the Municipal Assistance Corporation (MAC) sold $100 million of 10⅝-percent coupon bonds due in 2008 along with two-year warrants allowing their holders to purchase another $100 million at the same coupon rate and due in 2007. The warrants could be detached from the bonds and did trade in the secondary market in ways similar to "options" in the stock market. This financing arrangement was used by the issuer since the use of the warrants wed it to price its bonds at a lower coupon rate than would normally be the situation. In the example above, MAC saved approximately 75 basis points in its initial borrowing costs by issuing warrants.

---

[4] It should be noted that these warrants are not the same as tax warrants issued by state and local governments. The latter are usually short-term notes issued in anticipation of taxes. The term *tax warrant* is just another name for tax anticipation notes.

Credit Considerations

Warrants are issued in high interest-rate environments as a way to reduce interest costs for a bond issuer. If interest rates dramatically decline before the warrant's expiration date and the warrant holders exercise their warrants, the issuer then will have to issue bonds with coupon interest rates substantially above the current market levels. As an example, MAC in 1981 also sold bonds with two-year warrants to buy $59,505,000 in bonds with $12\frac{3}{4}$-percent coupons. When yields declined during the fall of 1982, investors began to exercise their warrants.[5] While MAC saved approximately $295,000 to $443,000 a year through the reduced interest on the original $12\frac{3}{4}$-percent issue, it will have to pay $1 to $1.2 million more annually on the $12\frac{3}{4}$-percent bonds that have been issued to the warrant holders.[6] This is because they were issued at a time when the market for MAC bonds was approximately 11 percent.[7] It should be noted that in 1986 these bonds were refunded.

Potential Financial Burden on the Issuer

Of the two major credit-quality considerations, the first credit concern is to determine how many warrants have been issued and the additional revenues required by the issuer for debt service if all the warrants are converted into bonds. Clearly, an issuer who sells substantial amounts of warrants at just the peak of a high interest-rate/inflation cycle could be exposing itself to substantial financial pressures in a lower interest-rate/stable-price environment. For a revenue bond issuer such a development could substantially reduce the net revenue coverage figures and thereby the credit worthiness of the underlying bonds. Because of this, in evaluating the credit worthiness of a warrant, the investor should determine the financial impact on the issuer if—in a worst-case scenario—all the outstanding warrants are exercised. If the exercise of the warrants results in substantially reduced credit worthiness, the attractiveness of the warrant clearly becomes less so.

---

[5] Municipal Assistance Corporation for the City of New York, *First Quarter Report Ending September 30, 1982,* Note 8—Commitments, November 4, 1982.

[6] Some Gimmicks Used to Sell Bonds Sour as Rates Fall, Inflation Slows," *The Wall Street Journal,* December 14, 1982, pp. 33, 43. Of course, it should also be noted that MAC saved investment-banking fees since holders exercised their warrants and bought additional bonds directly through the warrant agent, the United States Trust Company of New York.

[7] Interview with MAC bond trader in the Municipal Bond Department of Merrill Lynch, Pierce, Fenner & Smith, Inc., January 3, 1983.

Again turning to MAC, while (as noted above) the issuer did have to pay increased debt service as the result of its $12\frac{3}{4}$-percent bond warrants, it has averaged out its interest costs by selling warrants during various stages of the interest-rate cycle. Some warrants have become worthless to their purchasers, which of course is what the issuer wanted to see occur. This is true of many of the $10\frac{5}{8}$-percent bond warrants that expired in January 1983.[8]

Additionally, the amount of MAC warrants outstanding represented a very small percentage of MAC total debt. Clearly, if warrants are issued, it is desirable to see them issued at various stages of the interest-rate cycle and in amounts of relatively modest size.

Legality Concern

The second concern for the analyst or investor in evaluating the investment quality of a warrant is its legality. There must be a legal opinion rendered by a nationally recognized and experienced municipal bond attorney that the issuance and performance of the warrant will not violate any existing state and local governmental laws. This is particularly important since warrants are new to municipal finance and have not been directly addressed in state constitutions.

Warrants are relatively new in municipal finance with only one issuer, MAC, having issued them. Guidelines for the investor to use in evaluating their credit worthiness are twofold: First, what is the financial impact on the issuer's revenues if all the outstanding warrants should be exercised, and concurrently, has the issuer sold warrants during various stages of the interest-rate cycle so as to average out its interest-rate exposure? Second, is there a legal opinion by a nationally recognized municipal bond attorney clearly indicating that the issuer can issue and execute the warrants?

TAX, REVENUE, GRANT, AND BOND ANTICIPATION NOTES

Notes are temporary borrowings by states, local governments, and official jurisdictions to finance a variety of activities.[9] Usually, notes

---

[8] While the detachable warrants for the $10\frac{5}{8}$ percent bonds were for $100 million in additional bonds, warrants were exercised for $31,590,000 of the $10\frac{5}{8}$-percent bonds. Municipal Assistance Corporation, *Third Quarter Report Ending March 31, 1983.*

[9] Information on the note issues discussed in this chapter is derived from the official statements of the various issues. General analytical concepts are from Luther Gulick, "Debt Administration," in *Municipal Finance,* ed. A. E. Buck in collaboration with other staff members of the National Institute of Public Administration and the New York Bureau of Municipal Research (New York: Macmillan, 1926).

are issued for a period of 12 months, though it is not uncommon for them to be issued for periods of as short as 3 months and for as long as 3 years. There are two general purposes for which notes are issued—to even out cash flows and to temporarily finance capital improvements. Each is explained below.

Two Major Purposes of Notes

Evening Out Cash Flows. Many states, cities, towns, counties, and school districts, as well as special jurisdictions sometimes borrow temporarily in anticipation of the collection of taxes or other expected revenues. Their need to borrow occurs because while payrolls, bills, and other commitments have to be paid starting at the beginning of the fiscal year, property taxes and other revenues such as intergovernmental grants are due and payable after the beginning of the fiscal year. These notes—identified either as tax anticipation notes (TANs), revenue anticipation notes (RANs), or grant anticipation notes (GANs)—are used to even out the cash flows that are necessitated by the irregular flows of income into the treasuries of the states and local units of government. In some instances, combination tax and revenue anticipation notes (TRANs) are issued, which usually are payable from two sources.

Temporarily Financing Capital Improvements. The second general purpose for which notes are issued is in anticipation of the sale of long-term bonds. Such notes are known as bond anticipation notes (BANs). There are three major reasons why capital improvements are initially financed with BANs.

First, because the initial cost estimates for a large construction project can vary from the construction bids actually submitted, and since better terms are sometimes obtained on a major construction project if the state or local government pays the various contractors as soon as the work begins, BANs are often used as the initial financing instrument. Once the capital improvement is completed, the bills paid, and the total costs determined, the BANs can be retired with the proceeds of a final bond sale.

Second, issuers such as states and cities that have large, diverse, and ongoing capital construction programs will initially issue BANs, and later retire them with the proceeds of a single, long-term bond sale. In this instance, the use of BANs allows the issuer to consolidate various, unrelated financing needs into one bond sale.

The third reason why BANs are sometimes issued is related to market conditions. By temporarily financing capital improvements with BANs, the issuer has greater flexibility in determining the timing of its long-term bond sale and possibly avoiding unfavorable market conditions.

Security Behind Tax and Revenue Anticipation Notes

Tax anticipation notes are generally secured by the taxes for which they were issued. For counties, cities, towns, and school districts, TANs are usually issued for expected property taxes. Some governmental units go so far as to establish escrow accounts for receiving the taxes and use the escrowed monies to pay noteholders.

Revenue anticipation notes and grant anticipation notes are also usually, but not always, secured by the revenues for which they were issued. These revenues can include intergovernmental grants and aid as well as local taxes other than property taxes. In one extreme case, and as the result of the New York City financial crisis in 1975, RANs issued by New York City for expected educational aid from the state of New York provide for the noteholder to go directly to the state comptroller and get the state-aid monies before they are sent to the city's treasury, if that is necessary to remedy a default. Most RANs just require the issuer to use the expected monies to pay the noteholders once they are in hand. Additionally, it must be noted that most TANs, RANs, and GANs issued by states, counties, cities, towns, and school districts are also secured by the *general obligation pledge,* which is discussed later in this section.

Information Needed before Buying Tax or Revenue Anticipation Notes

Before purchasing a TAN, RAN, or GAN, the investor should obtain information in five areas in addition to what is required if long-term bonds are being considered for purchase. The five areas are:

1. Determining the reliability of the expected taxes and revenues.
2. The dependency of the note issuers on the expected monies.
3. The soundness of the issuers' budgetary operations.
4. The problems of "rollovers."
5. The historic and projected cash flows by month.

Each area is discussed below.

Determining the Reliability of the Expected Taxes and Revenues. If a TAN is issued in anticipation of property taxes, a question to ask is: What were the tax collection rates over the previous five years? Tax collection rates below 90 percent usually indicate serious tax collection problems. Additionally, if the issuer is budgeting 100 percent of the tax levy while collecting substantially less, serious problems can be expected.

If a RAN or GAN is issued in anticipation of state or federal grant monies, the first question to ask is if the grant has been legislatively authorized and committed by the state or federal government. Some RAN issuers, which included New York City prior to its RAN problems in 1975, would issue RANs without having all the anticipated grants committed by the higher levels of government. This practice may still be used by other local governments that are hard-pressed to balance their budgets and obtain quick cash through the sale of RANs. A safeguard against this is to see if the issuer has in its possession a fully signed grant agreement prior to the RAN or GAN sale.

Dependency of the Note Issuers on the Expected Monies. One measure of the credit worthiness of the TAN or RAN issuer is the degree of dependency of the issuer on the temporarily borrowed monies. As examples, some jurisdictions limit the amount of TANs that can be issued in anticipation of property taxes to a percentage of the prior year's levy that was actually collected. The state of New Jersey, which has one of the most fiscally conservative local government regulatory codes in the country, limits the annual sale of TANs and RANs by local governments to no more than 30 percent of the property taxes and various other revenues actually collected in the previous year. Many other states are more permissive and allow local governments to issue TANs and RANs as high as 75 to 100 percent of the monies previously collected or even expected to be received in the current fiscal year.

Soundness of the Issuers' Budgetary Operations. Another critical element of the TAN or RAN issuer's credit worthiness concerns determining whether or not the issuer has an overall history of prudent and disciplined financial management. One way to do this is to determine how well the issuer, over the previous five fiscal years, has maintained end-of-year fund balances in the major operating funds.

Problems of Rollovers. Key indications of fiscal problems are revealed when issuers either retire their TANs and RANs with the proceeds of new issues or issue TANs and RANs to be retired in a fiscal year following the one in which they were originally issued. Such practices are known as *rollovers,* and are sometimes used by hard-pressed issuers to disguise chronic operating budget deficits. To leave no doubt as to the soundness of their budgetary operations, many states, local governments, and special jurisdictions have established, either by statute or by administrative policy, that all TANs and RANs issued in one fiscal year must be retired before the end of that fiscal year. While such a policy reduces the flexibility of the issuer to deal with unexpected emergencies that may occur, it does help provide protection to the noteholders against TANs and RANs ever being used for hidden deficit financing.[10]

It must be noted that in some circumstances RANs and GANs can be properly issued for periods greater than 12 months. For an example, RANs of the Alabama Federal Aid Highway Finance Authority were issued in 1981 and were due two and a half years later in 1984. These RANs were in anticipation of the authority's receiving the federal share of its costs of certain interstate-highway construction projects. The Federal Highway Administration had established a 36-month reimbursement schedule. Therefore, in this instance the RANs must be outstanding for a period greater than 12 months.

The Historic and Projected Cash Flows by Month. The last area for investigation by the investor or analyst is the TAN or RAN issuer's cash flow history and projections. Initially, what is required here is a monthly accounting, going back over the previous fiscal year, which shows the beginning fund balances, revenues, expenditures, and end-of-month fund balances. In the analysis of this actual cash flow, the investor should determine how well the issuer has met its fiscal goals by maintaining at least a balanced budget and meeting all liabilities, including debt-service payments. The top portion of the exhibit on pages 106 and 107 is an historic monthly cash flow summary for TANs that were issued by a school district in New York state.

The bottom half of the exhibit is the projected monthly cash flows for the fiscal year in which the TANs were to be issued. Here, the investor should look to see if the issuer has included in the projections sufficient revenues to retire the TANs, and if the estimated revenue and expenditure amounts are realistic in light of the prior fiscal year's experience.

---

[10] It should be noted that this approach toward rollovers is contrary to the position of the late Jackson Phillips, former head of Moody's municipal department, who wrote in August 1975 that "the ability to refinance (rollover or renew) a maturing note has been regarded as a valuable backstop to notes of the revenue-anticipation type. . . . Evaluation of a note must, therefore, consider . . . the availability of refinancing through market rollover. . . ." "Liquidity of Temporary Loans," *Moody's Municipal Credit Report,* August 1, 1975. However, this policy statement was made before the New York City general obligation note crisis of 1975—which occurred largely because the use of the rollover mechanism had allowed the city to avoid retiring its notes and, instead, to annually increase its short-term debt until it had become unmanageable.

The Security behind Bond Anticipation Notes

BANs are secured principally by the ability of the issuers to have future access to the municipal bond market so as to retire the outstanding BANs with the proceeds of long-term bond sales. Additionally, it must be noted that most BANs issued by states, counties, cities, towns, and school districts are also secured by the general obligation pledge, which is discussed latter in this section.

Information Needed before Buying Bond Anticipation Notes

Two factors determine the ability of the issuers to gain market access; therefore, the BAN investors should obtain information in these areas:

1. The credit worthiness of the issuers.
2. Expected future market conditions and the flexibility of the issuers.

Credit Worthiness of the Issuers. Since the outstanding BANs are to be retired with the proceeds of long-term bond sales, the credit worthiness of the BANs are directly related to the credit worthiness of the underlying bond issuers. Therefore, the investor must obtain the same credit information on the BANs that he would if long-term bonds were being issued. In general, the stronger the bond credits, the greater the abilities of the BAN issuers to successfully complete their respective long-term bond sales. Additionally, the investor or analyst should also make a determination as to the probable market access and acceptance of the BAN issuer. That is, in the past how well have the bonds of the issuer been received in the marketplace? Has the issuer had to pay interest costs substantially higher than other bond issuers of similar credit worthiness? Answers to these questions will determine the credit risks involved when purchasing the BANs.

Expected Future Market Conditions and the Flexibility of the Issuers. While it is not possible for the BAN investor to know in advance the condition of the market when his BANs come due, it is safe to conclude that, if the issuer's credit worthiness is at least of investment-grade quality, there should usually be a market for that issuer's bonds. Of course, the weaker the credit worthiness and the larger the amount of BANs to be retired, the higher the rate of interest would have to be.

If the BANs come due at a time when the municipal bond market is experiencing rising interest rates, the BAN issuer should have the

LANCASTER CENTRAL SCHOOL DISTRICT
ERIE COUNTY, NEW YORK
TAX ANTICIPATION NOTES FOR 1985–1986 TAXES
Monthly Cash Flow—Actual and Estimated
(dollar amounts shown in thousands)

Dated: June 6, 1985

	July	Aug.	Sept.	Oct.	Nov.	Dec.	Jan.	Feb.	March	April	May	June
CASH FLOW 1984–1985 ACTUAL*												
Balance from Prior Month	$ 879	$3,979	$3,592	$2,926	$7,809	$7,962	$7,254	$6,171	$5,205	$3,847	$4,370	$4,650
CASH RECEIPTS												
Property Taxes	–0–	–0–	–0–	6,313	912	318	–0–	311	–0–	–0–	65	4
State Aid (Net)	–0–	–0–	535	580	558	–0–	–0–	–0–	–0–	1,621	1,650	1,640
Sales Tax	191	108	102	200	104	–0–	102	323	100	189	100	125
Other Revenues (a)	394	45	112	48	226	150	250	122	310	163	115	135
Note Proceeds	3,000	–0–	–0–	–0–	–0–	–0–	–0–	–0–	–0–	–0–	–0–	–0–
TOTAL AVAILABLE CASH	4,464	4,132	4,341	10,067	9,609	8,430	7,606	6,927	5,615	5,820	6,300	6,554
CASH DISBURSEMENTS												
Note Principal Repay	–0–	–0–	–0–	–0–	–0–	–0–	–0–	–0–	–0–	–0–	–0–	3,000
Note Interest Repay	–0–	–0–	–0–	–0–	–0–	–0–	–0–	–0–	–0–	–0–	–0–	–0–
Other Disbursements	485	540	1,415	2,258	1,647	1,176	1,435	1,722	1,768	1,450	1,650	2,800
TOTAL DISBURSEMENTS	485	540	1,415	2,258	1,647	1,176	1,435	1,722	1,768	1,450	1,650	5,800
MONTH END BALANCE												
FORWARD	3,979	3,592	2,926	7,809	7,962	7,254	6,171	5,205	3,847	4,370	4,650	754
CASH FLOW 1985–86												
Balance from Prior Month	$ 754(b)	$3,447	$3,005	$ 2,293	$7,758	$7,988	$7,508	$6,408	$5,258	$3,818	$4,368	$4,688
CASH RECEIPTS												
Property Taxes	–0–	–0–	–0–	7,000	1,000	485	–0–	350	–0–	–0–	–0–	–0–
State Aid (Net)	–0–	–0–	560	610	600	–0–	–0–	–0–	–0–	1,725	1,785	1,750
Sales Tax	150	115	110	200	110	110	150	160	110	200	110	125
Other Revenues (a)	43	43	118	55	220	150	250	125	300	125	125	125
Temporary Loans	3,000	–0–	–0–	–0–	–0–	–0–	–0–	–0–	–0–	–0–	–0–	–0–
TOTAL AVAILABLE CASH	3,947	3,605	3,793	10,158	9,688	8,733	7,908	7,043	5,668	5,868	6,388	6,688

CASH DISBURSEMENTS												
Temporary Loans Repaid	-0-	-0-	-0-	-0-	-0-	-0-	-0-	-0-	-0-	-0-	-0-	3,000
Other Disbursements	500	600	1,500	2,400	1,700	1,225	1,500	1,785	1,850	1,500	1,700	2,800
TOTAL DISBURSEMENTS	500	600	1,500	2,400	1,700	1,225	1,500	1,785	1,850	1,500	1,700	5,800
MONTH END BALANCE FORWARD	3,447	3,005	2,293	7,758	7,988	7,508	6,408	5,258	3,818	4,368	4,688	888(c)

* Cash flow is Actual to April 30, 1985; no assurance can be made as to estimates.

Notes: (a) Includes earnings on investments.
(b) June 30, 1985 balance.
(c) Projected balance as of June 30, 1986. Does not reflect $225,000, which amount represents a part of the District's investment in defaulted repurchase agreements with the Lion Capital Group. The District can not predict at this time if and when the $225,000 principal amount of said investment will be recovered. Accordingly, the 1985–86 cash flow projection assumes the unavailability of said $225,000. The matter is in litigation.

flexibility to retire the maturing BANs with a new BAN issue instead of issuing long-term bonds. Most state and local government finance regulations recognize this need for allowing BANs to be retired from new BAN issues. Also, the ability of the issuer to refund, in the municipal market, the maturing BANs with new BANs is directly related to the credit quality of the issuer. It should also be noted that, unlike most TANs and RANs, BANs can be refunded—that is, rolled over—into new BANs. However, prudent issuers usually are limited by local laws to having their BANs outstanding for no longer than five to eight years. If there is no limit as to how long the BANs can be outstanding, the temptation is great for the BAN issuer to avoid funding out the BANs with a bond issue.

Security behind the General Obligation Pledge

Many TANs and RANs issued by states, cities, towns, counties, and school districts are secured by the general obligation pledge. What this means is that the issuers are legally obligated to use, if necessary, their full taxing powers and available revenues to pay the noteholders. Therefore, if a tax anticipation note is issued by a city secured by property taxes as well as by the general obligation pledge, and if the city's property tax collection rate that particular year does not generate sufficient taxes to pay the noteholder, the city must use other resources to make the noteholder whole, including available monies in its general fund. Of course, the importance of the general obligation pledge is directly related to the diversification of the issuer's revenue base and lack of dependence on note sales, as well as on the soundness of its budgetary operations. Many BANs are also secured by the general obligation pledge of the issuer. If the overall credit quality, revenue structure, and market image of the underlying general obligation issuer are stronger than those of the agency or department that has issued the BANs, then the general obligation pledge would be a positive factor since it would strengthen market access either for a rollover of the BANs or for retiring them with the proceeds of a long-term bond sale.

CONSTRUCTION LOAN NOTES

There are five major credit risk areas that the investor should keep in mind when determining the degree of insulation from adversity of construction loan notes. These are short-term securities that are used to provide interim construction monies for multifamily housing projects. The areas of credit concern are:

1. Is federal insurance already in place during construction?
2. Is permanent financing escrowed or committed?
3. Is there adequate cash flow protection?
4. Are there adequate construction and certification periods?
5. How reliable are the CLN investment agreements?

Is Federal Insurance Already in Place during Construction? Before the construction loan notes are issued the investor should determine if there is Federal Housing Administration (FHA) mortgage insurance already in place. FHA insurance covers construction loan advances regardless of whether or not the project is completed. This provides comfort to the noteholders should the developer default on his interest or principal payments prior to the maturity of the notes.

Is Permanent Financing Escrowed or Committed? Another key element in the determination of the credit quality of a construction loan note is whether or not there is an approved permanent financing plan to take out the construction loan notes. There are generally two plans possible.

In one type of financing plan, bonds are originally sold at the same time as the notes. The bond proceeds are placed in escrow pending project completion, cost certification, and final endorsement for FHA insurance. Then, once these three events occur, the bond proceed monies can be released and used to pay the noteholders. Bonds that are simultaneously sold with construction loan notes are usually done so under HUD's Section 8–11 (b) program, which is primarily for local issuers.

In the second type of note takeout plan, the Government National Mortgage Agency (GNMA) is committed to provide cash—which along with other required monies such as contributions by the developer—is used to retire the construction loan notes. For the GNMA takeout to occur, the project must be completed, cost certified, and have received final endorsement for FHA insurance.

Is There Adequate Cash Flow Protection? Still another concern is to determine beforehand how well designed are the cash flow projections. For CLNs where bond proceeds are escrowed, and for GNMA issues, temporary investment earnings, interest payments by the developers, and construction payment drawdowns of the CLN proceeds should be based on worst-case assumptions so as to meet all CLN interest payment dates. The cash flow projections should be presented in a format that shows by month the total expected income and expenses. Additionally, the cash flow projections should show worst-case scenarios covering periods when mortgage insurance payments and other backup security features or liquidity enhancements may have to be depended upon. Of course, the combination of the investment earnings and interest payments that the developer makes on advanced monies should be the basis for the financing, though the note trustee should have immediate access to the other security structures as well.

There are additional concerns in the case of CLNs where a GNMA takeout is planned. Since the GNMA takeout only provides 97½ percent of the amount needed to retire the construction loan notes, the gap must be provided for in advance. The investor should make sure that expected investment earnings together with cash contributions by the developer are sufficient. Additionally, since the GNMA takeout could occur months before the actual maturity of the construction loan notes, the investor should check to see that investment agreements are in place for the temporary investment of the GNMA monies, or if there is a provision to call the notes following the GNMA takeout.

Are There Adequate Construction and Certification Periods? Because of possible construction delays and the time required by FHA/GNMA for the processing of the final mortgage documents, ample time should be allowed between the expected completion date of the project construction and the construction loan note maturity date. Generally, a six-month lag between targeted construction completion and note maturity is not sufficient. While there may not be a default by the mortgagor on the FHA-insured mortgage loan, a delay in construction or final FHA endorsement could have a negative impact on note security by preventing the timely release of permanent financing funds. Therefore, the issuer's financing plan should include a minimum period of approximately eight months between the expected construction completion date and the maturity of the construction loan note.

How Reliable Are the CLN Investment Agreements? Because many local issuers have limited backup resources available, and the projected investment earnings on the unspent note proceeds play a crucial role in the financing plan, the investment agreement is also of concern in the credit risk analysis. If the investment agreement is in the form of a contract with a commercial bank, the bank should be well capitalized and of high investment quality itself. If the investment agreement takes the form of a repurchase or "repo" agreement, the investor must examine certain other factors that are discussed in an earlier section of this chapter.

It should also be noted that construction loan notes issued by state housing agencies, as compared to local housing agencies, usually have additional security elements that make some of the above guidelines less applicable. This particularly pertains to the eight-month period between the date expected for project completion and the note maturity date. Generally, as compared to local housing issuers, state housing agencies have staffs that are capable of monitoring the construction progress; have demonstrated market access in the event rollover notes must be sold; and have general-fund balances, established lines of credit, and other reserves that can provide added liquidity to the project financings, if necessary. Nonetheless, it should be noted that construction loan notes, whether they are issued by state housing agencies or local housing agencies, and which are well secured in all of the five above areas, are usually of high credit quality and present very little credit risk to the investor.

10

Investment Features of Selected Local Bond Securities

Under our federal system of government, states in the first instance determine the security structures for local municipal bonds. This is accomplished in their respective state constitutions, statutory laws, and court decisions. Because of the diverse nature of states, the security structures for local bonds sometimes differ significantly from state to state. General obligation bonds issued by school districts in one state may have additional bondholder protections that school bonds issued in another state may not have. Yet, many investors are unaware of the differences. The purpose of this chapter is twofold. First, it is to describe some of the distinguishing differences between the more important local bonds. The second is to highlight those that have special strengths as well as those that have weaknesses.

In this chapter are 13 specific sections. The first five are on MAC bonds, North Slope, Borough, Alaska bonds, San Francisco BART bonds, New York City housing authority bonds, and certain other New York City double-barreled bonds. The respective strengths and weaknesses of these five specific bonds are described. The next seven sections are on the respective security enhancements created by specific states to further secure whole generic groups of local bonds most of which are general obligations. They include the Texas "Guaranteed" school bonds, the Texas State University Constitutional Appropriation Bonds, the Pennsylvania School District "Act 150" Bonds, school bonds in New York State, New Jersey's "qualified" school and city bonds as well as its "insured" school bonds, and Michigan's "qualified" school bonds. The last section of this chapter discusses the strengths and weaknesses of "MUD" bonds issued in the state of Texas. In selecting bonds to be discussed in this chapter, we have primarily focused on those that are of the larger supply in the industry.

MAC'S "SECOND RESOLUTION" BONDS

The Municipal Assistance Corporation (MAC) was created by the state of New York in 1975 to provide financing for the city of New York for capital improvements as well as for funding out the city's budget deficit. As of 1986, it has issued over $9 billion in municipal bonds under two separate bond resolutions. Under the First General Resolution approximately $1.682 billion have been issued and are outstanding; and under the Second General Resolution approximately $6.505 billion have been issued and are outstanding.[1] This section focuses on the larger of the two bond security structures, MAC's Second Resolution bonds.

The Security

Pledged revenues are defined as annual appropriations from the state legislature of: (1) general revenue-sharing monies (Per Capita Aid) due the city of New York; (2) sales tax revenues collected by the state from a 4-percent sales tax imposed within the city on most retail sales; and (3) stock-transfer tax revenues collected by the state on the transfer of stock and certain other securities.

Annual debt service, operating expenses, and reserve requirements on MAC's First General Resolution bonds have a prior lien on the sales tax and stock-transfer tax revenues. After MAC expenses are met, including debt service on the bonds, the remaining monies flow to the city of New York's general fund.

The Flow of Funds

Sales taxes *plus* stock-transfer taxes collected *less* operating expenses of MAC, *less* maximum annual debt service (DS) payable on the outstanding First Resolution bonds *plus* available Per Capita Aid *pays*

---

[1] These amounts include bonds that could be issued in connection with MAC's commercial paper program.

debt service on the Second Resolution bonds. Below is a table that shows the flow of funds and debt service coverage on the Second Resolution bonds.[2]

Sales taxes	$1,815,000,000
Stock-transfer taxes	$1,055,000,000
MAC operating expenses	(11,000,000)
DS on First Resolution bonds	(344,000,000)
Net available	$2,515,000,000
Available Per Capita Aid	399,000,000
Total available for DS on Second Resolution bonds	$2,914,000,000
Maximum DS on Second Resolution bonds	$ 885,000,000
DS coverage	3.29 times

Note: For 12 months ended October 31, 1985.

Although stock-transfer taxes are still available for debt service payments, if they are not required for debt service payments, they are rebated back to stock-transfer taxpayers. Full rebates have been made since October 1, 1981.

The Additional Bonds Test

Second Resolution bonds can be issued only if available revenues cover maximum annual debt service on the old and to-be-issued Second Resolution bonds by two times. Additionally, no more than $10 billion in total MAC bonds can be issued. Available revenues used for the additional bonds test are derived from:

1. The *lesser* of either the sales and stock-transfer taxes collected over the previous 12 months; or, the amounts estimated to be collected over the next 12 months.
2. The amount of Per Capita Aid paid to MAC during the current year.
3. *Less* maximum annual DS on the First Resolution bonds and MAC operating expenses for the current year.

---

[2] Preliminary official statement for $123.75 million. Municipal Assistance Corporation Series 56 Bonds, dated December 2, 1985.

The Capital Reserve Aid Fund

A debt-service reserve is to be funded at 1.00 times the amount of debt service to be paid in the succeeding calendar year on Second Resolution bonds outstanding and to be issued. This fund is subject to the legislative makeup provision, the so-called moral obligation. (For additional information about the moral obligation, see Chapter 8.)

Credit Worthiness Strengths

Below are six aspects of the bond security that provide comfort to the investor.

3.29 Times Maximum Annual DS Coverage. Available revenues in 1985 would have covered maximum annual DS in 1988 of $885 million on outstanding and new Second Resolution bonds by an estimated 3.29 times.

It should also be noted that a more conservative formula for determining the maximum annual DS coverage on the Second Resolution bonds is to take the DS on the First Resolution bonds, add it to the maximum DS on the Second Resolution bonds, and then divide that number into the available revenues. Using this formula, the coverage would be 2.64 times.

Almost One Year's Maximum Annual DS Reserve. There is a Capital Reserve Aid Fund for the Second General Resolution bonds that, on September 30, 1985, held securities valued at $828.0 million. Maximum annual DS on all the bonds—including bonds that conditionally are obligated to be issued—was estimated to be $885 million (in 1988).

Insulation from New York City. Annually, the pledged revenues cannot pass to the city of New York until the DS on the bonds has first been provided for.

It should also be noted that while a legal test of the MAC security structure in a worst-case senario (*i.e.,* a New York City bankruptcy) has not occurred, the authority of the state to appropriate the earmarked monies to MAC has been upheld by the highest state court, and the bond attorneys have opined that the earmarked monies are legally insulated from any possible suits from creditors of New York City or the city itself.

The State's Moral Obligation Pledge. If the Capital Reserve Aid Fund should have to be used, the state must be notified and may replenish it if the legislature makes an appropriation. While this makeup provision is not mandatory, the state of New York has assisted all other moral obligation bonds where the need occurred.

Issuance Test for First Resolution Bonds. There is an issuance test for the First Resolution bonds that limits annual DS to $425 million. (Maximum annual DS in 1985 is $344 million.)

Strong Coverage Test Required for New Bond Issues. A two times coverage test of available revenues for maximum annual DS on the old and to-be-issued Second Resolution bonds is required. It should be noted that under existing statutes, MAC is not authorized to issue additional debt, excluding refunding bonds, after December 31, 1984.

Credit Weaknesses

Below are four aspects of the bond security that are potential weaknesses to the credit quality.

Monies Must be Annually Appropriated. While the state legislature has appropriated Per Capita Aid, the sales tax, and the stock-transfer tax to MAC since 1975, under the state constitution the legislature cannot be legally obligated to do so. Future budgetary problems of the state could adversely influence the amount of Per Capita Aid that is appropriated.

Second Lien Bonds. The First General Resolution bonds have a prior lien on the sales and stock-transfer tax revenues. However, the Per Capita Aid is not so pledged.

Elastic Revenue Base. The sales and stock-transfer tax revenues are very elastic and could decline in a prolonged economic recession.

Conclusion

In summary, the credit worthiness of the Second Resolution bonds is strengthened by the high coverage of maximum annual debt service (3.28 times); the substantial debt reserve fund ($828 million); the insulation of MAC revenues from the city of New York; the state's moral obligation pledge; and the strong two-times coverage test for additional bonds.

The credit worthiness is weakened by the need for the state legislature to annually appropriate the earmarked monies, the prior lien of the First Resolution bonds, the elasticity of the pledged tax revenues, and the uncertainty concerning both the state's and the city's budgetary operations.

NORTH SLOPE BOROUGH, ALASKA SELLS EXCESSIVE AMOUNTS OF BONDS*

With a population of 10,171, the Borough has an amount of general obligation bonds and notes outstanding similar to the city of Philadelphia, with a population of 1,665,382. The Borough, while encompassing an area of 88,281 square miles, is located north of the Arctic Circle; its small population is distributed among eight villages and communities. It was initially incorporated in 1972 so that the native population would benefit directly from the considerable wealth generated from Prudhoe Bay and the oil pipeline.

Since that time, the Borough has embarked on a massive bond issuance program that has been greatly inflated by the sheer remoteness of its location. A prime example is the allocation of more than $55 million for the acquisition of local gravel for use in various construction projects. The six-year bond issuance program is also swelled by the broad range of development activities (such as building homes for school teachers) undertaken in each community. As an example, the village of Wainwright, containing 483 people, is scheduled to receive $82.3 million in capital projects including construction of 14 housing units, a school, community facility, water and sewer facilities, an electric generation system, and an airport. Additionally, the debt issuance program, according to the Borough itself, is not primarily designed to broaden the economic base of the Borough, but does serve as the primary source of employment in many of the villages.

The Borough has greatly accelerated its debt issuance since 1982; the outstanding debt at the end of fiscal year 1982 was $587.4 million, increasing to $955.7 million (including $200 million BANs) one year later and $1.2 billion, at the close of fiscal year 1985. Debt factors are extremely unfavorable with an 11.9 percent debt burden and a debt per capita of $118,320.00. Debt service accounted for 54 percent of expenditures in 1983. Although debt issuance for the remaining capital projects appears to be minimal in future years, according to Borough documents there is a strong indication that the only major constraint on future borrowing would be the 20-mill tax levy, which is the maximum amount of local taxes paid by oil companies that can be credited against their state of Alaska tax liabilities. Clearly, the bonds can only be considered as being of low investment quality over the long term.

---

* Coauthored with William E. Oliver of the Municipal Bond Research Department, Merrill Lynch, Pierce, Fenner & Smith, Inc.

The Borough's vast tax base, derived from oil and gas exploration activities and pipeline transmission, continues to provide adequate security for the bonds. Recent refundings have brought principal maturities more in line with the expected life of the Borough's oil and gas reserves. Of course, it should also be noted that current bondholders could have some of their bonds refunded, which of course increases the credit quality of their investment substantially.

SOME UNUSUALLY WELL-SECURED SAN FRANCISCO BAY AREA RAPID TRANSIT DISTRICT (BART) BONDS

The purpose of this section is to provide information on the unique features of the San Francisco Bay Area Rapid Transit District (BART) general obligation bonds. BART was established by the state of California to build and operate 71 miles of double-track urban rail transit routes serving San Francisco, the cities of Berkeley, Oakland, and Daly City,[3] and suburban areas within Alameda and Contra Costa counties. These have been financed by issuing debt, including general obligation bonds, which have been authorized by the electorate, and which are secured by unlimited ad valorem taxes on the full value of all taxable property within the BART boundaries.

Who Collects the Property Taxes?

Annually, the Directors of BART are required by state law to determine the amount of property taxes necessary to pay BART G.O. bond debt service and certain operating expenses.[4] They then levy the taxes, and the tax collectors of the counties that BART overlaps include the BART levies in their tax bills.

How Strong Is This Security?

The bond counsel to BART has indicated that there are no mechanical or legal procedures that he is aware of that make the BART unlimited property tax pledge any weaker than the pledge behind individual county general obligation bonds.[5] If some taxpayers, for whatever rea-

---

[3] Daly City property owners are not subject to the BART levy.

[4] State of California Public Utilities Code, Sections 28500, 29121, 29122, and 29128 (1957, and amended thereafter).

[5] Interview with C. Richard Walker, Orrick, Herrington & Sutcliffe, San Francisco, February 24, 1978.

son, do not pay their property taxes, foreclosure proceedings are initiated, and in the meantime, the tax levy is raised to make up the difference. If a county tax collector should ever refuse to levy and collect the property taxes for BART, a mandamus can be obtained by the bondholders or by BART, commanding the county officials to collect the taxes and turn them over to BART.

Did the 1978 Jarvis Tax-Reduction Law Weaken the Security?

No. The Jarvis tax-reduction law of 1978 limited ad valorem property taxes to 1 percent of full value. However, taxes levied to pay debt service on voter-approved general obligation bonds (which included the BART G.O.s) were specifically excluded from the limitation.

OLD NEW YORK CITY HOUSING AUTHORITY BONDS THAT ARE NOW FEDERALLY BACKED

Since 1968, certain bonds issued by the New York City Housing Authority that were originally secured only by authority revenues and the guarantee of the city of New York have been converted to a federal program. Because of the strong security features of the federal pledge, such converted bonds are of the highest credit quality. This section identifies those bonds that are now federally secured and explains how Public Housing Authority bonds are secured.[6]

Background

The New York City Housing Authority (NYCHA) was established in 1934 by the city of New York to construct and operate public housing projects for persons of low income. It is the nation's largest and oldest public housing program. Financing for these housing projects has been primarily from three sources. Most projects were financed from proceeds of authority bond sales in which the bonds were secured by a contractual pledge of annual contributions from HUD to be applied first to the payment of principal and interest on

---

[6] Data sources for this case study include: New York City Housing Authority Annual Fiscal Report, dated 12/31/79; calendars of the New York City Board of Estimate, dated 9/18/80, 6/26/80, and 5/29/80; interview with the general manager of the New York City Housing Authority on 9/17/80; interviews with the comptroller of the New York Housing Authority on 9/17/80 and 9/22/80; and New York City Housing Authority Consolidated Financial Statements, dated 12/31/84.

the bonds. The annual monies from Washington were paid directly to the paying agent for the bonds, and the bondholders were given specific legal rights to enforce the pledge. These bonds, known as either Public Housing Authority, or New Housing Authority bonds, are of the highest credit quality because of this federal pledge.[7] The second source of financing for the authority came from loans made to it by the state of New York. The third source of financing for the housing projects came from the authority's selling its own bonds that were guaranteed only by the city of New York. Each housing project constructed by the authority was financed under either the federal program, the state program, or the city program.

Conversion to the Federal Program

Under the federal laws, beginning in the late 1960s certain authority housing projects that had been financed through the sale of authority bonds originally guaranteed only by the city of New York were incorporated into the federal program. Debt service on authority bonds issued for the housing projects named in Exhibit 1 is now paid by the federal government (HUD) directly to the paying agent for the bonds.

Conclusion

In terms of bond security, the above bonds now have the same security features as the ones that had originally been issued as Public Housing Authority or New Housing Authority bonds and are of the highest credit quality.

NEW YORK CITY BONDS THAT HAVE TWO LAYERS OF PROTECTION

Unlike other general obligation bonds of New York City, those issued for elementary and secondary schools have a double-barrel security feature. Besides being general obligations and thus payable out of

---

[7] These bonds are not to be confused with the authority's $27.12 million Section 8 assisted mortgage revenue bonds that were issued in 1978, and which are *not* guaranteed by the U.S. government, though they do receive federal subsidies under certain circumstances.

EXHIBIT 1 New York City Housing Authority
Bonds that Have Been Converted
to the Federal Program

Year of Change	Project Name on Bond
1968	Colonial Park
	Consolidated City
	(Eastchester City
	Sheepshead Bay, South
	Beach, Woodside)
1972	Elliott
	Dyckman
	Lexington
	Ravenswood
	Riis
	Sedgwick
1979	Arverne
1980	Gun Hill
	Parkside
	Nostrand
	Glenwood
	Todt Hill
	Pelham Parkway
	Berry
	Pomonok

general-fund revenues and real estate taxes, the bondholder can turn to the state comptroller for direct payment in the event of default by New York City. In this section this security feature is described as well as the specific New York City general obligation bonds that are double-barreled.

How the Security Structure Works

Under Section 99–b of the New York State finance law, the bondholder can, in a default, file a claim with the state comptroller. This security program is also discussed in another section of this chapter in terms of how it relates to school districts in New York State.

It is the duty of the state comptroller to immediately investigate the circumstances of the alleged default to determine if it indeed has occurred. If it has, the state comptroller must deduct and withhold from the next succeeding "state aid to education" payment an amount sufficient to pay the bondholders. As of June 30, 1984, outstanding New York City general obligation bonds issued for "school purposes" totaled $671,289,814, and state-aid-to-education payments made in fiscal year 1984 were $907,722,297.[8]

Bonds that Qualify

Some New York City general obligation bonds issued for school purposes are for higher education, and not for elementary and secondary schools. Since the city does not distinguish on its printed bonds the specific school purpose, the differentiation of the elementary- and secondary-school-purpose bonds from the higher-education bonds is not readily possible visually. It is, however, essential to make such a distinction. If even a small fraction of the bonds of a particular issue are for higher-education purposes, questions may be raised as to whether the entire issue qualifies under Section 99–b.

Exhibit 2 lists New York City general obligation school bonds that are limited to elementary- and secondary-school-construction purposes. It should be emphasized that, in order for a New York City general obligation bond to be double-barreled, it must not only have the correct date of issue, coupon rate, and maturity date, but also it must state on the face of the bond that it is for school purposes. If it does not, then it does not qualify under Section 99–b.

Drawbacks

Drawbacks of the Section 99–b mechanism in regard to the New York City general obligation bonds are twofold. First, the Section 99–b mechanism only becomes operational when a bond default has already occurred. That is, it is a remedy for a default, but does not prevent one from occurring. Second, state-aid-to-education payments are made only at specified times of the year. Therefore, a default may occur at a time when the state comptroller does not have any appropriated state funds available for the eligible New York City general obligation bondholders. Nonetheless, the mechanism does provide the bondholder with added protection that other New York City general obligation bonds do not have.

---

[8] City of New York comptroller's report for fiscal 1984. It should also be noted that the New York City Educational Construction Fund Revenue Bonds, 1972 Series A, also share this security feature. As of June 30, 1984, no more than $37.650 million of the original $51.15 million bond issue remained outstanding.

EXHIBIT 2 New York City General Obligation Bonds: Elementary and Secondary Schools Only*

Date of Issue	Coupon	Serials Through
October 15, 1971	7.40	April 15, 1983–87
July 15, 1972	6.50	January 15, 1983–87
January 1, 1973	5.25	July 1, 1984–87
August 1, 1973	6.90	February 1, 1987–88
August 1, 1973	7.00	February 1, 1984–87
November 1, 1973	5.50	May 1, 1985–88
February 1, 1974	5.80	August 1, 1986–87
February 1, 1974	5.50	August 1, 1987–88
March 1, 1974	6.00	September 1, 1983–88
August 1, 1974	8.00	February 1, 1985–89
October 15, 1974	8.00	April 15, 1983–89
February 15, 1975	7.50	August 15, 1989

* The identification of the double-barreled bonds is derived from: notice of sales for the specific bonds involved; section 99-b of the New York State Finance Law titled: "Withholding of state aid for school purposes upon default in payment of obligations of the prospective recipient;" city of New York comptroller's reports for the years: 1947–50 and 1965–75; review of the capital budget working papers for the specific bond issues involved.

TEXAS "GUARANTEED" SCHOOL BONDS*

The Texas School District Bond Guarantee Program was authorized by an amendment to the State constitution approved by voters on November 7, 1983. The amendment permits the use of the assets of the Texas Permanent School Fund, currently at $5 billion, for the guarantee of principal and interest payments on qualified school district general obligation bonds. The program will have a capacity to guarantee bonds of up to twice the cost or market value, whichever is less, of the Permanent School Fund, as estimated by the state board of education and certified by the state auditor. The objective of the guarantee program is to reduce borrowing costs for school building projects.

What Is the Texas Permanent School Fund?

The Permanent School Fund is composed of revenues generated by oil and gas royalties from state lands endowed in a trust fund created

---

* This section was written by William E. Oliver.

in the 1876 constitution for the purpose of benefitting Texas public schools. The fund's assets are invested in a restricted group of corporate bonds and equities, U.S. Treasury securities and cash. Interest and dividends from the fund historically have been used to provide state financial aid to school districts.

How the Bonds Qualify

In order to qualify, a school district must be deemed to be in sound financial condition by the commissioner of education, following a review of the purpose of the bond issue, its consistency with the district's five-year plan for accreditation, and the historical and projected financial operations of the district. Once approved, a statement relating the constitutional and statutory authority for the guarantee and the endorsement of the commissioner will be printed on the bonds. The guarantee is not effective until certification has been given by the attorney general. It is anticipated that most school districts will utilize this program for bond issuance.

How the Guaranteed Bond Procedure Would Work

The bonds would initially be secured by the taxing powers of the local school district. However, if the school district is unable to make principal and/or interest payments on its guaranteed bonds, it must notify the state commissioner at least five days prior to maturity. Upon notification, the commissioner will authorize a transfer of the amount required for debt service from the Permanent Fund to the district's paying agent. The state comptroller will then be directed to withhold the amount of the payment, plus interest, from the first state monies payable to the school district and deposit these funds to the Permanent Fund's credit.

Conclusion

Clearly, these bonds are of the highest credit quality. This is because of:

1. The significant size of the endowment supporting the program, as well as the acceptable, though varying credit quality of the Permanent School Fund's investments.
2. Strong statutory regulations restricting the utilization of the Permanent Fund's assets and the protections built into the guarantee that precludes overleveraging.

3. Provisions for detailed review and analysis of the participants' credit worthiness.
4. The establishment of a mechanism designed to ensure timely payment of debt service prior to an actual default occurring.

TEXAS STATE UNIVERSITY "CONSTITUTIONAL APPROPRIATION" BONDS*

What Are Constitutional Appropriation Bonds?

On November 6, 1984, a proposal to appropriate $100 million annually for ten years to support higher education at these universities was approved by the voters.

Under the provisions approved by voters, and contained in Article VII, Section 17 of the Texas Constitution, the state will make a continuing Constitutional appropriation of $100 million each year for 10 years, beginning on September 1, 1985. These bonds are payable from the first monies coming into the state treasury not otherwise appropriated by the Texas Constitution. The bonds must be in serial form, subject to competitive bidding and scheduled to mature by August 31, 1994. No more than 50% of the annual appropriation can be pledged for debt service payments; the remaining monies must be used for capital improvement projects. Although this formula is subject to change by a two-thirds vote of the state legislature in 1990, the legislature may not reduce appropriations in such a way as to impair the payment of debt service obligations.

How Does the Program Work?

In order to participate, each university must adhere to provisions of the Excellence in Higher Education Act of 1985. The bonds must be issued in accordance with the structure detailed above, and approved by the attorney general. Following certification by the state comptroller that sufficient monies have been appropriated, the state university's board of trustees must file a claim in compliance with procedures established under Texas law (Article 4357, Vernon's Texas Civil Statutes as amended). The Comptroller then issues a warrant directly to

---

* This section was written by William E. Oliver.

the bond paying agent/registrar at least 15 days prior to the due date for principal and interest.

How Are the Funds Allocated?

The appropriations are allocated according to a formula established in the Excellence in Higher Education Act of 1985. This formula takes into consideration the condition of facilities and their utilization, the programs offered by the institutions, the existence of medical facilities and compliance with the Texas desegregation plan. Annual appropriations are to be made to the state universities as follows:

East Texas State University	$ 3.3 million
Lamar University	7.2 million
Midwestern State University	1.7 million
North Texas State University	10.9 million
Pan American University	3.1 million
Stephen F. Austin State University	5.1 million
Texas College of Osteopathic Medicine	2.2 million
Texas State University System	19.5 million
Texas Southern University	6.8 million
Texas Tech University	10.7 million
Texas Tech Univ. Health Sciences Ctr.	4.3 million
Texas Woman's University	3.6 million
University of Houston System	15.7 million
University of South Texas System	3.6 million
West Texas State University	2.3 million
TOTAL	100.0 million

Conclusion

These bonds, like the Texas "Guaranteed" Bonds are of the highest credit quality. This is because of:

1. The constitutional authorization for appropriations, allocating first monies not otherwise appropriated by the Texas Constitution to be used for the payment of debt service.
2. The commitment to improving higher education demonstrated by the government in the creation of the Excellence in Higher Education Act of 1985 and the voters in approving an Amendment to the Texas Constitution authorizing an annual appropriation of $100 million.
3. The provision that the formula allocating 50% of annual appropriations for debt service cannot be changed by the legislature so as to impair the repayment of debt.
4. The structuring of all bonds to be retired within 10 years.

PENNSYLVANIA SCHOOL DISTRICT "ACT 150" BONDS*

Bondholders of Pennsylvania School District bonds receive additional security under the so-called "Act 150" provisions, amending Section 633 of the Pennsylvania School Code. The act provides that in the event of nonpayment of debt service by a school district, the Secretary of Education will withhold any portion of the state appropriation due the school district and will pay those monies directly to the trustee. However, these provisions only assure the ultimate repayment of principal and interest and do not either prevent a default from occurring or necessarily ensure timely repayment of debt. Investors thus should be cognizant of the underlying credit quality of the issuer in order to avoid certain secondary market risks which could arise, either during a period of severe fiscal strain experienced by the district or in a default situation. It is also important to examine the district's cash flow to determine that adequate appropriations are available when debt service payments become due.

State Aid to School Districts

Education subsidies to Pennsylvania School Districts are determined by utilizing a complex reimbursement formula which is based on enrollment statistics and district expenditure totals. Although assistance is based in part on pupil count, the Public School Code provides that subsidies in any given year may not be less than the amount realized in the previous year. This protects districts which have declining enrollments. The principal forms of the state aid subsidies are the instructional subsidy for general operations and the debt service subsidy for certain bond issues deemed eligible for reimbursement by the state. However, the state maintains additional subsidies for smaller school districts and for special education, transportation, and vocational and remedial education. State subsidies are a major source of funding for school districts, in some cases, accounting for greater than 50% of annual revenues.

Monitoring by The Department of Education

The Department maintains a computerized database which is used to annually monitor the fiscal stability of each district based on approxi-

---

* This section was written by William E. Oliver and Christopher J. Mauro, Municipal Bond Research Department, Merrill Lynch, Pierce, Fenner & Smith, Inc.

mately 20 early warning signals of financial distress. Additionally, the Pennsylvania Public School Code provides that the state may appoint a special three member Board of Control if the district meets one of seven predetermined conditions of fiscal instability. The board is appointed to assume control of the operations of the school district. Among the many special powers granted to the board, it may increase levies and suspend professional employees if necessary to bring about a sound financial condition. These procedures provide some protection against municipal bond defaults.

Act 150 Withholding Provisions

A certain degree of bondholder protection is provided by the provisions of Section 633 of the Pennsylvania Public School Code of 1949 as amended by Act 150 of 1975. These provisions provide that, in the event of nonpayment of principal or interest on any indebtedness of the school district, the Secretary of Education shall withhold from the state appropriations due to the school district an amount equal to the unpaid debt service and will forward that amount directly to the trustee. Appropriations available for debt service consist of monies due the school district during the entire fiscal year. The schedule of appropriations is tied to the state's fiscal year which closes on June 30th.

Act 150 Drawbacks

1. The Act 150 provisions only become effective when a bond default has already occurred. That is, it is a remedy for a default but does not prevent a default from occurring.
2. While the Act 150 safeguards provide for the repayment of interest and principal, the available funding is derived from state appropriations which are tied to the budget process. The Act is not a form of state guarantee. Although emergency mechanisms can be put into place to provide the necessary funding, the availability of appropriations may be subject to timing problems, particularly during periods of budgetary stringency at the state level.
3. The special withholding measures are not a part of any contractual obligation with the bondholder and are based on statutory provisions which can be modified or repealed by the legislature at any time. However, Act 150 has been in place since 1975 and appears unlikely that its provisions will be significantly altered.

TWO SPECIAL STRENGTHS OF SCHOOL BONDS IN NEW YORK STATE

There are two special security features of New York school district general obligation bonds. The first is that any uncollected taxes are reimbursed to the school district by the county, thereby assuring 100 percent school tax collections by the end of the fiscal year. The second is that, if necessary, state aid due the school districts must be used to pay the bondholders.

School Districts in New York State

School districts in New York State are units of local government created to operate public schools, authorized to levy real estate taxes, and authorized to issue debt including both general obligation bonds and notes. Under the state constitution this debt is payable, if necessary, from the levy of ad valorem taxes on the full value of all taxable property within the boundaries of the respective school districts. For school districts that are in cities with populations under 125,000, there is a debt limit of 5 percent of the issuer's assessed valuation. Within other districts, the debt limit is 10 percent as determined by the state legislature. There is no limit on the taxes that can be levied for payment of the debt.

Why Is the Tax Collection Rate Always 100 Percent for Most School Districts?

Tax collectors of the school districts collect the school tax levies, except that in cities of 125,000 or more the city tax collectors also collect the school levies. In towns of less than 125,000 people, the same arrangement can be made by mutual agreement. Under New York State law the school districts receive delinquent school tax payments from their respective county treasurers. In this way the school districts receive 100 percent of their annual tax levies, and the counties themselves are responsible for collecting the unpaid taxes. It should also be noted that generally there are two exceptions to this procedure: school districts in Westchester County and school districts located within cities.

Additional Bond Security

If a school district does not pay its debt service, the bondholder (under a New York State law enacted in 1959) can file a statement with the state comptroller, who must deduct and withhold from the next succeeding state-aid payment any amount sufficient to pay the bondholder. The security feature is Section 99-b of the State Finance Law.

How Important to the School District's Budget Are the State-Aid Payments?

New York State first began to provide local school districts with annual aid in 1925, when the state began to assist in paying for physical improvements. In 1962 the state began providing school districts with annual aid for operating expenses as well. The state-aid monies are derived from a special formula that is based on weighted average daily attendance in the respective school districts compared to the statewide average daily attendance. Some school districts receive up to 85 percent of their revenues from the state of New York; many depend on state-aid programs for at least 50 percent. In many if not all school districts, the total amount of annual state aid is substantially more than the annual debt service.

Section 99-b Drawbacks

There are three aspects of the Section 99-b security structure that the investor should be aware of.

1. The Section 99-b mechanism only becomes operational when a bond default has already occurred. That is, it is a remedy for a default but does not prevent a default from occurring.

2. State-aid-to-education payments are made only at certain times of the year. Therefore, a default may occur at a time when the state comptroller does not have any appropriated state funds available for the specific school district.

3. Where a school district has defaulted in the payment of interest or principal due upon school bonds, the comptroller is first required to withhold and pay from state funds appropriated for the support of common schools the employer's contribution to the New York State Teachers' Retirement System, before payments to the holders of the delinquent bonds can be made.

Additional Case-Law Support

Security for bonds of all New York State issuers, including school districts, was further strengthened in November 1976 when the New York State Court of Appeals declared the New York State Emergency Moratorium Act invalid. This was the state law that allowed New

York City to postpone redeeming its general obligation notes in November 1975.

NEW JERSEY "QUALIFIED" SCHOOL AND CITY BONDS

In 1976 the governor of New Jersey signed into law two bills (known as "qualified bond" acts) that provide additional security for certain general obligation bonds issued by New Jersey issuers. The chief characteristic of the two laws (one is for municipalities and the other is for school districts) is that selected state-aid monies, normally paid directly to the municipality or school district, will be paid directly by the state treasurer to the bond-paying agent.

Revenue Features

Municipal Qualified Bonds. The selected state-aid monies pledged for debt service are the business personal property tax replacement revenues (Public Law 1966, c. 135), state revenue sharing funds (Public Law 1976, c. 73), and state urban aid funds (Public Law 1971, c. 64). The latter state-aid program is available to 24 New Jersey urban municipalities. While these state-aid programs could be eliminated or changed, the law provides that any future state-aid programs that provide funds in substitution of the above would be pledged as security for the qualified bonds.

School Qualified Bonds. Under this law, state-aid monies pledged for debt service are those available under the Public School Education Act of 1975 (Public Law 1975, c. 212) and four other state-aid programs. As with the municipal qualified bonds, the law specifies that, while the specific state-aid programs may be eliminated or changed, any future substitute state-aid programs would be pledged as security for such qualified bonds.

Bond Paying Procedures

After the bonds are sold, the issuer certifies to the state treasurer the name and address of the paying agent, the maturity schedule, the interest rate, and debt-service payment dates. The state treasurer is then required to withhold from the amount of state aid due the issuer an amount sufficient to pay the debt service on the qualified bonds, and to make this payment directly to the paying agent. The issuer still must include the debt-service requirements in its annual budget since the diversion of cash does not represent additional state aid to the issuer, but merely a diversion of cash flow to ensure that the principal and interest on the qualified bonds will be paid promptly.

Bond Strengths

The three strengths of New Jersey qualified bonds are:

1. Debt-service payments are made directly by the state treasurer to the paying agents.
2. The State Local Finance Board reviews and authorizes all qualified bond sales under the two laws in order to ensure that state aid more than covers the anticipated debt service.
3. The qualified bonds are also general obligations of the issuing municipalities and school boards.

Conclusion

The original purpose of the qualified-bond acts was to assist municipalities and school districts (particularly those in urban centers) that had had problems issuing bonds as a result of New York City's fiscal difficulties in 1975. In the opinion of the attorney general of New Jersey, once the qualified bond issue has been approved by the State Local Finance Board and certified to the state treasurer, the earmarked state-aid funds cannot be used for any purpose by or on behalf of the issuer other than to pay the required debt service on the qualified bonds.

It should also be noted that future New Jersey legislatures are not necessarily bound by prior legislation, though several of the state-aid programs pledged under the qualified-bond acts have been in existence for several years.

NEW JERSEY'S OWN INSURANCE PROGRAM FOR LOCAL SCHOOL BONDS

Certain general obligation school bonds issued by local governments in New Jersey have a layer of security that is known as a school bond reserve.[9] This reserve, administered by the state treasurer, is to be used to pay debt service on the school bonds if the local govern-

---

[9] Data sources for this section include: state of New Jersey Assembly Bill No. 10706 (introduced May 19, 1980, by Assemblymen Burstein, Karcher, Doyle, Bennent, and by Assemblywoman Garvin); interview with David T. Beale, executive director, New Jersey Department of the Treasury, on August 7, 1980; interviews with Elias Abelson Esq., Division of Law, state of New Jersey, on August 18, 1980, and June 8, 1983; interview with George Tuttle, Director of Finance, city of Paterson, New Jersey on August 11, 1980; and the report of the "Trustees for the Support of Free Public Schools Funds," November 27, 1984.

ments themselves should ever be unable to do so. This section describes the reserve, how it works, and which local school bonds are now secured by it. It should be noted that accounting and budget controls for local governments in New Jersey are stringent, and that this reserve adds yet another layer of security to the school bonds.

The New Jersey School Bond Reserve Act

This law, passed in July 1980, contractually pledges a portion of the existing New Jersey Fund for the Support of Free Public Schools for paying debt service on certain outstanding, and to be issued, local government general obligation school bonds. Known as the "school bond reserve," this reserve receives revenues from compensation paid to the state for its riparian (i.e., tidewater) lands. These lands, which are now or were formerly covered by the mean high tide, are located around the state and include areas of the Hackensack Meadowland and some Atlantic City resort properties. The school bond reserve is to contain an amount equal to at least $1\frac{1}{2}$ percent of all outstanding and eligible local government school purpose bonds.

Under the law, if a local government anticipates that it will be unable to make its regular debt-service payment, it is obligated to notify the state at least 10 days prior to the payment date. If the local school bonds qualify, the state treasurer shall use monies in the school bond reserve to pay the debt service as it comes due. If monies in the reserve are so used, the state treasurer at least once a year must replenish the reserve with new monies from available riparian-rights revenues to bring the reserve back up to its 1.5 percent requirement. At June 30, 1985 the market value of the reserve was $16,473,929, and the market value of the Fund for the Support of Free Public Schools was $45,250,553.

Local General Obligation Bonds Covered by the School Bond Reserve

Under the law, the principal and interest on bonds issued since December 4, 1958, by New Jersey counties, municipalities, and school districts and that were for elementary and secondary school purposes are covered by the reserve. County community-college bonds are not affected. Additionally, under the law, each bond so covered and issued subsequent to the effective date of the act (which was July 16, 1980) shall bear the following legend:

Payment of this obligation is secured under the provisions of the New Jersey School Bond Reserve Act in accordance with which an amount equal to 1½ percent of the aggregate outstanding bonded indebtedness (but not to exceed the moneys available in the fund), of New Jersey counties, municipalities and school districts for school purposes as of September 15 of each year, is held within the state fund for the support of free public schools as a school bond reserve pledged by law to secure payments of principal and interest due on such bonds in the event of the inability of the issuer to make payment.

Allowed Investments of the Assets of the School Bond Reserve

Under the law the assets of the school bond reserve are composed entirely of direct obligations of the U.S. government or obligations guaranteed by the full faith and credit of the U.S. government. Additionally, at least one third of the securities in the reserve shall mature within one year of their dates of issuance or purchase. On or before each September 15, the state treasurer shall review the investments in the reserve to see that they meet the requirements of the law.

Future Available Revenues from the State's Riparian Rights

While the school bond reserve as of June 30, 1984, held $19.5 million, it has a claim to all future revenues derived from the state's riparian rights. It should be noted that, while the state estimates potential revenues as being as high as $100 million, there had been attempts through state referenda and court cases to restrict the state's riparian rights and the amounts that the state can collect on the sale of its rights as well.

Strengths and Weaknesses of the Security Structure

While the school bond reserve (as an insurance reserve and from actuarial insurance aspects) provides additional protection to the eligible general obligation bonds, there are certain aspects of this security structure that should be noted. First, the school bond reserve is only reviewed annually (September 15 of each year) to determine if its holdings equal at least 1½ percent of the outstanding local school bonds. Second, responsibility for notification of a potential default rests with the issuer. Third, the monies generated by the riparian rights are relatively small when compared to the total debt service payable on the eligible bonds.

It should be noted that because of this reserve, Standard & Poor's gives its AA to all school bonds for which a rating is requested.

"QUALIFIED" SCHOOL BONDS IN MICHIGAN

Since 1955 the state of Michigan has had a financial aid program for school districts in which the school district is allowed to borrow and the state is required to lend to it an amount necessary for the school district to avoid a default on its own general obligation bonds, or to reduce the local property tax levy that is being used to pay debt service. The amounts borrowed are to be paid back with interest. The qualification for participation in this program is done by the state government prior to the original bond sale. If necessary, the state is required to use monies in its own general fund to pay the debt service. The money goes from the state treasurer to the school district's debt-service fund.

Because of this special security backup with the state, school-district bonds in Michigan are of stronger credit quality. There are over 400 school districts in Michigan with "qualified" bonds outstanding. These bonds were usually rated one notch below the state's ratings by Moody's. However, following a number of changes in the state's ratings since 1980, many of the existing ratings on qualified school bonds no longer reflect this approach.

TEXAS MUNICIPAL UTILITY DISTRICT (MUD) BONDS

Municipal Utility District (MUD) bonds in Texas are issued by special districts to finance the construction of certain capital improvements in unincorporated areas of the state. Such MUDs are created by the Texas Water Commission and are subject to the continuing supervision of the Texas Department of Water Resources and the Texas Water Commission. The capital projects are usually water and/or sewer systems located within the specific MUDs that are undergoing residential and commercial development. Some MUDs are purely residential, some are purely commercial (such as for shopping centers), and some are a combination of the two.

How Are the Bonds Secured?

MUD bonds generally are secured by the pledge of unlimited property taxes on all taxable property, if necessary, that is located within the MUD. Additionally, the net revenues of the water and sewer systems, if there are any, are usually pledged to the MUD bondholders. Of course, while a MUD bond is legally secured by unlimited property taxes, how likely it is that the planned development will occur within projections determines the credit worthiness of the specific MUD bond issue.

Credit risk is in two stages. First, there is the initial risk that the specific public improvements—that are financed by the proceeds of the bond sale—neither will be completed on schedule nor at projected, reasonable cost. Such occurrences may throw into doubt the overall economic soundness of the development plan for the MUD.

The second stage of the credit risk is the ability of the MUD developer to properly construct, market, and sell residential homes or commercial properties in the improved MUD. This is necessary in order to create a strong property valuation base that can be taxed at a moderate to low tax rate to pay debt service on the bonds.

Questions to Ask Concerning the General Credit Risk

The following are some of the questions that should be asked by the investor before purchasing a MUD bond.

Who Is the Developer of the MUD? The investor must evaluate the competitive ability of the developer to build and effectively market the development. The developer must be judged in terms of his ability both to construct the public utilities (streets, water, and sewer systems) and to build and sell homes in the MUD to the public, or in the case of a commercial MUD, to attract quality commercial tenants. A developer with a long history of successful experience with such projects and strong financial resources in the business is clearly preferred. This is particularly the case since the U.S. Bankruptcy Court has the power to stay tax collection procedures against the developer. Clearly, a MUD that is being developed by a wholly owned subsidiary of a major corporation such as the Exxon Corporation is a stronger credit than one in which the developer is less substantial.

How Conservative Is the Developer's Construction Program and Schedule? The investor must determine if the developer's construction schedule and financing costs are realistic. Has the developer determined his total construction costs and does the developer's financing plan include enough capitalized interest to cover potential construction delays? If additional bonds had to be issued to complete the installation of the public utilities, the property tax burden on the property owners, of course, would be increased.

What Is the Maximum Impact on MUD Property Tax Rates? Assuming the successful issuance of the MUD bonds, the investor must determine the maximum and annual projected debt-service requirements and what the projected tax rate would be per $100 of assessed valuation. If the projected tax rates are substantially higher than rates currently levied in competing areas, the rate of development within the MUD could be adversely impacted.

In this regard it should be noted that, in general, commercial MUDs require less public services—such as police and fire facilities—than do the residential MUDs. Therefore, the tax burdens of the commercial MUDs sometimes are lower.

What Is the Socioeconomic Target Market? An important element in the determination of the credit quality of a residential MUD bond is the socioeconomics of the population that will be purchasing property and living in the specific MUD. The more economically upscale the target population is, the more insulated the MUD should be from low property tax collection rates that would be caused by recessionary forces. A critical indication of the socioeconomics of the MUD is the median home values projected by the developer.

Of course, it also should be noted that during periods of relatively high interest rates, it may be difficult for high-priced homes to be sold in the purely residential MUDs. In this regard, commercial MUDs, such as those for shopping centers, could be stronger credits if the developer and commercial tenants are financially sound.

Where Is the MUD Located? Because of the lack of mass-transit systems in many suburban areas, the actual location of the MUD in relationship to major population centers, medical facilities, churches, fire stations, interstate highways, and environmental amenities such as recreational facilities is important; it could affect the successful development of the MUD.

How Reliable Is the Legal Opinion? The MUD bond issue should have two unqualified legal opinions to the effect that the bonds are valid and legally binding obligations of the MUD. The first should be of the attorney general of Texas, and the second of a recognized and experienced municipal bond attorney.

Is the MUD Located within the "Extraterritorial Jurisdiction" of a Major City? Some MUDs are located within the exclusive extraterritorial jurisdiction of a major city that could annex the MUD. If this were to occur the MUD bonds would become general obligations of the larger, annexing city. One city that has a history of annexing MUDs is the city of Houston. While a MUD that is located within the exclusive extraterritorial jurisdiction of Houston cannot be assumed to be ultimately annexed by Houston, there is the potential that this could happen. Conversely, the city of Dallas does not have a strong history of annexing MUDs that are located within its extraterritorial jurisdiction. Also, it should be noted that even if the MUD is located within the extraterritorial jurisdiction of Houston, it may have other characteristics (as discussed above) that make the MUD bond a speculative investment.

Conclusion

The credit worthiness of Texas MUD bonds ranges all the way from the speculative category of risk to investment grade. By asking and obtaining answers to the questions discussed above, the prudent investor should be able to distinguish MUD bonds that are strong credits from those that are not.

11

Some Bonds that Either Have Gone Belly-Up or Had Near-Misses and Related Problems

While most municipal bonds and notes have not defaulted, over the past 25 years there have been significant defaults and near-misses. What is particularly distressing to investors is that even bonds and notes that were considered at issuance by some to be the safest municipal bond investments later either defaulted or have been on the brink. As examples, the major commercial rating agencies, Moody's and Standard & Poor's, gave ratings of triple A and A–1, and triple A and A+, respectively, to the $8 billion of the troubled Washington Public Power Supply System bonds. It was when these commercial ratings were in effect that underwriters sold and investors bought the bonds. Over $2.5 billion of these bonds have now defaulted.

In this chapter, 14 specific bond issues are discussed. Each bond that defaulted or was a near-miss was defective in its structure. For some, the project feasibility studies and revenue projections were overly optimistic, for another the projected construction costs were too low, for another the enforceability of an innovative legal structure was incorrectly assessed by the bond attorneys, for another the basic legal question of whether or not the issuer could sell general obligation bonds for the stated purpose was not properly researched by the bond attorney, and for still another political conflicts brought about the default. While all of these defaults and near-misses have special aspects that created the respective crisis, they also provide the student with a rich background for understanding why there is a need today for municipal bond research.

THE OKLAHOMA WATER RESOURCES BOARD TRIES TO SELL BONDS THAT ARE UNCONSTITUTIONAL

In early 1984 investors were presented with an opportunity to purchase a new bond from an agency of the state of Oklahoma. It was a $50 million *State Loan Program Revenue Bonds, Series 1984* issue of the Oklahoma Water Resources Board. The Preliminary Official Statement indicated that the bonds would be offered for sale, subject to the approving legal opinions of the Attorney General of the state of Oklahoma as well as of a local, though nationally recognized, municipal bond attorney. The bonds were to be insured by MGIC Indemnity Corporation which would fully reinsure this policy with AMBAC and were to be given a AAA municipal bond rating by Standard & Poor's. The bonds were priced and marketed in February of 1984.

The Oklahoma Water Resources Board is a state administrative department that was to loan bond proceeds to local governments for the development of water and sewage systems in Oklahoma. In addition to the MGIC bond insurance, the bondholder security had three basic components. First, the participating local governments were obligated to make loan repayments. Second, they were obligated to adopt rate covenants sufficient to repay their respective loans from the Oklahoma Water Resources Board and to provide net revenues available for debt service that are at least equal to 125 percent of the maximum annual debt-service requirements. Third, the Board had established a debt-service reserve fund with a minimum required balance of not less than $7.5 million. This reserve fund was funded from monies appropriated by the Oklahoma legislature through a "revolving fund."

This security structure was innovative and was seen by some as an attractive safeguard for bondholders.[1]

While the bonds were priced, marketed, and physically printed, actual delivery was not made. In February, the mayors of three Oklahoma cities and the city managers of two other towns challenged the legality of the bond issue.

In early April of 1984 the Supreme Court of Oklahoma ruled that the bond issue was unconstitutional. The court held that:

> The terms of the instant bond resolution would require an unconstitutional assumption of debt by the State on behalf of the local entities. . . . We cannot uphold the validity of this bond resolution for the reason that the pledge of collateral or security of the monies in the Revolving

---

[1] For an example, see "Oklahoma Seeds Water Projects," Standard & Poor's *Credit Week,* January 30, 1984, p. 2,317.

Fund amounts to a pledge or lending of the State's credit in violation of Section 15 of Article X.[2]

Clearly, the Supreme Court of Oklahoma was unambiguous in refusing to approve the bond issue. As the result of the court's decision the bonds were not sold or delivered.

It should be noted that in August of 1984 the Oklahoma voters approved by a vote of 397,272 to 206,488 a State constitutional amendment that permitted the State to pledge monies in a state-managed revolving fund as collateral for revenue bonds issued by the Board. In May of 1985 the Board successfully sold the first bond issue under the security structure.[3]

THE CASE OF THE CITY OF GAHANNA'S BOND ANTICIPATION NOTES

Over the years, several cities in Ohio, including Cincinnati, Cleveland, Columbus, and Dayton, have sold general obligation bonds that have been issued for "urban redevelopment" purposes.

These bonds were sold with approving legal opinions and were given investment grade ratings by Moody's or Standard & Poor's, or both. However, in the fall of 1983, the highest court in Ohio agreed to hear a challenge to one of such general obligation debt issuances that had been initiated by an irate taxpayer. The court case was *James M. Ryan* v. *City Council of Gahanna* (Case No. 83–763, Supreme Court of Ohio), which was decided on February 1, 1984.

While there were other legal issues raised, the one that was of most concern to bondholders was the allegation that general obligation bonds issued for urban redevelopment projects (with private interests involved) did not qualify as a public purpose under the Ohio constitution and, therefore, could not be secured by property taxes. The challenge was based upon a strict interpretation of the state constitution.

On February 1, 1984, the highest court in Ohio in an unanimous 7–0 decision held in the Gahanna case that:

> A municipal corporation may not enter into a joint venture with, nor extend credit to, a private corporation or association where such venture or extension is supported by the issuance and sale of bonds or notes

---

[2] *Reherman, et al.,* v. *Oklahoma Water Resources Board,* 679 p. 2d 1296 (Okl. 1984). Rehearing on the Court's majority opinion was denied May 8, 1984.

[3] This is reported in *Resources In Review,* November, 1984, p. 14; and in the Preliminary Official Statement, dated May 30, 1986 for $50,000,000 Oklahoma Water Resources Board, State Loan Program Revenue Bonds, Series 1986, pp. 32–33.

guaranteed by earmarked tax revenue of the municipal corporation. (State ex rel *Ryan* v. *City Council of Gahanna,* 9 Ohio St. 3d 126, 459 N.E. 2d 208, [Sup Ct Ohio, 1984]).

This case involved limited property-tax general obligation bond anticipation notes (BANs) issued for urban redevelopment purposes by the city of Gahanna, Ohio. The court determined that Gahanna's purchase of blighted land and redevelopment of such land, as opposed to the "preferred form" of redevelopment through a "community urban redevelopment corporation," constituted under Ohio law a joint venture between the city and private developers.

The court said that a provision in the authorizing ordinance requiring that "funds derived from a tax levy were to be placed in a separate and distinct fund for payment of the obligation" was unconstitutional, and that the deletion of that provision from the debt authorization ordinance would cure any constitutional defect. The court specifically approved the issuance of Gahanna urban redevelopment bonds backed only by the full faith and credit of the city, but restrained the city from further issuing bonds or notes until such obligations could clearly state on their face that they were "not guaranteed by or payable from specially designed tax moneys."

On February 9, 1984, $735,000 of the affected Gahanna urban redevelopment general obligation bond anticipation notes came due. They were not presented for payment and remained unpaid for several months. Eventually, they were retired with the proceeds of another bond issue, which was not a general obligation, property-tax secured issue.

Did the Decision Affect Outstanding Limited Property Tax General Obligation Bonds?

While the court was specifically speaking to the Gahanna BANs, there is a question as to whether the rationale of this decision could be applied to outstanding urban redevelopment and urban renewal bonds and notes issued by other cities in Ohio such as Columbus, Cleveland, Cincinnati, and Dayton that are also secured by a pledge of limited property taxes. Cities such as Cleveland and Cincinnati had hundreds of millions of dollars in such bonds outstanding, with some of them rated Aa by Moody's.

The major bond attorneys in Ohio who in the past have written legal opinions upholding the legality of such issues have indicated that the Gahanna decision does not legally affect their outstanding bonds. As an example, the chairman of the administrative committee of Peck, Shaffer & Williams in Cincinnati, has stated that:

The Supreme Court speaks prospectively in a particular case. Presently outstanding urban redevelopment bonds and notes may contain unnecessary language but they remain secured by the full faith and credit of the specific municipality. Additionally, all outstanding bonds and notes, of course, are protected by the contract clause of the United States Constitution. (Press release of Peck, Shaffer & Williams, received February 3, 1984).

While the Ohio court has said that proceeds of specifically designed taxes cannot be legally pledged to the bondholders when a joint venture with private enterprises exists, it also has said that the issuer can pledge its full faith and credit to the bondholders. What this appears to mean is that the issuer can in an operating sense use property tax revenues, among other revenue sources, to pay bondholders, but cannot legally pledge specific tax revenues to the bondholders. In a stressful budgetary environment, the holders of other limited property tax general obligations of the same issuer might argue that they have a claim to the available limited property tax monies and should be paid prior to holders of obligations not having such a claim. Such claimants could include the holders of limited-property-tax-supported general obligations issued for municipal parks and libraries and where no joint venture is present. Such an argument, if it were to legally prevail, could weaken the security for urban redevelopment general obligations that are similar to Gahanna's. Of course, it should be noted that not all other limited tax general obligations issued for urban redevelopment purposes have the same characteristics as those issued by Gahanna and therefore may not be negatively impacted by the court's decision. Holders of any bonds or notes thought to be affected by the Gahanna decision might be well advised to consult with their counsel as to any possible effect upon their holdings.

UPGRADING NEW YORK CITY'S CREDIT RATING, 1970–1973: A HORROR STORY*

In August 1977, as part of the "fallout" from New York City's fiscal collapse, the Securities and Exchange Commission (SEC) issued its

---

* This section was written by Judge Theodore Diamond, New York City Civil Court. It reveals how New York City successfully devised and implemented a political and mass media campaign for pressuring the rating agencies into raising their credit ratings on its debt. The author, who is now a civil court judge in Kings County, New York, was research counsel and director of the research unit of the New York City comptroller's office between 1970 and 1974 and was intimately involved in these events.

staff report on New York City securities.[4] The 31-page chapter on credit rating agencies included only a few pages about the upgraded ratings in 1972–73. But how did the ratings go up when financial conditions were getting worse? About the 1970–75 period, SEC stated generally:

> The agencies appear to have failed, in a number of respects, to make either diligent inquiry into data which called for further investigation, or to adjust their ratings of the city's securities based on known data in a manner consistent with standards upon which prior ratings had been based.[5]

• • • • •

> During the period covered by the investigation, as shown below, billions of dollars of New York City's securities were sold or traded predicated upon ratings that were based largely upon unverified data and information furnished by the city to the rating agencies involved. Indeed, the agencies expressly disclaimed any responsibility for the accuracy of the information upon which they acted. Nor did they apparently recognize a responsibility to make diligent inquiry even in the face of adverse facts which came to their attention.[6]

The report emphasized that, while the city supplied data for each sale including a "Notice of Sale" and "Supplementary Report of Essential Facts," it did not have a "Report of Essential Facts" until 1975. This was irrelevant! The data for such a report are available, and substitutes for "Essential Facts" had been issued in the past. But an interesting question not addressed by the SEC was the extent to which the 1972–73 upgrading was a signal to city officials that they could pressure or bluff the agencies and even the market, and thus enjoy a license for continued irresponsibility in the future.

The *Staff Report* stated that, early in 1972, two New York congressmen held a hearing on credit ratings, and a proposal to impose federal regulation on rating agencies.[7] A December hearing was sched-

---

[4] U.S. Congress, House of Representatives Committee on Banking, Finance and Urban Affairs, Subcommittee on Economic Stabilization, *Securities and Exchange Commission Staff Report on Transactions in Securities of the City of New York* (95th Congress, 1st Session, August 1977). Hereafter cited as *Staff Report.*

[5] Ibid., "Introduction and Summary," p. 9.

[6] Ibid., Chapter 5, "The Role of the Rating Agencies," p. 1f.

[7] Ibid., p. 10, footnote 2. Such reports had been issued in 1967, 1968, and 1969. The February 1972 Credit Rating Report (see footnote 18), p. 5, was the same as a "Report of Essential Facts."

uled by the New York State Senate Select (Goodman) Committee to Investigate the Rating of Tax-Exempt Bonds, and Moody's raised the rating from Baa–1 to A the day before.[8] While Moody's did provide some reasons for its action, the report demonstrated that many fiscal and economic factors were getting worse.[9]

In September 1973, city officials from budget (David Grossman), finance (John Fava), comptroller's office (Sol Lewis) met with Standard & Poor's (S&P), and delivered a written report outlining various improvements in the city's financial, socioeconomic, and accounting areas. After discussion of the report and other documents, and review of the comptroller's Annual Report for 1972–73 in November, S&P determined that an increase in the rating was warranted; and, in December, it was increased from BBB to A.[10] The SEC said that S&P analysts were aware that the data supplied by the city were to some extent a product of fiscal gimmickry (providing six examples), but S&P was "assured" by the city officials that these abuses were being corrected.[11]

What Really Happened, and How?

1964–70. In 1964, City Comptroller Beame issued a report, "New York City Bonds—A Prime Security," arguing for an improved rating from A to AA. In July 1965, Moody's lowered the city's rating from A to Baa. Dun & Bradstreet (D&B) rated bonds in eight categories, with 22 levels of credit risk. It downgraded New York City from "good" to "better medium," from risk category 9 to 10. A year later, S&P dropped the rating from A to BBB. In 1968, Moody's subdivided the Baa rating level; and the city got Baa–1, for the best credits in the Baa rating. In 1971, D&B's municipal rating service was merged into Moody's—unfortunately, because D&B reports were more complete.

In 1967 and 1968, City Comptroller Procaccino issued editions of "Essential Facts and Supplementary Information for Investors," about 35 pages long, half filled with financial schedules. In 1969, an election year, the office produced a slick, 50-page report entitled "New York City, An Investment Opportunity; Essential Facts for Investors," which was similar to publications by industrial development agencies.

---

[8] Ibid., p. 14, footnote 5.
[9] Ibid.
[10] Ibid., p. 15.
[11] Ibid., p. 16f. Also, see footnote 1 on page 17.

In the general national prosperity of the late 1960s and the "go-go" years on Wall Street, there appeared to be improvements in the city's financial position. "In the two-year period ending June 30, 1969, the city managed to reduce its net funded debt by $24 million. . . ."[12] In his 1969 book, *The City,* Mayor Lindsay said, "I've seen a bankrupt city become fiscally sound in the space of three years."[13]

Comptroller Beame returned to office in 1970. On January 20, he said, "The city originally lost its A rating because the rating agencies were concerned we were using borrowed money to pay for some day-to-day expenses." Jac Friedgut of Citibank noted (in 1975) that Beame indicated such practices had ceased.[14] In June 1970, the third deputy comptroller advised me, as chief of the comptroller's research unit, to work on the credit rating. Because I had done a 1969 campaign position statement on city finances that identified some major problems, I replied that:

> Any attempt to improve the credit rating should be a long-term effort. . . . If we define an overall program, the banks and credit agencies might be more agreeable to our efforts. More important, if at the end of a year or two we have been able to achieve some of these things, all the more reason why they should go along with us.[15]

1971. In 1971, I indicated that we had to make improvements in the legal requirements and administrative factors that protected bondholders, because we couldn't rely on improvements in the financial and economic well-being of the city, its people, or institutions.

> I believe it unlikely that the general situation will improve in the next decade. No reason for improvement appears on the horizon. The city's master plan projections are quixotic. The results of the 1970 census will be released soon, providing clear and convincing evidence that vast sections of the Bronx and Brooklyn are disaster areas.[16]

However, we developed a strategy after reading all the literature on credit ratings, their purpose, what they measured, the key factors, and the measures used to evaluate each municipality. I was advised by a municipal analyst that factors usually cited as the basis for bond

---

[12] *Staff Report,* Chapter 3, "Role of the City and its Officials," p. 18.

[13] John V. Lindsay, *The City* (New York: W. W. Norton, 1969), p. 17.

[14] *Staff Report,* Chapter 1, "Chronology of Events," p. 162.

[15] Author's memo to Third Deputy Comptroller Julian Buckley, June 23, 1970, p. 1.

[16] Author's memo to Comptroller Beame, January 25, 1971, p. 1.

ratings were so extensive that no rating organization could have the time to go into all of them for the thousands of rated bonds.[17] Although rating agencies were competent to adjust a credit up or down based on what was happening in that municipality, their weakness was that they pretended to be able to do more than that—and could not! The strategy called for: (1) a report on the fiscal and economic strength of the city, to be the focus of our efforts; (2) criticizing the validity of the rating system in general; (3) identifying differences between rating agencies about various municipalities; (4) publicizing embarrassing errors by rating agencies; (5) providing situations where rating agencies might express inconsistent statements about what they were doing; (6) calling for government regulation of credit rating agencies.

I still believed that a fiscal improvement program was necessary. I was wrong. No program was ever mentioned, or needed!

Although the comptroller kept asking for the credit rating report in 1971, he did not publicize the issue much. However, he was getting increased pressure from his Technical Advisory Committee on City Debt Management, who indicated that they needed more "help" if they were to *"move* all this city paper."[18]

We resolved that the report would not be a "puff piece" like the "Essential Facts" issued in the 1960s, and we did not repeat silly arguments about how much New York City spent for various services. After all, if New York City spent $3 billion annually on education and the schools were a disaster, that wasn't persuasive! We decided to have lots of text, especially on administrative, social, and economic factors—where we could build up arguments. We were willing to identify problems and discuss them. We made old arguments in new ways, and new arguments. We knew that financial factors had deteriorated badly between January 1970 and June 1971.

Chapter I, a short introduction, described city ratings changes and set forth rating definitions. We did not pretend to be neutral.

> The purpose of this study is to show that New York City's credit rating was unfairly and unnecessarily downgraded. . . . The study will support the city's claim for a higher rating . . . we believe careful study by the rating agencies of the material in this report justifies an upward adjustment. . . .[19]

---

[17] Author's discussion with J. Sheafe Satterthwaite, Summer 1971.

[18] Remark to the author by Third Deputy Comptroller Melvin Lechner.

[19] New York City Office of the Comptroller, *The Case For Upgrading New York City's Credit Rating,* (February 1972), "Introduction," pp. 1–1, 1–3. Hereafter cited as *Credit Rating Report.*

Chapter II, "City Debt Structure," was four pages long. It identified the funded debt outstanding on December 31, 1971, and on December 31, 1960. It pointed out that four kinds of funded debt had decreased, two kinds increased; total increase was $1.8 billion. We also identified eight kinds of temporary debt as of December 31, 1971, but without the 1960 comparisons that had appeared in the first draft. The original Chapter II had been entitled "Factors Considered by Rating Agencies," and was 14 pages long. This did not appear in the final report but had been useful in developing our strategy.

Chapter III, 32 pages long, was entitled "Factors Applied to New York City." Originally 26 pages long, it had been largely rewritten by Alice Rubin and included material on: security behind the debt, real estate, construction, changes in attitude, tax collection, socioeconomic factors, headquarters capital, commercial development, port of New York, public assistance, per capita income, recreation capital, and so on. About 25 percent were quotations from reputable organizations.[20] Another 25 percent were tables that didn't really prove anything but looked good.

Chapter IV, "Comparison of New York City with Other Cities," originally 8 pages, had been immeasurably fortified and expanded by Julie Holtz to 34. This section became a treasure trove of material used in Beame statements during 1972–73. We took the 20 largest cities, added Newark (26th), and compared S&P, Moody's, and D&B ratings. This chapter included sections on repayment, credit reports, description, basic data, and key ratios. It listed favorable quotes about New York City in recent rating reports, and compared them with unfavorable quotes about other cities, arguing that New York City should have been rated as well as other cities with higher ratings. (Incidentally, this does *not* mean that a logical "scoring" system could not be devised and applied—only that the rating agencies didn't have one).

An early draft included a Chapter V, "Effects of the Present Rating," (four pages) that emphasized higher interest costs and eligibility for investment. The one-page Chapter V, "Conclusion," included:

> There can be no doubt that the bonds of many of these cities have been rated higher than New York City bonds, even though New York City's economic strengths and its ability to repay its obligations are stronger.

---

[20] Publications cited were from: Chase Manhattan Bank, Regional Plan Association, New York State Budget Division, First National City Bank, U.S. Census Bureau, Economic Development Council, etc.

• • • • •

The refusal of the rating agencies to respond favorably to the comptroller's repeated requests for a just upgrading of the city's credit rating has prompted him to call for federal action in this regard. What is needed is the establishment of uniform federal standards in the rating of all municipal obligations in the country, and federal regulation and/or supervision of the rating agencies.[21]

This was followed by an appendix, with 21 financial schedules.

In other words, the report was an attorney's brief—defining the issues in terms most helpful to our client, making our points, undercutting the arguments and credibility of opponents. It was entitled *The Case for Upgrading New York City's Credit Rating.* That implied that an opposing case could be made—for downgrading. True, but no one made *that* case; in fact, it would have been an easier case!

1972. The report was issued on February 17. (The cover page of the report is shown in Exhibit 1.) Letters were sent to Senator Sparkman (Banking, Housing, and Urban Affairs) and Congressman Patman (House Banking and Currency), asking for federal supervision and regulation of credit rating agencies. "I've thought that New York City ought to be at least A," said Beame.[22]

On February 24, he told the Municipal Forum that city bonds were a "top-drawer, blue-chip investment," and "no matter what political, fiscal, or social troubles beset city hall, there is virtually no risk in buying city bonds." Beame said it was riskier to invest in any major corporation in the country.[23]

Beame spoke to the Rockaway Rotary Club on March 1, confident that Congress would supervise rating agencies like the SEC supervised securities, and mentioned the high interest costs resulting from the bad rating.[24]

On March 16, after S&P had reduced the rating of New York State bonds to AA (Moody's had done this in 1964), the state senate appointed a committee to investigate the credit rating of tax-exempt bonds.

On March 27, a few Democratic congressmen from New York City organized a hearing on credit ratings. Carey had to stay in Wash-

---

[21] *Credit Rating Report,* p. V–1.

[22] Comptroller press release 72–36, February 17, 1972; *New York Times,* February 18, 1972, p. 48.

[23] Comptroller press release 72–39, February 24, 1972. Also see release 72–68 of March 27, which repeated these statements.

[24] Comptroller press release 72–42, March 1, 1972.

EXHIBIT 1

THE CASE FOR . . .

UPGRADING
NEW YORK CITY'S
CREDIT RATING

THE CITY OF NEW YORK
OFFICE OF THE COMPTROLLER

ABRAHAM D. BEAME
COMPTROLLER

FEBRUARY, 1972

ington, and Koch sent a staff aide, but Congressmen Podell and Murphy were present. Before a friendly group, Beame's rhetoric soared. "Before 1965, my position was that New York City bonds merited a rating of at least AA if not AAA." He charged that agencies "compared different cities without uniform standards and wind up with ratings which do not accurately reflect relative fiscal strengths." He compared New York City and Newark, with one agency rating Newark higher, one lower, one equal. He called for federal supervision or regulation.[25] Representatives of rating agencies, in testimony, differed on whether lower ratings caused higher interest costs, or whether

---

[25] Comptroller press release 72–68, March 27, 1972; transcript of congressional hearing before Congressmen Bertram Podell and John Murphy, March 27, 1972 (Coast Guard Hearing Room, Old Customs House, New York City).

fiscal problems caused both. Podell suggested that there might be collusion between agencies and underwriters, who would make more money on lower-rated issues. He pointed out that hearings had been held on this subject in the 1960s.[26]

We were also helped because stories about municipal bond sale irregularities were in the news, leading to calls for regulation.

In August, Beame criticized S&P for rating the city's Housing Development Corporation (HDC) better than the city itself, while Moody's rated them one notch *lower*. Beame argued that HDC was a creation of the city; while S&P said there was a state "makeup" provision. A *New York Times* story said, "Privately, however, rating men were dismayed that the two principal services disagreed so much about the quality of the corporation's bonds."[27]

In October, Beame pointed out that, despite poor ratings, New York City bonds had outperformed the market generally in seven out of eight sales over two years.[28] That month, an L. F. Rothschild and Company municipal bond report said of city bonds, "We are of the opinion that the above bonds are entitled to higher ratings than those assigned by the two major investment rating services."[29]

On December 1, Beame called the Moody's Baa–1 rating "an insult to the credit of New York City."[30]

A *New York Times* editorial on December 7, entitled "NYC: Good Risk," seemingly endorsed Beame's position, referring to "the unfairly low credit ratings . . . arbitrarily assigned to this city's offerings."[31]

On December 12, John Nuveen & Company had a large advertisement in the *New York Times* entitled, "There are at least eight good reasons to invest in New York City bonds."[32]

Moody's caved in on December 17, raising the rating from Baa–1 to A. Mayor Lindsay called it a "marvelous Christmas present." Chairman Merola of the City Council's Finance Committee said it was "long overdue."[33] The following day, at a hearing before the State

---

[26] *New York Post,* April 1, 1972, p. 12; March 28, 1972, p. 67; *New York Times,* March 28, 1972, p. 59.

[27] Comptroller press release 72–145, August 10, 1972; *New York Times,* August 11, 1972, p. 40.

[28] Comptroller press release 72–192, October 18, 1972, a speech at a dinner of the New York City Study Trip for Investors.

[29] Report dated October 23, 1972, p. 1.

[30] Comptroller press release 72–233, December 1, 1972.

[31] *New York Times,* December 7, 1972, p. 36.

[32] *New York Times,* December 12, 1972, p. 73.

[33] *New York Times,* December 18, 1972, pp. 1, 69. Moody's Vice President Phillips stated, "New York City has not developed the trend of funding current expenditures we once feared," *Daily News,* December 19, 1972, p. 81.

Senate (Goodman) Committee to Investigate the Rating of Tax-Exempt Bonds, Beame declared, "We are entitled to a higher credit rating, and we demand it." Beame asked now for an AA rating, attacked S&P's BBB as "outrageous, unfair, inaccurate, undeserved, and arbitrary; and something must be done about it." He attacked S&P for rating New York State Urban Development Corporation two grades higher than the city. He said that the city's fiscal position had improved since 1971.[34] A former head of S&P's municipal rating activities denied they were arbitrary or capricious, but admitted "ratings are nothing but opinions."[35]

1973. On January 11, Beame complained that S&P had given an improperly high rating to Evergreen Valley bonds, erroneously stating that they were backed by Maine. Evergreen Valley had defaulted.[36]

In March 1973, the city's total debt went over $10 billion. *The Wall Street Journal* defended the rating agencies in an editorial entitled "Roughing the Scorekeeper," and identified some deteriorating factors.[37]

On March 13, a bill to regulate credit rating agencies was introduced in Congress. Beame spoke about it at a speech in Chicago on March 16: "For almost a decade, my argument . . . has been that the rating analysts either don't know what they are doing, or have irrelevant standards; or when their standards *are* relevant, they do not apply them uniformly."[38] A city bond sale for $285 million at just over 5 percent led Beame to announce that the city had outperformed the market. He pressed for an AA rating.[39]

On April 17, Beame criticized an A rating for the United Nations Development Corporation, which had no guarantees and no certain revenue sources.[40]

---

[34] *New York Post,* December 19, 1972, p. 13; *The Bond Buyer,* December 20, 1972; comptroller press release 72–249, December 19, 1972. For the organization of the Goodman committee, see *New York Times,* March 16, 1972, p. 40.

[35] *The Bond Buyer,* December 20, 1972.

[36] Comptroller's letter to John Pfeiffer of S&P, January 11, 1973; *New York Times,* February 20, 1973, p. 42.

[37] *The Wall Street Journal,* March 12, 1973.

[38] Comptroller press release 73–65, March 16, 1973; press release 73–60, March 13, 1973.

[39] *New York Times,* April 12, 1972, p. 52.

[40] Comptroller press release, 73–93, April 17, 1973, citing a *New York Times* column of April 16 on "Credit Markets," p. 61; *New York Times,* April 18, 1973, p. 43.

Things became ridiculous! The student senate of The City University of New York voted to support Beame's campaign for a higher rating. An employee in the graduate school business office got 2,600 signatures on a petition.[41]

On June 1, Moody's gave a city note sale its second highest rating, MIG–2. The city said this "was expected to prepare the climate for a double A rating."[42]

A *New York Times* article on August 19 anticipated regulation of municipal bond sales—to stop fraudulent operations.[43] Wall Street spokesmen were getting nervous at all the talk of regulation. Wallace Sellers of Merrill Lynch, in the *New York Law Journal* of December 10, wrote: "The fact that our issuers are public bodies with little incentive to make misstatements of facts regarding security, and with great incentive to keep issuing costs down, certainly justifies our exemption from the 1933 Act."[44] But he recognized that something had to be done about the bucketshops, and admitted that many less sophisticated people were in the municipal market now in comparison with the past when bonds were bought by institutions or by sophisticated wealthy people with good advisors.

On December 14, S&P raised the city's rating from BBB to A. S&P said, "The financial condition has improved in each of the last two fiscal years, showing an amazing resiliency to withstand budget difficulties."[45] A *New York Times* editorial concluded:

> The city has won its long fight to have its bonds upgraded to A status by both of the country's major credit rating agencies. . . . The improvement . . . climaxes a joint effort by Mayor Lindsay and by Mr. Beame, in his capacity as comptroller, to demonstrate that the fiscal health of New York is strong and getting stronger.[46]

New York City's *Credit Rating Report* may have been the greatest work of fiction in the 20th century. *Less than two years after its bond ratings were upgraded, New York City defaulted on its outstanding general obligation notes.*

---

[41] Comptroller press release 73–61, March 14, 1973; press release 73–93, April 17, 1973.

[42] *New York Times,* June 2, 1973, p. 41.

[43] *New York Times,* August 19, 1973, Financial Section, p. 1.

[44] *New York Law Journal,* December 10, 1973. p. 35. See comptroller press release 73–60, March 13, 1973, quoting SEC Chairman Casey. For the Beame position, see *the Bond Buyer,* December 10, 1973.

[45] Standard & Poor's statement of December 14, 1973; *New York Times,* December 15, 1973, p. 43.

[46] *New York Times,* December 20, 1973, p. 38.

HOW FEASIBLE WAS THE FEASIBILITY STUDY FOR THE WASHINGTON PUBLIC POWER SUPPLY SYSTEM BONDS?*

Uncritical acceptance of revenue forecasts has come home to roost, perhaps most dramatically, with the Washington Public Power Supply System's (WPPSS) nuclear Projects 4 and 5. An epitaph for investors in the Projects 4 and 5 revenue bonds could well say, "They believed everything they read in the feasibility study and in the official statement."

WPPSS told those investors from the time of its earliest Projects 4 and 5 bond sales that power from the two plants would be necessary to meet the future energy needs of the Pacific Northwest.[47] In July 1976, in a warning regularly cited to the bond market, the federal Bonneville Power Administration (BPA) told the region's utilities that, without the electricity from the two projects, the Northwest could face an energy shortage by mid-1983.[48] The forecasts were grossly wrong. Power from the two projects, it is now estimated, will not be needed in the region until the end of the century.[49]

Unwanted, plagued by cost overruns and construction delays, the two projects were abandoned in January 1982. By 1983, the supply system was struggling to resolve a financial crisis that threatened default on $2.25 billion in construction bonds sold before WPPSS, its participating utilities, and the bond market finally recognized their mistakes.

The now-terminated projects were planned as the final stage of a two-step effort by WPPSS to build five nuclear plants in Washington

---

* This section was written by Howard Gleckman of *The Bond Buyer.*

[47] Washington Public Power Supply System, Generating Facilities Revenue Bonds, Series 1977A (Nuclear Projects Nos. 4 and 5) Official Statement, March 1, 1977, pp. 15 and 25; also pp. A–9 and A–15 containing letter from R. W. Beck and Associates.

[48] Bonneville Power Administration, *Notice of Insufficiency,* July 24, 1976.

[49] This is based upon the consensus of three 1982 load-growth forecasts for the region. All three projected a most-likely or mid-range annual growth rate of 1.5–1.7 percent through the end of the century. The forecasts cited are the Washington state legislature's "Independent Review of WPPSS Nuclear Plants 4 and 5" (Hinman Report), March 15, 1982; the draft report of the Northwest Power Planning Council, adopted January 7, 1983; the Bonneville Power Administration's "Forecasts of Electricity Consumption in the Pacific Northwest, 1982." The legislative study suggested the two projects "or a substitute for them" would be needed between 1992 and 1999. The power-council draft report suggests that thermal power for the end of the century should come from coal-fired projects rather than WPPSS Projects 4 and 5. The Bonneville forecast suggested the projects might be needed by the early to mid-1990s.

State. The power from the two plants was sold to 88 public utilities, which promised to purchase the entire generating capacity of the projects, whatever its cost. Linked with those agreements, called *take-or-pay contracts,* predictions of the region's need for Projects 4 and 5 power became the underpinning of the plants' feasibility and their bonds' security.

However, the load-growth forecasts cited in the supply system's official statements were not the only projections available by 1977, when WPPSS began its massive borrowing in the tax-exempt market for the two plants. Other estimates, including at least two commissioned by the federal government, projected that conservation generated by rising energy prices would reduce demand far below the forecasts cited by the supply system. Questions about projections relied upon by WPPSS were also raised by the U.S. General Accounting Office (GAO) in a mid-1978 report.[50]

In its March 1, 1977, official statement, WPPSS cited a forecast that projected a 5.5-percent average annual growth rate in energy demand over 15 years. That official statement for the supply system's first major tax-exempt borrowing for construction of the two plants included several charts showing potential energy shortages both for the region and for WPPSS 4 and 5's participating utilities.[51] The March 1 official statement said, for example, "Early in the 1970s, it became apparent that . . . (WPPSS nuclear Projects 1, 2, and 3) would not provide adequate generating resources to supply the region's growing demand for electrical power beyond the early 1980s."[52] The same forecasts were also used by Bonneville to justify its 1976 warning of a mid-1983 energy shortage unless Projects 4 and 5 were built. How could these forecasts have been so wrong? How could the supply system investment bankers, rating agencies, and investors have ignored what, in hindsight, were key factors of energy price elasticity and economic uncertainty?

Part of the answer may lie in their source. Until 1976, the region had few independent estimates of future power needs. Instead, the primary source of load growth forecasts came from the Pacific Northwest Utilities Conference Committee (PNUCC), a group that represents the utilities themselves. Until 1977, the group's forecasting

---

[50] General Accounting Office, "Report to Congress: Region at the Crossroads—The Pacific Northwest Searches for New Sources of Electric Energy," August 10, 1978.

[51] WPPSS, Official Statement, pp. 15, A–9, A–15.

[52] Ibid., p. 25.

method was simple. It merely added up the load forecasts of Bonneville and each of the region's 7 investor-owned and 113 public utilities. The sophistication of each of those individual estimates, of course, varied widely. Some utilities provided detailed projections. Others, according to energy officials knowledgeable about the process, merely made "seat of the pants" guesses based on prior historical trends. Although BPA and PNUCC staffs offered technical assistance in preparing the projections, the individual power-company forecasts were, in the end, accepted as part of the overall estimate.

That total, called the sum of the utilities projection, in turn became the official regional forecast. It found its way into supply-system official statements and Bonneville's own projections. In 1976, it was the basis for BPA's warnings about energy shortages. The forecasts depended on three key assumptions. The first was that the projections should be based, in part, on once-in-a-lifetime "critical water years," when drought sharply reduced hydroelectric power generation. The second was that the region's booming economy of the 1960s and early 1970s would continue without letup for as long as 20 years. The third was that power, then available for less than 1 cent a kilowatt hour, would remain so inexpensive that ratepayers would not reduce consumption in response to higher prices. Although the PNUCC recognized that nuclear- and coal-generated electricity would be more expensive than hydropower—the region's primary source of energy—it took many years before the group expected enough of a cost increase to noticeably affect consumption.

Ironically, much of the increase in electric rates from 1979 to 1983, and the reduced consumption it generated, can be directly attributed to WPPSS's own construction program. The least expensive of the WPPSS plants, Project 1, is expected to deliver electricity at about 2.4 cents a kilowatt hour. The most expensive, the now-terminated Project 5, would have provided power at almost 3.5 cents had it been completed at cost estimates made in 1981.[53]

Beginning in 1977, PNUCC did use a computer model to supplement its estimates, but its projections still basically tracked the results of the sum of the utilities method. "The problem with these models is that you need a lot of data, and we just didn't have it," said David Hoff, manager of corporate planning for Puget Sound Power & Light Company and former chairman of PNUCC's forecasting committee.[54]

---

[53] Northwest Power Planning Council, "Development of Resource Targets Issue Paper," November 29, 1982, p. 29.

[54] Northwest Power Planning Council, "Northwest Energy News," April 1982, p. 8.

The PNUCC forecasts, however, contained strong evidence that the group's early estimates may have been overstated about the region's future need for power. After 1974, every annual PNUCC growth estimate declined. Conservation, virtually ignored in early PNUCC estimates, was a factor after 1977. In 1974, for example, PNUCC estimated that utilities in the region would need 17,339 average megawatts of power by 1979–80. In 1977, the group projected 1979–80 energy needs at 15,687 megawatts. The difference was more than the projected output of WPPSS Projects 4 and 5. In 1979–80, utilities in the region actually used 14,866 average megawatts.[55]

The PNUCC forecasts, however, were not the only projections available to WPPSS and BPA, although both agencies chose to discount others. In the spring of 1976, the consulting firm of Skidmore, Owings & Merrill prepared a report at Bonneville's request that concluded that increased conservation in the Northwest would reduce, or even eliminate, the need for all five WPPSS nuclear projects.[56] In October 1976, after a spate of press leaks, BPA made the Skidmore, Owings report public. However, BPA released, at the same time, its own internal analysis that criticized Skidmore, Owings' findings and suggested the projected conservation would never be achieved. Three months later, a second study confirmed many of the Skidmore, Owings, conclusions about conservation.

A January 31, 1977, report by the Natural Resources Defense Council (NRDC), a San Francisco-based environmental group, projected the region would only need 14,000 average megawatts of power annually by 1995, two and one-half times less than estimated by PNUCC.[57] The report, with assumed "vigorous" conservation, was funded by the Federal Energy Research & Development Administration, now part of the Department of Energy. According to NRDC's Ralph Cavanagh, the report was "widely distributed and widely publicized" in the region. The study results were reported in both major Seattle daily newspapers on February, 25, 1977.[58] WPPSS's first major Projects 4 and 5 bond sale was a $100 million offering in July 1975

---

[55] Washington Energy Research Center, "Independent Review of Washington Public Power Supply System Nuclear Plants 4 and 5. Final Report to the Washington State Legislature," March 15, 1982, p. 77.

[56] Skidmore, Owings & Merrill, "Bonneville Power Administration Electric Energy Conservation Study," July 1976.

[57] Natural Resources Defense Council, "Choosing an Electrical Energy Future for the Pacific Northwest," January 31, 1977.

[58] "An Alternative Energy, Scenario," *Seattle Times,* February 25, 1977, p. A–8; "Regional Energy Plan Keyed to Conservation," *Seattle Post-Intelligencer,* February 25, 1977, p. A–10.

to finance the preliminary engineering. WPPSS did not initiate its heavy borrowing to finance construction until February 23, 1977, after both the Skidmore, Owings and the NRDC studies were completed.

Similar, though less dramatic, conclusions about the region's potential for conservation were reached by the U.S. General Accounting Office, an arm of Congress, in August 1978.[59] The GAO reviewed both the PNUCC estimate of a 4.8-percent energy growth rate through the year 2000 and a second "conventional" 1977 projection by the Northwest Energy Policy Project (NEPP), a group sponsored by the federal government and the states of Washington, Oregon, and Idaho. The accounting firm of Congress said NEPP's midrange forecast of 2.7-percent annual energy growth rate through 2000 was "considered most likely to occur."[60] If that projection was accurate, GAO said, the region showed a strong potential for conservation. GAO recommended a "go slow" attitude towards new thermal projects, including nuclear, and a "thorough assessment" of alternatives.[61]

There were other clues as well. In 1976, the city of Seattle's municipal utility, City Light, decided not to join the construction consortium for Projects 4 and 5, although it was a major participant in WPPSS nuclear Projects 1, 2, and 3. A major factor in its decision was the conclusion of an internal study, called "Energy 1990," which projected that price-induced conservation would dramatically reduce energy demand in the region.[62]

As late as 1979–80, the market and the rating agencies seemed to ignore the growing evidence that the region would not need the power from the two plants in the foreseeable future. Instead, until the market finally closed to Projects 4 and 5 after March 1981, they stressed that the bonds were secured by their take-or-pay contracts even if the power was not actually purchased or used. Some investors apparently were convinced that take-or-pay would, in effect, absolve the supply system of its sins. The bonds would be repaid by the utilities that signed take-or-pay agreements, even if the projects' power was not needed or the plants were never completed, argued many on Wall Street.

When originally issued, WPPSS Projects 1, 2, and 3 bonds received Moody's Investors Services' very highest credit rating of Aaa, and the Projects 4 and 5 bonds its A–1 rating. While lower in credit

---

[59] GAO, "Region at the Crossroads."

[60] Ibid., p. iv.

[61] Ibid., p. v.

[62] Seattle City Light, "Energy 1990," 1976.

quality, A–1 was designated by Moody's as having the "strongest investment attributes" within the "upper medium grade" of credit worthiness. Standard & Poor's Corporation initially gave WPPSS Projects 1, 2, and 3 bonds its highest rating of AAA, and the Projects 4 and 5 bonds its rating of A+ (which is comparable to Moody's A–1 rating). By 1986 Moody's had no ratings on any of the bonds. Standard & Poor's only rated the defaulted Projects 4 and 5 bonds. Its rating was D, for default.

The result of the WPPSS forecasting trap is a $2.25 billion debt for what appears to be a dry hole. A debt that, perhaps predictably, WPPSS's utilities in 1986 were seeking every legal means to avoid.

WHAT REALLY WENT WRONG IN CLEVELAND IN 1978?

While New York City, Detroit, Boston, and Cleveland all had similar crisis-prone financial problems, only in Cleveland was the municipal government paralyzed and unable to avoid defaulting on December 15, 1978, on a relatively small $15.5 million note loan.[63] New York City's default in December 1975 was on $2.419 billion in notes. Other than Cleveland, no major city in recent memory has presented the public with such macabre scenes as the elected president of the school board being arrested for improper conduct; the local electric utility sending U.S. marshals to attach city assets so as to assure payment of its bills; and part-time city councilmen defiantly boycotting council meetings called by the mayor to deal with urgent city business. While much attention has been paid to the combative personalities of the mayor and city council president as well as the day-to-day verbal posturings of the various political actors at city hall and in the organized labor and business establishments, Cleveland may have defaulted on its notes primarily for one reason. Its mayor lacked the institutional resources to be an effective chief executive who could manage political conflict.

Restrictive Powers

In actual practice, because of restrictive Ohio state laws and the city's own 1913 charter, policymaking in Cleveland city government resem-

---

[63] Data for this case study is drawn from: selected back issues of the *Cleveland Plain Dealer;* phone interviews with the city's acting budget administrator, Bert Bastock, on January 2 and 8, 1979; phone interviews with the executive director of the Ohio Municipal League on December 29, 1978, and January 3, 1979; preliminary Official Statement (Proof #6) for $25,165 million City of Cleveland Limited Tax Bond Anticipation Note Sale of July 1978, dated June 21, 1978.

bled government by mob caucus. At times the mayor was nothing more than a figurehead of power and executive leadership. In fact, the members of the city's school board had terms of office twice as long as that of the mayor. Cleveland's mayor lacked the traditional big-city "carrots and sticks" of unlimited four-year terms of office, extensive appointment and removal powers in the bureaucracies, and strong taxation and budget powers—all of which are used by effective mayors to reward friends and intimidate enemies.

Between 1970 and 1978, Cleveland had operating budget deficits caused by a declining population, stagnant economic resources, and the inability of city hall to bring the budget in line with its limited revenue resources. Unlike nearby Detroit and Pittsburgh—which had even more serious economic and budgetary problems—Cleveland took the easiest political course of action by paying off last year's budget deficit with this year's borrowed monies. As a consequence, Cleveland in 1978 budgeted $28.9 million for paying interest and principal on its bonds, and also was required to retire $40 million in notes. With a general fund budget of $147 million in 1978 and without a new bond sale, voluntary rollover agreements by the noteholders, or default, Cleveland would have had to use 27 percent of its general-fund revenues for the retirement of its notes.

While Cleveland's mayor in 1978, Dennis Kucinich, was elected in a citywide election in November 1977 with 93,172 votes, he had been frustrated in many of his policies by a largely part-time city council in which the average councilman was elected by about 2,500 votes. The council president, when he last had a contest in his ward in 1975, was elected to public office with only 3,665 votes. In strong mayoral cities such as New York, Detroit, Chicago, and Boston, recalcitrance en masse by similar part-time politicians is unheard of. In Cleveland, because of the weakness of the mayor's office, it was an acceptable norm.[64]

Two-Year Term of Office

A major weakness of Cleveland's mayor in 1978 was that each term of office was for only two years. This hardly provided the incumbent with sufficient time to establish his own policies and to develop a citywide constituency before he must focus on reelection strategies.

---

[64] It should be noted that, since 1978, the city's charter has been amended to provide a four-year term of office for the mayor as well as for the members of the city council.

The shortness of his term served as an open invitation for political opposition, as his potential rivals could count on the mayor constantly having to divert his energy and resources to reelection concerns while they could hope that they would not have to face punishment by the incumbent if he lost the election. Additionally, unlike other large cities, Cleveland had a unique recall mechanism that allowed his opponents to force him to undergo the pressures of electoral approval even during his two-year term. The mayor survived one such recall vote in August 1978 by a slim margin of a little over 300 votes.

Limited Appointment and Removal Powers

Another limitation of the mayor's power was that he had no control over many of the city's essential services or over who provided them to Cleveland's residents. The school system was entirely independent of city hall, with its own governing body of seven members who were elected every four years. Mass transit, sewage operations, port development, and welfare were all either county or special district functions. While the city financed the costs of its municipal court system, the mayor had no judicial appointment powers, and court administration was entirely in the hands of an elected clerk. Also, even in the 10 city departments that were nominally under the mayor's control (such as police and fire), he faced well-entrenched bureaucracies supported by 24 public employee unions and a civil service commission that restricted his managerial powers as well.

Limited Taxing Powers

Because of restrictive state laws, the mayor was required to seek electoral approvals for increased property and personal income taxes that were above state-allowed levels. These requirements no doubt greatly weakened the mayor's ability to deal quickly and effectively with budgetary problems as they occurred. The mayor's powers were further weakened by his having to obtain city council approval before a tax resolution could even be placed on the ballot. Vote authorizations were only approved by the city council after much rancorous politicking and bickering with the mayor. As a contrast, in New York City, stringent opposition en masse to the mayor's revenue programs by local legislators would be discouraged by that mayor's ability to punish his enemies through his extensive appointment powers and his control of city programs and services. While as a result of the Jarvis-Gann initiative in California many communities embraced the belief that more curbs on local taxing powers were desirable, Cleveland showed the potential negative results of such restrictions. It is because of these tax restrictions that, at times, government in Cleveland most nearly resembled chaotic policymaking.

Limited Federal and State Support

Still another weakness of Cleveland that further compounded the basic institutional weaknesses of the mayor was that the city, as the result of its declining population, was losing its political influence on the state and national levels as well. The population declined from 914,808 residents in 1950 to an estimated 638,793 in 1975. In 1978, out of a 23-member Ohio congressional delegation, only two members had predominately Cleveland-based constituencies, whereas the congressional delegation from New York City totaled 18 members. Possibly, this difference was an important factor in Washington's refusal to help Cleveland avoid its note default in December 1978; it was stated by a Treasury Department spokesman at the time that, unlike New York City's budgetary problems, Cleveland's were "local" in nature.

On the state level, the situation for Cleveland was much the same. Out of 99 state assemblymen and 33 state senators in 1978, only six assemblymen and two senators were predominately from the city.

Conclusion

Other governing bodies contemplating weakening the institutional powers of their own chief executives, such as Cleveland already had done, may well look to this city to see what they can expect. Cleveland's political saga may be a lesson well worth pondering.

ALL THAT GLITTERS MAY NOT BE AN ENFORCEABLE AND VALID OBLIGATION: THE CASE OF THE WEST VIRGINIA STATE BUILDING COMMISSION BONDS*

During the latter half of the 19th century, the municipal bond market was faced with various states and local governmental bodies repudiating their obligations on municipal bonds, based upon legal technicalities or outright desire not to pay certain obligations. In response to such problems, the municipal bond market began requiring not only specific legislation or court decisions determining the validity of municipal

---

* This section was written by James E. Spiotto of Chapman & Cutler.

debt obligations but also opinions by bond counsel as to the validity and enforceability of such debt. As simple as the proposition may appear in the abstract, from time to time municipal-financing parties struggle with the question of whether or not bonds in the hands of bondholders are the valid and binding obligation of the issuing body.

The West Virginia State Building Commission Bonds, Series 1968, in the principal amount of $24.2 million is an example of financing where the question of the validity of the bonds proved fatal to the originally structured debt obligation. While there was support by decisional law from other states, the bonds were invalidated by the Supreme Court of West Virginia after millions of dollars of bonds were issued and sold. Fortunately, the bonds were later reaffirmed by the state of West Virginia pursuant to a new financing method. However, there was no legal obligation on the part of the state to do so.

Facts

The principal question raised by the 1968 West Virginia financing was whether the bonds violated constitutional debt restrictions as to the permitted general obligations of the state, since the bonds were issued by the State Building Commission to finance the construction or the acquisition of government buildings and were payable from a fund created by lease payments that, in turn, were paid for by annual state appropriations to various governmental agencies.[65] Indiana, Michigan, Rhode Island, and Oklahoma have in the past upheld similar financing, while New Jersey, Oregon, Georgia, and Wyoming have invalidated statutes which provide for such transactions.

Section 4 of Article X of the constitution of the state of West Virginia provides in relevant part:

> No debt shall be contracted by this state, except to meet casual deficits in the revenue, to redeem a previous liability of the state, to suppress insurrection, repel invasion or defend the state in time of war; but the payment of any liability other than for the ordinary expenses of the state, shall be equally distributed over a period of at least 20 years.

---

[65] Constitutional debt limitations were placed in numerous state constitutions in the latter half of the 19th century, after numerous state repudiations of excessive debt obligations. The limitations were intended to protect both the states' citizens and bondholders from unnecessary and extravagant debt and bond default. States that repudiated general obligation debt in the 19th century include Florida, Alabama, Louisiana, Mississippi, North Carolina, South Carolina, Georgia, Arkansas, Tennessee, Minnesota, Michigan, and Virginia.

In 1968, the legislature of the state of West Virginia reenacted and amended Article 6 of Chapter 5 of the State Code, thereby creating the State of West Virginia Building Commission and empowering the commission to finance the cost of a project by the issuance of state building revenue bonds, the principal of and interest on such bonds to be payable solely from a special fund. Section 10 of the statute provided that nothing in the article should be construed or interpreted to authorize or permit the incurring of state debt of any kind or nature as contemplated by the provision of the constitution of the state of West Virginia in relation to state debt.

Thereafter, on March 11, 1968, the legislature adopted and approved by resolution the issuance of the bonds, not to exceed the total principal amount of $25 million, for the purpose of acquiring land and constructing new state office buildings and parking facilities. The resolution of the building commission authorizing the bonds specifically provided that no part of the costs of construction were to be paid from any funds, grants, or gifts to be received from the U.S. government or from any other source except the proceeds of the sale of the bonds.

By resolution, the building commission covenanted with the bondholders that the buildings constructed with the proceeds of the bonds would at all times be leased to state agencies under leases sufficient to produce revenues equal to but not less than 130 percent of the average annual principal and interest payment on the bonds and 100 percent of the operating expenses of the system. The resolution of the building commission further provided that no lease or agreement for the use of the system or any of its facilities should pledge the credit or taxing power of the state for the payment of rentals or fees provided for in said leases or agreements.

The bonds themselves specifically provided as follows:

> This bond and the coupons appertaining hereto are payable solely from and executed by a lien upon and pledge of the revenues derived from the operation and management of the project and do not constitute an indebtedness of the state of West Virginia of any kind or nature as contemplated by the provisions of the constitution of West Virginia in relation to state debt and the state shall not be obligated to pay this bond or the interest thereon except from the revenues of the system as provided in the constitution. The credit or taxing power of the state shall not be deemed to be pledged to nor shall a state tax ever be levied for the payment of the principal or interest on this bond.

By contracts of lease dated April 1, 1970, the building commission as lessor leased to the state of West Virginia, as lessee for and on behalf of various departments and agencies of the state, office space in the office buildings at a monthly rate of rental that totaled the sum of $2.9 million annually.

Each lease provided that it should continue from "fiscal year to fiscal year" and that it should be considered "renewed for each ensuing fiscal year during the term of the lease, unless it is terminated or modified by agreement of both lessor and lessee." Each lease further provided that "this lease shall be considered canceled, without further obligation on the part of the lessee, if the state legislature or the federal government should subsequently fail to appropriate sufficient funds therefor or should otherwise act to impair the lease or cause it to be canceled."

The entire bond issue of $24.2 million was purchased by an underwriter. The issue was given an A rating by Moody's. The bonds of the series were to mature annually beginning with the year 1972 and ending with the year 1993.

The Lawsuit

In 1970, the owners of certain real estate to be acquired through condemnation and included in part of the project sought and obtained a writ of prohibition in the Supreme Court of West Virginia halting any further action in the eminent domain proceedings. Their basis was that the bonds issued pursuant to the 1968 statute[66] constituted a debt of the state of West Virginia in violation of Section 4 of Article X of the state constitution in view of the fact that rental payments to be used in retiring the bonds would be derived almost exclusively from monies to be appropriated by the legislature to various state agencies and departments.

Although the West Virginia Supreme Court noted that there was a split of authority with respect to the issue of whether such financing created a state debt,[67] the court found that the rental payments were a debt that would necessarily be paid by appropriations in annual installments over a period of years and by successive legislatures from

---

[66] Apparently, State Building Revenue Bonds, Public Safety Series, in the principal amount of $2.5 million and State Building Revenue Bonds, Science and Cultural Center Series, in the principal amount of $1.5 million were also issued and sold pursuant to the statute; but such bonds were not directly questioned by the initial suit. However, such other bonds would be subject to the same constitutional infirmities as the $24.2 million issue.

[67] The court found that the "special fund doctrine" was inapplicable, as the fund for payment of the bonds was maintained by neither a special excise tax nor a self-liquidating facility.

fiscal year to fiscal year. For this reason, the court determined that the statute pursuant to which the bonds were issued was unconstitutional and created a state debt in violation of the constitution of the state of West Virginia. According to the court, if by its decision the state were embarrassed financially, it was not the fault of the court:

> The parties should have known that this was a questionable procedure and the matter of the validity of these bonds and the question of whether they were general obligations or revenue bonds could have been tested in a proper proceeding in a court of competent jurisdiction before the building commission proceeded to the point where, admittedly, chaos may result because of the decision of the court in this case.[68]

Given the fact that the bonds were sold and the project was basically completed, the court was correct that chaos could have ensued.

Subsequent History

The decision of the West Virginia Supreme Court was decided on December 15, 1970, and a rehearing was denied on January 18, 1971. That same year, the state statute was amended to comply with the court's decision. In enacting the amendment, the legislature specifically found that the purpose of the amendment was, inter alia, "to accord statutory recognition to the existing rights, legal and equitable, of the holders of the bonds heretofore issued by the commission, to afford security for the payment of the obligations evidenced thereby, and to provide a special fund for the payment of those obligations.[69]

In the mandamus case that the state quite properly required following the amendments, the West Virginia Supreme Court determined that payment of rent from the state road fund and from a fund to be created and maintained from the sale of alcoholic liquors by the state would not unconstitutionally create state debts in violation of the provisions of the constitution. In the mandamus case, the court also authorized the payment of overdue interest on the Science and Cultural Center Series bonds that had not been paid during the litigation. Therefore, while a default had occurred, no bondholder dollars were lost.

Conclusion

The lesson to be learned from the West Virginia case is basic. In order to ensure that a valid and binding debt is being created, if legal

---

[68] *State ex rel Hall* v. *Taylor,* 178 S.E. 2d 48, 59 (W. Va. 1970).
[69] W. Va. Code § 5–6–2 (f) (1971).

questions are raised that cannot be answered with certainty, it is advisable to have such questions resolved by a court of competent jurisdiction prior to issuing the bonds, rather than run the risk of their invalidity. This is particularly true since such invalidation could jeopardize the issuer's ability to obtain further credit in the marketplace.

THE PROBLEM BONDS OF THE MIDLANDS COMMUNITY HOSPITAL, SARPY COUNTY, NEBRASKA*

On January 3, 1983, Midlands Community Hospital in Sarpy County, Nebraska, retired $320,000 in bonds.

The payment was only a small portion of the $19.7 million in bonds outstanding, but it marked the first time the hospital has made a principal payment on schedule since it entered the tax-exempt market 10 years ago.

The payment was also a sign, the hospital's management said, that a three-year drive to solve the hospital's financial problems was succeeding.

Midlands' troubles began during the planning stages, although they were not apparent until after the hospital's construction.

In the mid-1960s, the board of directors of the Doctors Hospital, an aging 100-bed facility in downtown Omaha plagued by declining patient use and outdated equipment, decided to build a new hospital.

The board selected Papillion, a city situated 12 miles from Doctors Hospital, as the site for the new Midlands Community Hospital. With a population growth rate of 112 percent in the 1960s, Papillion seemed an ideal place to set a new facility. This notion was supported by a feasibility study done by the accounting firm of Arthur Young & Company.

The study estimated patient use according to projected population figures in the area the hospital would serve. It projected occupancy percentages of 59 percent in 1976, the hospital's first year, 71 percent in 1977, and 84 percent by 1978.

Of greater importance to the board, however, was a questionnaire sent by the accounting firm to 562 physicians and 252 dentists in Omaha and Sarpy County that found that 106 physicians and 12 dentists would seek appointment to the staff at Midlands, enough to provide adequate debt coverage.

With these findings in hand, the board decided to proceed with construction.

---

* This section was written by Kent Pierce.

The study on the surface appeared to be thorough and professional; but as events later proved, the study was terribly flawed.

When the hospital opened in January 1976, there were only three doctors available to admit and treat patients.

Later that same year, a serious revenue shortfall occurred due to an occupancy rate of 30 to 40 patients per day, less than half the rate projected in the feasibility study. It became apparent that revenues and reserves would not be adequate to cover the scheduled debt-service payments over the next couple of years. As a result, Midlands was put into receivership by order of the Sarpy County District Court in October 1976. On January 3, 1978, the hospital missed its first principal payment to the bondholders.

"Depending on the medical staff to move 12 miles from Omaha to Sarpy County" was the weak link in the feasibility study's projections, said Morris Miller, former chairman of the board of the Omaha National Bank and now the receiver of the hospital.

"A lot of doctors said they would move, but when the chips were down, they realized that their patient pool was not in Sarpy County but back around their offices in Omaha," he said.

The doctors who had indicated a willingness to practice at Midlands had signed letters of intent. The letters, however, were not legally binding; the physicians could not be forced to work at Midlands.

An additional tactical error was made by the hospital board in its decision to build the hospital before building office space for the doctors. Doctors who were considering a practice at Midlands quickly realized that they would be forced to commute between Papillion and their offices in Omaha. This error did little to attract doctors to Midlands.

Based on faulty assumptions, the hospital's financial foundation quickly crumbled. A review of Midlands' credit-rating history illustrates this point.

Moody's originally assigned an investment quality (conditional) Baa rating to both the $19.2 million hospital bond 1973 series and the $2.5 million project-completion bond issue of 1976. Offered through the Hospital Authority No. 1 of Sarpy County, Moody's subsequently downgraded the bonds twice. They bottomed out in February 1977 at Caa—which is below investment grade.

Midlands' rating scorecard at Standard & Poor's reflects similar setbacks. After receiving a BBB (provisional) investment grade rating in 1973 and again in 1976, the hospital's credit standing was dropped to D.

By 1983 the hospital's finances appeared to have improved, but not to the point where its debt was investment grade. The hospital's basic problems are a lack of working capital and the depletion of security accounts, such as the bond reserve fund and the operation and maintenance reserve fund.

Midlands' financial problems have resulted in a negative funds balance. At the end of the 1982 fiscal year (June 30, 1982), the hospital's total funds balance was a negative $3.5 million. Although this figure was down $400,000 from 1980–81 fiscal year figures, it was still a horrible ratio between total assets and total liabilities.

Not surprisingly, investors have shown little interest in the bonds. The bonds traded in 1983 at 60 to 70 cents on the dollar but not in great volume. This estimate reflects some gain in price from a low of 38 cents on the dollar, a discount offered during the hospital's most difficult times in the late 1970s.

From this stumbling start, Midlands has slowly progressed toward financial recovery. To conserve funds, more than half of the original staff has been laid off, and the receiver has hired Hospital Corporation of America, a management company that has 145 hospitals in its fold, to run Midlands' day-to-day operations.

Calvin Bremmund, assistant administrator in charge of financing for Midlands, said that the hospital's improved financial condition is due, in part, to the steady growth of "patient days" since the hospital opened in 1976.

Daily bed occupancy rates are indicators of hospital revenues. At Midlands it has risen from a first-year average of about 40 to a 1982 average of 84.

Mr. Bremmund said revenues accumulated from the increased patient days over the last three years have been sufficient to pay back defaulted principal payments dating back to the initial principal payment due in January 1978. With the $320,000 payment on January 3, 1983, Midlands is back on the debt-service schedule projected back in 1973.

Another bright note is that the hospital has never missed a semiannual interest payment on either the Series 1973 or the 1976 bonds.

The number of doctors practicing at the Sarpy facility has risen from the dismal figure of 3 in 1976 to 33 in 1983. Also, the geographic area serviced by the hospital is expected to grow by 30 percent this decade. The hospital today has 208 beds, the same number it opened with.

It would be premature to lift the hospital's receivership for at least another 24 months, declared Mr. Miller who is the receiver of the hospital. He explained that during this period, the hospital management plans to rebuild depleted reserve funds and pay about $1 million in debt remaining from the late 70s. The latter figure can be broken down into bills owed various long-time creditors, such as the utility companies and the general contractor. Mr. Miller hoped that some sort of payback arrangement could be developed involving 10-year bank notes.

When these goals are achieved, he said that a recommendation to lift the receivership will be forthcoming.

In the meantime, Mr. Miller remains optimistic. He predicts that the hospital will succeed because Omaha's metropolitan area is expanding and with it the population of Sarpy County. The more people, the more patients, the better off the hospital.

"Midlands Community Hospital," he said, "was a good idea that took hold before its time."

It should be noted that as reported in the Standard & Poor's Craftweek publication of April 21, 1986 the hospital had become current on all principal and interest payments, had replenished the incentive reserve funds, and had terminated the receivership.

DEFAULT OF THE BEAUFORT COUNTY, SOUTH CAROLINA, HOSPITAL FACILITIES GROSS REVENUE AND FIRST MORTGAGE BONDS (HILTON HEAD HOSPITAL)*

Beaufort County, South Carolina, sold $11.2 million of hospital facilities gross revenue and first mortgage bonds dated June 1, 1974, for the Hilton Head Hospital. The issue consisted of $1.125 million of serial bonds due January 1, 1979, through January 1, 1985, and $10.075 million of 8¼ percent term bonds due January 1, 2005. When these bonds were issued, they had been given medium-grade credit ratings by Moody's of Baa (conditional) and by Standard & Poor's of BBB (provisional). Proceeds from the bond sale were used to construct a 40-bed acute care hospital, a 40-bed skilled nursing facility, and an ambulatory care facility. Construction of the project began March 1, 1974; while completion was originally scheduled for October 1, 1975, the facility began operating a little earlier on August 8, 1975.

Hilton Head Island is a resort area and retirement community off the coast of South Carolina. According to population estimates done by the Sea Pines Company (a local community developer and resort operator), population on Hilton Head more than doubled be-

---

* This section was written by George Yacik of *The Bond Buyer.*

tween 1970 and 1974 to 7,900.[70] The hospital's feasibility study, which was done by Booz, Allen & Hamilton, Inc., took this estimate into account and thus said that such a medical facility would be needed and economically feasible by 1975. It based its projected utilization rate on a projected population on the island of 19,600 by 1980.[71]

However, population growth on Hilton Head began to slow. A special census conducted in April 1975 found that the actual population for 1974 was 6,500, not 7,900 as previously estimated.[72] In addition, the island was hit hard by the national economic recession of 1974–75.

As a result, the hospital's actual patient utilization rate fell far below the estimates in the feasibility study. For example, in March and April 1976 only 50 percent of the acute care beds in the facility were occupied. The failure of the hospital to attract patients occurred not only because of the slow development on Hilton Head but because of the lack of a full-time cardiologist on the hospital's staff, which resulted in a loss of patients to hospitals in nearby Savannah, Georgia.[73] At the same time, staffing levels at Hilton Head Hospital were above those at other comparable hospitals in South Carolina.

In late January 1976, Hilton Head Hospital informed the bonds' trustee, Bankers Trust of South Carolina, that its gross revenues would not cover its operating expenses. For the first 11 months of operation ending June 30, 1976, the hospital incurred an operating loss of $2.19 million.[74] Money in the debt-service reserve fund was sufficient to meet coupon payments through July 1, 1977.

The hospital went into technical default when it failed to pay to the trustee on April 1, 1976, one sixth of the bond interest due on July 1, 1976. The reserve fund was fully exhausted in order to meet the July 1, 1977 coupon payment; the coupon payment on January 1, 1978, was not met. The hospital was also in default of a $153,493 note due in February 1977 that was held by the trustee, with interest at 1½ points above the prime rate, and a $52,665 unsecured note held by the Island Investment Corporation.[75]

---

[70] The official statement for the $11,200,000. Beanfort County, South Carolina, Hospital Facilities Gross Revenue and First Mortgage Bonds, Series 1974, dated May 31, 1974, p. A–5.

[71] Ibid, p. A–8.

[72] Standard & Poor's, *Fixed Income Investor,* November 26, 1977, p. 54.

[73] Moody's Investors Service, *Municipal Credit Report,* March 22, 1976.

[74] Report of the accountant, McKnight, Frampton, Buskirk and Co., Hilton Head, S.C., September 8, 1977.

[75] Moody's Investors Service, *Municipal Credit Report,* December 18, 1978.

At that time, the trustee advised that it was in the bondholders' best interest that the hospital remain in operation. The hospital then implemented some staffing and cost-cutting measures, such as moving from a data processing accounting system to a manual system and purchasing drugs and medical supplies from a central supply purchasing bureau. It also began a fund-raising drive.

THE URBAN DEVELOPMENT CORPORATION DEFAULTS ON ITS NOTES*

In 1968, the New York State Urban Development Corporation (UDC) was established by the state legislature to construct subsidized housing in urban renewal areas as well as undertake economic development projects. Less than seven years later, the UDC was on the brink of bankruptcy after defaulting on $100 million in bond anticipation notes on February 25, 1975. With its credit standing ruined, UDC was unable to gain access to the market to refinance the defaulted notes, past-due bank loans, operating expenses, and (most critically) funds to complete construction of half-finished projects. These items totaled almost $700 million. If the projects underway could not be completed, UDC bondholders—$1.1 billion outstanding—would have to look to the state's moral obligation pledge for repayment of debt service.

An invasion of the UDC debt-service reserve fund and subsequent replenishment by the state had not been contemplated when the moral obligation device had been developed. Moreover, the magnitude of UDC's debt-service requirements was difficult for the state to absorb because of its own budgetary difficulties due to the 1975 recession and the rapidly developing New York City financial crisis. The UDC note default was subsequently cured by the state (in May 1975), and a new state agency (the Project Finance Agency) was formed to complete the financing of the unfinished UDC projects.

Nonetheless, although its solvency has since been assured by the state, the UDC crisis shook the world of municipal bond investors.

---

*This section was written by David Herships of Ehrlich-Bober & Co., Inc. The author has drawn information for this case study from the New York State Moreland Act Commission on The Urban Development Corporation and other State Financing Agencies, *Restoring Credit and Confidence* (1978). Mr. Herships was a consultant to the commission. The author's views are his own and do not represent those of Ehrlich-Bober & Co., Inc.

An agency of a major state had defaulted on its obligations, thereby calling into question the credit worthiness of the public-authority debt structure of New York as well as other states. In addition, the accountability and the very purpose of public authorities were questioned as well. It should be noted that in recent years, the UDC has been able to meet its obligations without dependence on state aid and its financial statements have received an unqualified auditor's opinion.

Origins of UDC

Faced with deteriorating conditions in the inner cities in the mid-1960s, the governor of New York State, Nelson A. Rockefeller, recommended to the state legislature that it establish a new agency to meet urban housing needs and facilitate economic development as well. The state already had set up the Housing Finance Agency (HFA) in 1960 to finance rental housing at below-market rates after voters had repeatedly rejected a general obligation bond program for the purpose. The HFA bonds were also secured by the so-called moral obligation of the state. The HFA, however, proved to be conservative and would only undertake those housing projects—largely middle-income—which were financially sound. As a result, the riskier, inner-city, low-income housing and urban renewal projects envisioned by the state were not built.

Legislation was enacted creating the UDC in the emotionally charged atmosphere following the assassination of Dr. Martin Luther King, Jr., in April 1968. The role of the UDC, however, while including the financing and construction of low-income subsidized housing, also was unique in that it included unprecedented responsibilities for urban renewal, commercial and industrial development, and the role of developers of so-called new towns.

The UDC was set up to be self-sufficient: that is, project revenues would be applied to payment of principal and interest on the bonds. During the start-up and construction period, however, expenses were to be financed from first-instance state appropriations, and later from capitalized interest. Because of the long delay until project revenues would be available, in order to market the bonds, the state's moral obligation pledge was included in the UDC's financial structure. The moral obligation pledge was the security in part necessary to satisfy the investment community and the rating agencies of the bonds' credit worthiness. As a result, both agencies gave UDC bonds investment grade ratings for the first bond sale in 1971. The ratings may have been partially due to the sound track record established by the HFA since its inception in 1960 as well as to the view that the state, particularly under Governor Rockefeller's leadership, would support its agencies if necessary.

One factor bears special mention. These long, 40-year bonds were not secured by individual project revenues, of which there were many, but were general purpose bonds secured only by the agency's general creditworthiness. In part, this was because of the long lead time of many of the agency's projects and because, during construction, project revenues were not available.

UDC's intent was to finance construction by long-term bond sales as construction progressed. Its first bond sale—for $250 million—occurred in 1971. Both Moody's and Standard & Poor's rated the bonds A—clearly of investment quality in their eyes. UDC subsequently sold $675 million in long-term issues in the market: a $150 million issue in 1972, two issues totaling $300 million in 1973, and two issues for $225 million in 1974. In addition, there was a $200 million private placement of long-term bonds with New York City banks in 1974. This was a substantial amount of debt to be publicly marketed, given the large competing demand for funds by New York City, the HFA, the New York Dormitory Authority, and other New York borrowers, as well as the start-up, speculative nature of the projects.

Nonetheless, even these funds raised from the sale of long-term bonds were insufficient to meet all construction needs, and UDC turned to the short-term market. Short-term bank loans were first made in February 1973. Later, in July 1973, $75 million in one-year bond anticipation notes (BANs) were sold. On February 26, 1974, UDC sold $100 million in BANs rated MIG–2 (of "high quality") by Moody's. These are the notes that were not redeemed at maturity in 1975, defaulting instead.

With bond proceed monies in hand, UDC quickly embarked on a very large-scale construction plan. By 1972, however, financial problems began developing. Simply stated, management had committed for new construction programs that outstripped UDC's ability to raise funds in the market, even though the rating agencies gave the bonds investment-quality ratings. As a result, cash flow problems developed and UDC had to scramble to raise funds. The first external warning sign was when UDC's 1972 financial statements carried disclaimers from their accountants because of the uncertainty of receiving Federal Section 236 housing subsidies, the large amount of deferred projects costs, and concerns whether reserves for mortgage losses were sufficient.

Internal financial controls, weak to begin with, were not adequate to the growing size of UDC's myriad activities. As a result, financial planning and forecasting was inadequate during a critical period of UDC's expansion. New projects were started and construction commitments made based on unrealistic assumptions. Projects were undertaken that later proved to be economically unsound.

UDC's problems grew. By 1973, UDC estimated it needed to borrow $800 million just to complete the $1.2 billion in construction projects then underway. Over half of this amount had to be borrowed by the spring of 1974.

The 1975 Bond Anticipation Note Default

During 1973 and 1974, several developments occurred that set the stage for the BANs default. First, in 1973 the legislatures of both New York and New Jersey repealed the port authority covenant that limited that body's involvement with mass transit, thereby raising questions in investors' minds whether the state would support its moral obligation debt in time of trouble. Second, while still maintaining its investment-quality rating, in the fall of 1973 Moody's did reduce its rating on the UDC bonds a half a notch from A to Baa–1, thereby giving some indication that it was aware of the seriousness of UDC's financial problems. Third, in December 1973 Governor Rockefeller resigned, ending a 15-year tenure and thus removing a driving force from state government. Fourth and last, in the spring of 1974, a major Wall Street underwriter—Morgan Guaranty Trust Company—dropped out of the UDC account as a managing underwriter, because of its concerns over UDC's deteriorating finances.

Due to the above factors as well as tight money market conditions, in May 1974, UDC was unable to market $100 million in short-term notes at reasonable rates, thereby effectively losing a critical source of financing. It was only after long and arduous negotiation with the New York banks that a financing package was assembled in September 1974 that enabled the UDC to raise enough cash to last the balance of the year.

In early 1975, Governor Carey was inaugurated, and his administration began negotiating with the New York banks to resolve the UDC financial crisis. The talks took place amid New York City's deteriorating finances and the uncertain viability of the UDC projects. The UDC's cash needs, estimated at almost $700 million for the next 24 months, proved to be too large an obstacle to be overcome in the few short weeks between the governor's taking office and February 25, 1975, the maturity date of the $100 million in short-term notes. As a result, the UDC was unable to roll over the maturing notes and the default occurred.

THE 21-YEAR DEFAULT OF THE WEST VIRGINIA TURNPIKE COMMISSION REVENUE BONDS*

The original $96 million of the West Virginia Turnpike Commission revenue bonds were sold in early 1952. These are the 3¾ percents dated March 1, 1952, and due December 1, 1989. Because of higher than anticipated construction costs, unanticipated engineering difficulties, higher than estimated real estate costs, and design changes, $37 million in additional bonds had to be sold in 1954. These are the 4⅛ percents dated March 2, 1952, and due December 1, 1989.[76]

While interest on the bonds was capitalized through June 1, 1956, the turnpike opened in October 1954. The turnpike commission agreed to charge tolls adequate to pay all expenses, including debt service. However, revenues were insufficient to pay coupons on a timely basis. The first interest default began with the coupon due June 1, 1958, which was subsequently paid four months later. Also, on March 24, 1959, the West Virginia Supreme Court ruled that bondholders must be paid interest on the defaulted coupons at the same rate as on the bonds. For the next 21 years, the turnpike commission continued to default on all its coupon payments. By June 1, 1969, for example, coupon payments were four years in arrears. The default period ended on December 1, 1979, when the interest coupon was paid when due plus the penalty interest.

The turnpike, when originally built, was approximately 88 miles long. It was a two-lane highway extending from Charleston on the north to a junction with U.S. routes 219 and 460 close to the southern border of the state. When the turnpike was planned, it was assumed that connecting highways to the north and south would also be built and that the turnpike would facilitate highway travel between the Midwest and the Southeast.

The turnpike did not attract the amount of long-distance traffic that had been projected. In its early days, the West Virginia Turnpike was anything but a key unit in a network of superhighways. Several miles of the toll road south of Charleston could be avoided by using parallel local roads. Also, connecting interstate highways were not ready. Finally, the traffic engineer overestimated initial commercial

---

* This section was coauthored with Charles T. Noona. Mr. Noona is with Bear, Stearns & Co.

[76] Data for this case study are from the Annual Report prepared by Peat, Marwick, Mitchell and Company for December 31, 1985 and dated February 31, 1986; and the monthly report covering the period from January 1, 1986, through May 1, 1986, prepared by the West Virginia Turnpike Commission, dated June 4, 1986.

vehicle usage. Expected traffic was slow to develop because of the delayed completion of Interstate 77 over the Virginia mountains to the Carolinas.

In the 1970s, the economics of the turnpike began to change in three ways. First, in 1970, the Federal Highway Administration and the West Virginia Department of Highways agreed to provide for, on a respective 90-percent–10-percent financing basis, the upgrading of the turnpike to four-lane federal interstate standards. While the improvements were paid for by the federal and state governments, the tolls were to remain in effect until all the outstanding revenue bonds had been retired. Second, in 1976 Interstate 77 (I77) was opened to traffic from Cleveland, Ohio, to the northern terminus of the turnpike. From the turnpike to the south, I77 was completed through Virginia and North Carolina to South Carolina. Finally, in 1979, Interstate 79 was opened to traffic from Charleston to I90 at Erie, Pennsylvania.

With the completion of the connecting interstate highways and the upgrading of the turnpike, traffic on the turnpike was increased. For example, traffic has improved from 4,433,706 vehicles in 1977 to 6,385,849 in 1982 to 9,909,700 in 1985. The trend has continued in 1986 with traffic up 20% for the first five months of the year.

Net revenues in 1985 amounted to $15.3 million at 3.8 times annual interest of approximately $4 million. Net revenues are expected to decline to about $9.2 million in 1986 reflecting self insurance costs of about $5 million. It should also be noted that, while the turnpike is at the time of this writing current in its semiannual coupon payments, the $90.7 million term maturities are due on December 1, 1989. Although the turnpike commission has since 1982 been retiring bonds through secondary market purchases, it is doubtful that the turnpike will generate sufficient revenues to retire all the term bonds by the scheduled maturity date of December 1, 1989. About half of the bonds are expected to be retired by 1989; the balance will have to be refinanced.

THE DEFAULTED CHESAPEAKE BAY BRIDGE AND TUNNEL DISTRICT, VIRGINIA, SERIES C, 5¾-PERCENT, THIRD-PLEDGE REVENUE BONDS*

In August 1960, $200 million in revenue bonds were sold in order to refund an earlier issue of bonds as well as to build a two-lane,

---

* This section was coauthored with Charles T. Noona.

17.5-mile bridge-tunnel in the lower Chesapeake Bay between the southern tip of the Delmarva Peninsula and Chesapeake Beacon near Norfolk, Virginia. The project was completed and opened to traffic on April 15, 1964.[77]

There are three separate bond securities, each with a final maturity of July 1, 2000. The $70 million Series A bonds have a coupon rate of 4.875 percent and have a first lien on the bridge and tunnel net revenues. The $30 million Series B bonds have a coupon rate of 5.50 percent and have a second lien on the net revenues. The $100 million Series C bonds have a coupon rate of 5.75 percent and a third lien on the net revenues.

Although there is not a formal rate covenant, the traffic engineers are to make recommendations in the schedule of tolls so as "to produce the maximum net revenues possible," and the district will revise its tolls in accordance with the recommendation.[78]

By July 1, 1970, the facility's reserves had been exhausted and the interest on the third-lien, Series C bonds was not paid. The toll road was scheduled to be completed in October 1963. Interest was capitalized in bond proceeds until March 7, 1965. Net revenues were projected to be $11,115,000 in 1964 compared with debt service of $10,812,000. Instead, completion occurred on April 15, 1964. Net revenues for the year ending April 30, 1965 were $6,881,626. Annual bond interest was $3,412,500 on the Series A 4⅞, $1,650,000 on the Series B 5½, and $5,750,000 on the Series C 5¾. However, only $1,819,126 was available for the Series C interest.

The coverage for interest on the Series C bonds remained very low through 1974, a period of nine years, when only $1,838,644 was available for that purpose. It was not until 1979, 15 years after operations began, that Series C interest ($5,750,000) was earned with a slight margin. Since then there has been steady improvement. Net revenues in fiscal 1985 amounted to $18,450,000 for 1.5 times coverage of interest on the three Series of bonds and amortization of the Series A & B bonds. Also, with the aid of a real estate sale, the District

---

[77] Data for this case study are from the official statement for $200 million Chesapeake Bay Bridge and Tunnel District Revenue Bonds, dated August 1, 1960; annual audit report for fiscal year ended June 30, 1985, for the Chesapeake Bay Bridge and Tunnel District, dated August 27, 1985; annual audit report for fiscal year ended June 30, 1981, for the Chesapeake Bay Bridge and Tunnel District, dated August 14, 1981; and an interview with William Oliver, author of *Moody's Credit Report* of September 19, 1982.

[78] Official statement for $200 million Chesapeake Bay Bridge and Tunnel District Revenue Bonds, p. 26.

gained $2,566,000 which enabled five Series C coupon payments to be made in fiscal 1985. The Series C bonds are now current in coupon payments and are expected to remain current. Some Series C bonds may be retired as early as late 1987 or early 1988. As of June 30, 1986 the reserve maintenance fund exceeded $3,000,000. An additional $4,000,000 is planned to be deposited into the fund in fiscal 1987.

Three reasons can be suggested for the default. First, at the time of construction it was hoped that the 17.5-mile, two-lane series of bridges and tunnels would attract a heavy volume of traffic and serve as a major link in the north–south highway system along the Atlantic seaboard. However, competition with the toll-free inland Interstate 95 highway, which includes Maryland's John F. Kennedy Memorial Highway, has been keen. As a result, it primarily serves the Delmarva Peninsula community. Automobile traffic tends to be highly seasonal, with the transportation of farm crops during the summer a major factor.

It is interesting to note that at the time of the 1960 bond sale the traffic engineers (Wilbur Smith and Associates of New Haven, Connecticut) had concluded that the project would be successful because of "the desires of motorists to bypass the larger metropolitan areas, and the attractiveness of the flatter topography closer to the Atlantic coastline to commercial vehicles. Both of these advantages are also provided by the Ocean Highway of which the proposed fixed crossing will be a part."[79]

A second reason for the default may be that, due to the numerous collisions by water traffic, the toll facility has had to be closed for long periods of time while repairs were being made to the two-lane structures. Besides increased insurance costs, the closing also resulted in uneven income flows.

A third reason for the default was that the traffic engineers for several years did not believe that a toll increase would be productive. Toll rates eventually were raised several times and as of July 22, 1986, were at a minimum of $9 for passenger cars and light trucks.

THE MUIR HOUSING PROJECT STRUGGLES TO COME BACK FROM DEFAULT*

On a 10.8-acre lot in Martinez, just outside Oakland, California, there stands the shell of a 100-unit housing project for the low-income elderly

---

[79] Ibid., Appendix I, p. 1–4.
* This section was written by Kent Pierce.

that is one month away from completion. The project has been one month away from completion since June 1982. And it would stay one month away from completion for some time to come unless its developer, Muir California Health Recreation and Retirement Facilities, Inc., could pull it out of the financial mess it fell into when it defaulted on a bond interest payment June 1, 1982.

"The whole issue has been a disaster," said Charles L. Gunther, president of Gibralco Inc., the Santa Monica, California, firm that underwrote the $4.2 million bond issue sold to finance the project. "We have been hurt as much or more than anyone else by this affair." Gibralco's reputation has been tarnished, he said, and the company has put considerable time and money into working on the various proposed settlements.

Mr. Gunther's complaint got very little sympathy, however, at a meeting in November 1982 of more than 100 Muir bondholders in Los Angeles. The meeting was called by the Bank of America, trustee for the bonds sold to finance the project, to discuss alternatives to foreclosure on the project as well as the possibility of foreclosure itself. The bondholders at the meeting—mostly individual investors ranging from doctors and investment counselors to a retired truck driver—represented over $1 million of the $4.2 million bonds sold for the project. It was their first official chance to speak since the bonds went into default, and they took full advantage of it. The meeting ran more than two and a half hours past the scheduled close of 8:30 P.M. as angry investors had their say about the project's past and their concerns about its future.

"We went into the project attracted by the tax exemption and planned to sit back and collect interest as the bonds matured," one bondholder complained. "Now that this is not happening, we do not want to sit back and listen to the verbal gymnastics of attorneys and watch them collect attorney's fees. We have to get the bondholders involved because it is the bondholders who have their own best interest at heart." Toward that end, the investors ended the meeting by nominating a seven-member bondholder committee to meet with officials of Muir, Bank of America, and the underwriters.

In the circumstances surrounding the Muir default, there are a number of undisputed facts that form the crux of the problems and the focus of all the negotiations.

In May 1981, Muir (a nonprofit health corporation) issued $4.2 million of tax-exempt serial bonds from 1984 to 2009 at yields running from 10 percent to 14 percent. Some of the proceeds were set aside in an interest reserve fund to pay for the first two interest payments in December 1981 and June 1982, and the rest went into buying land, paying bond attorneys, underwriting fees, and construction.

On June 1, 1982, when the project was approximately 80–85 percent complete, the bonds went into technical default because the interest reserve fund came up $60,000 short of the scheduled interest payment. Gibralco and Muir tried to come up with the $60,000, but gave up when it was disclosed that the project was suffering from more serious difficulties. The construction fund was $600,000 short of what it needed to finish the project, and the project's revenue projections were found to be 50 percent too high. With annual revenues originally designed to provide 1.01 to 1.28 times the amount of the bonds due over the first five years of the project, it became readily apparent that the future interest and principal payments could not be made unless the project's finances were restructured.

At that point, Bank of America, acting as trustee, moved to freeze the estimated $590,000 left in the construction fund account and the estimated $220,000 remaining in the interest reserve account. According to Paul Webber, an attorney for the bank, the money has since been reinvested and used to pay for security services, patch holes in the roof, continue insurance coverage, make a project appraisal, and (presumably) pay the bank's attorneys.

Explanations for what caused Muir's various financial problems are fairly simple. At the November meeting of the bondholders, Mr. Webber said that the June 1 interest payment was missed because the project was not generating the funds needed to augment the interest reserve fund.

Why the delay in construction? In an interview, James Snow, secretary-treasurer of Muir, said that construction had been put off and new expenses incurred because of the harsh 1981–82 winter and because of retroactive offsite and onsite requirements placed on construction by the city of Martinez. Bondholders at the November meeting were told that construction costs were running about 20 percent over the original $2.55 million projection.

As for the faulty revenue forecasts, Prefecto Villarreal, director of the Contra Costa Housing Authority (the agency slated to manage the project), explained that the project's success hinged on its appeal to elderly residents with Section 8 rent certificates from the federal Department of Housing and Urban Development. Those certificates are good for rent subsidy money from HUD, the amount of which is based on fair market rental rates that HUD sets for various regions of the country. The feasibility consultant for the project had based his revenue projections on the project being in a region where the

1982 base rental rate was $509; but HUD said that the project was in a region where the rental rate was $347. This mistake, Mr. Villarreal said, meant that the project's forecast of approximately $600,000 in revenues a year was about $200,000 too high.

Various proposals have been made to straighten out the project's financing. A couple of months after the default, Gibralco presented a plan that called for contributions from the bondholders, the county housing authority, and the contractor, Carlo Zocchi. According to Gibralco's calculations, the project could be completed if the housing authority paid for operating the project for five years and for a $121,000 sewer hookup fee, Mr. Zocchi deferred payment of about half of his remaining construction costs for 10 years without interest, and the bondholders agreed to take a 400–basis point reduction on bond repayments. The bondholders eventually would receive full payment on the bonds; and the housing authority would eventually control the project.

It appeared in late summer 1982 that the housing authority might accept the Gibralco proposal. But the political opposition in Martinez and Contra Costa County to the plan convinced the authority to come up with a counterproposal. That plan called for a pooled management fund to pay for the project's operating needs over five years, to which all the major participants could contribute.

Despite some resistance to this plan as well, the county board of supervisors authorized an interest-free loan of $100,000 to the authority to put in the management fund as a substantial gesture of good faith. Additionally, the Martinez council on community development approved a loan from federal community-development block-grant money to pay for the sewer hookup. With this money in hand, the authority believed it had the bargaining authority to hammer out a settlement.

Bank of America's solution for Muir's problem is to get a grant from HUD to pay for the project's completion—a highly unlikely event—or foreclose on the project. Attorney Webber said the bank feels that the bondholders are innocent bystanders in this affair and should not accept any settlement, including Gibralco's, at their expense. The bondholders' position on all of the preceding proposals remains unclear, though those present at the November gathering expressed an overwhelming desire to take some sort of action.

While the bondholders gave the proposed settlements a relatively sympathetic reception, their mood leaving the Los Angeles hotel was bitter. One investor, who wished not to be named, asked: "Where were all these guys—where was the underwriter, the bond counsel, the Muir people—when all the trouble was taking place? Why weren't the problems—these problems over rental rates, construction costs, and the interest reserve fund—picked up before the bonds were sold to us?"

Said William Jackson, an underwriter at Gibralco: "I think the germ of failure is that a deal can only stand so many things going wrong; and this one just had too many things go wrong."

THE BELLEVUE BRIDGE DEFAULT*

The Bellevue Bridge Commission in Bellevue, Nebraska, is paying back coupons 14 years behind schedule.

The commission was established in 1943 to construct, operate, and maintain a bridge across the Missouri River from Bellevue to Council Bluffs, Iowa. Though the bridge carries traffic to and from Iowa, the commission has no jurisdiction outside of Nebraska. In 1950, it issued $2.83 million of revenue bonds to construct the bridge. The bonds were secured solely by toll revenues on the bridge.[80]

The commission began paying interest out of construction funds, having issued enough bond principal to cover three years of interest payments. The bridge was completed on schedule, but five miles of access roads leading to the bridge on the Iowa side were not constructed as the commission had anticipated.[81] As a result, the commission defaulted on its May 1, 1954, interest payment. None of the scheduled semiannual interest payments were made again until June 1, 1972, when the May 1954 coupon was paid. Interest payments have been made sporadically since then;[82] as of November 1982 the Omaha National Bank, the commission's paying agent, paid coupons due May 1, 1968.[83]

The access-road problem was rectified when Shields & Company of New York paid $233,000 to pave the five miles of Iowa roads. But the commission's problems were still not over.[84] The commission had estimated that 350 vehicles would cross the bridge each day. In 1957, average daily traffic totaled about 100 vehicles.[85] Then in 1970,

---

* This section was written by Mark Fury.

[80] Moody's *Municipal & Government Manual,* 1981, p. 2112.

[81] Ibid.

[82] Ibid.

[83] Interviews with officers at the Omaha National Bank.

[84] Moody's, *Manual,* p. 2112.

[85] Ibid.

Interstate 29 opened five miles north of Bellevue. It provided transportation across the river free of charge.[86]

The 1950 bonds were intended to be 30-year maturities and pay 4-percent coupons. As of early 1985, coupon payments were 14 years behind and no principal had been retired.[87]

CHICAGO AND ITS DEFAULTED CALUMET SKYWAY REVENUE BONDS

The original $88 million of the city of Chicago's Calumet Skyway Toll Bridge revenue bonds were sold in December 1954. These are the 3¾ percents dated January 1, 1955, and due January 1, 1995. Because of increased construction costs, $13 million in additional bonds were sold in May 1957. These are the 4⅜ percents dated January 1, 1955, and due January 1, 1995.[88]

The six-lane skyway is about 7.75 miles long connecting the Indiana Toll Road to the Dan Ryan Expressway (I94) in the center of Chicago. It passes over the Calumet industrial district of river barges, drawbridges, heavy industrial plants, and railroad freight sidings. At the time of the bond sale in the 1950s the traffic engineers, Coverdale & Colpitts of New York City, estimated that the skyway would divert traffic away from other congested routes leading to downtown Chicago. The traffic engineers projected an annual volume of 23 million vehicles using the skyway by 1973. In 1973, traffic volume was only about 9 million vehicles.

In the early 1960s, competing toll-free highways were opened that had the result of diverting traffic away from the skyway. Because of the erratic traffic usage and the projected traffic volume never materializing, Chicago defaulted on its July 1, 1963, coupon payments and all additional payments thereafter. The payments generally have been made two to four years after the due dates, and have included penalties of 5 percent per annum on past-due interest coupons from the date of the defaults to the respective payment dates. For example, as shown

---

[86] Interviews with officers of the Bellevue Bridge Commission.

[87] Interviews with Omaha National Bank officers.

[88] Data for this case study is from the official statement for $88 million city of Chicago Calumet Skyway Toll Bridge revenue bonds, dated December 22, 1954; official statement for $13 million city of Chicago Calumet Skyway Toll Bridge revenue bonds, dated April 10, 1957; and *Moody's Credit Report* of November 25, 1980. The author would also like to thank Marilyn Madden of the Merrill Lynch municipal research department for her assistance.

EXHIBIT 2

NOTICE TO HOLDERS OF ALL
CITY OF CHICAGO, ILLINOIS
Calumet Skyway Toll Bridge Revenue Bonds

All bond holders are hereby notified that the Depositary, American National Bank and Trust Company of Chicago, 33 North LaSalle Street, Chicago, Illinois, will pay as of December 5, 1984, the interest coupons due January 1, 1982, on the above bonds with interest on these past due coupons from January 1, 1982 to December 5, 1984, at the rate of 5% per annum, as follows:

	Coupon Rate	Interest on Past Due Interest	Total Payment
3⅜% bonds	$16.88	$2.47	$19.35
4⅜% bonds	21.88	3.20	25.08

and an equivalent amount to the holders of the fully registered bonds.

Holders should present said coupons to one of the Paying Agents, American National Bank and Trust Company of Chicago, or The Chase Manhattan Bank, N.A., in New York City.

WALTER K. KNORR
CITY COMPTROLLER
CHICAGO, ILLINOIS

Source: *The Wall Street Journal,* May 27, 1986.

in the exhibit below, the interest coupons due January 1, 1984 were paid on June 18, 1986. (Exhibit 2)

Additionally, it should be noted that, while there is a 1.2-times rate covenant and tolls have been raised over the years, the erratic traffic volume and lack of a maintenance fund have required the payment of necessary maintenance charges out of current gross revenues. In 1985 the accumulated deficit of the skyway was over $40 million. This included the defaulted interest coupons, the 5-percent penalty per annum on the defaulted coupons, the unpaid sinking fund installments, and $2 million borrowed from the city of Chicago for interest payments.

12

Investment Considerations and Strategies

In this chapter we shall discuss investment considerations in selecting municipal bonds and strategies that can be employed by the individual investor.

TREASURY YIELDS VERSUS MUNICIPAL YIELDS

Because of the tax-exempt feature of municipal bonds, the yield on municipal bonds historically has been less than that on Treasuries with the same maturity. Exhibit 1 shows the yield levels and the ratio of municipal yields to Treasury yields for four maturities on February 1984, January 1985 and November 21, 1985. As can be seen, the yield ratio changes over time. Exhibit 2 shows the yield ratio of municipal yields to Treasury yields for maturities of 1 year, 5 years, 10 years and 20 years from mid-1974 to 1982.

DETERMINING IF THERE IS A YIELD ADVANTAGE BY BUYING MUNICIPALS

Before buying municipal bonds, an investor must determine whether his present and *expected future* tax brackets are high enough to warrant purchasing municipal bonds for his portfolio. Some brokerage firms publish tables showing for each tax bracket the "taxable equivalent yield" from owning a municipal bond. Exhibit 3 is an example of such a table. (For a more comprehensive discussion of the impact of the 1986 tax law on taxable equivalent yields see Appendix A.) The taxable equivalent yield is the yield an investor would have to earn

EXHIBIT 1 Yield Levels and Ratios (early February 1984, January 10, 1985, and November 21, 1985)

Issue	February 1984			January 10, 1985			November 21, 1985		
	Municipal Yield	Treasury Yield	Yield Ratio	Municipal Yield	Treasury Yield	Yield Ratio	Municipal Yield	Treasury Yield	Yield Ratio
3 year AAA G.O.	6.25%	10.75%	.58	6.75%	10.30%	.65	5.60%	8.75%	.64
5 year AAA G.O.	6.90	11.40	.60	7.25	11.00	.66	6.25	9.17	.68
10 year AAA G.O.	8.00	11.60	.69	8.25	11.45	.72	7.10	9.60	.74
30 year AAA G.O.	9.00	11.75	.77	9.25	11.50	.80	8.25	9.94	.83

SOURCE: Merrill Lynch, *Bond Market Comment* 8, no. 2 (January 11, 1985) and *Bond Market Comment* 8, no. 47 (November 22, 1985).

before taxes on a taxable bond in order to produce an equivalent after-tax yield offered on a municipal bond. By comparing the taxable equivalent yield to the yield offered on taxable bonds of the same credit quality and maturity, an investor can determine if municipal bonds will enhance a portfolio's after-tax return.

When a brokerage firm offers a municipal bond, it usually provides

EXHIBIT 2 Ratio of Yields on Municipals to Yields on Treasuries

Ratio of Yields on 1-Year Municipal Notes to Yields on 1-Year Treasury Bills

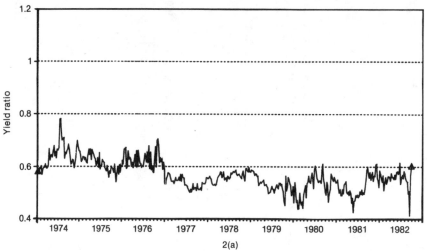

2(a)

Ratio of Yields on 10-Year AAA G.O. Bonds to Yields on 10-Year Treasury Notes

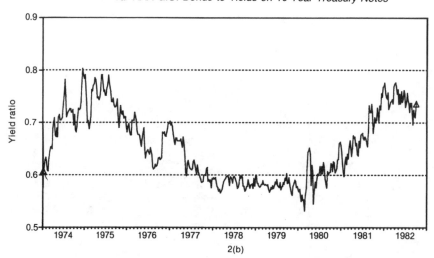

2(b)

EXHIBIT 2 (*Continued*)

Ratio of Yields on 5-Year AAA G.O. Bonds to Yields on 5-Year Treasury Notes

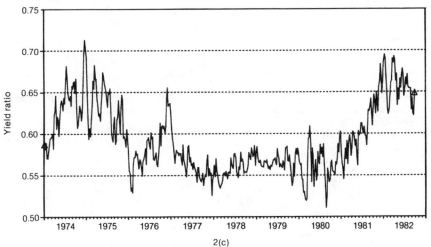

2(c)

Ratio of Yields on 20-Year AAA G.O. Bonds to Yields on 20-Year Treasury Bonds

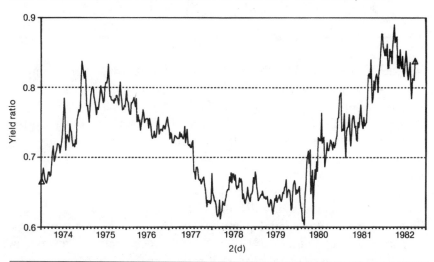

2(d)

SOURCE: James L. Kochan, "Analyzing Cycles in Municipal Yields: An Institutional Approach," in *The Municipal Bond Handbook: Vol. I,* eds. Frank J. Fabozzi, Sylvan G. Feldstein, Irving M. Pollack and Frank G. Zarb (Homewood, Ill.: Dow Jones–Irwin, 1983), pp. 334–35.

EXHIBIT 3 Tax-Exempt/Taxable Equivalent Yield (individual income brackets) Under the 1986 Tax Law for 1988

Single Return 1 exemption	$0 $17,850	$17,851 $43,150	$ 43,151 $100,480	$100,481 —
Joint Return 4 exemptions	$0 $29,750	$29,751 $71,900	$ 71,901 $192,930	$192,931 —
Tax Bracket	15%	28%	33%	28%
Tax Exempt Yields				
5.0	5.9	6.9	7.5	6.9
5.5	6.5	7.6	8.2	7.6
6.0	7.1	8.3	9.0	8.3
6.5	7.6	9.0	9.7	9.0
7.0	8.2	9.7	10.4	9.7
7.5	8.8	10.4	11.2	10.4
8.0	9.4	11.1	11.9	11.1
8.5	10.0	11.8	12.7	11.8
9.0	10.6	12.5	13.4	12.5
9.5	11.2	13.2	14.2	13.2
10.0	11.8	13.9	14.9	13.9
10.5	12.4	14.6	15.7	14.6
11.0	12.9	15.3	16.4	15.3
11.5	13.5	16.0	17.2	16.0
12.0	14.1	16.7	17.9	16.7

two yield measures. The first is the yield-to-maturity. For example, in mid-November of 1984, Fairfax County, Virginia, 4.90s general obligation bonds due October 1, 1992, sold for 76.25 percent of par for a yield-to-maturity of 9.25 percent. The second is the yield-to-maturity assuming a certain capital gains tax. The reason for this second yield measure is that only the interest, not the capital gain from holding a municipal bond, is exempt from federal income taxes. For certain municipal bonds purchased at a discount from par, there is a potential capital gains liability if the bond is held to maturity. Since the maximum capital gains tax at the time of this writing is 20 percent, yield-to-maturity after a 20-percent capital gains tax is quoted. In the case of the Fairfax, Virginia, general obligation bonds, although the yield-to-maturity was 9.25 percent, the yield after an assumed 20-percent capital gains tax was 8.73 percent.

Investors in at least the 35-percent tax bracket have been able to enhance the return on their portfolio by investing in municipal bonds. An investor should *not* hold a municipal bond in an IRA or Keogh Plan since it is tax-exempt by its structure.

SELECTING THE COUPON RATE

Municipal bonds come in a wide variety of coupon rates. The coupon rate will have an important impact on the investor's after-tax return and risk exposure.

Impact on After-Tax Return

A property of all bonds is that the lower the coupon rate relative to prevailing yields in the market, the greater the discount on the bond. A bond must sell below its par value so that an investor may realize the prevailing yield through coupon interest plus capital appreciation. For example, suppose that interest rates in the marketplace are 10 percent and that two municipal bonds, Muni-A and Muni-B, both with 15 years to maturity and a $5,000 par value have coupon rates of 10 percent and 3 percent, respectively. Muni-A would sell for its par value of $5,000. Muni-B, on the other hand, would sell for $2,310. The holder of Muni-B would realize a capital gain of $2,690 if the bond is held to maturity. The annual coupon interest of $150 (.03 × $5,000) plus the capital gain of $2,690 are the two forms of return that the investor will realize in order to achieve a 10-percent return.

Although two municipal bonds may offer the same yield, only the interest income, not any capital gain, is exempt from federal income taxes.

Since the coupon rate will determine whether the bond is selling at a discount and therefore whether there will be a taxable capital gain, the investor should carefully examine the yield after an estimated capital gains tax when comparing municipal issues.

Impact on Interest-Rate Risk

When interest rates rise, municipal bond prices decline. The possibility that an investor may have to sell his bond when interest rates have increased and bond prices have declined is known as interest-rate or market risk. Not all municipal bonds have the same degree of interest-rate risk. The lower the coupon rate, the greater the interest-rate risk.

To illustrate this, consider our two hypothetical municipal bonds, Muni-A and Muni-B. Let's look at what happens if interest rates rise from 10 percent to 12 percent the day after the bonds are purchased. For Muni-A, the 10-percent coupon bond selling at par ($5,000), the price of the bond will decline to $4,311. Thus, there would be a loss of $689 or 14 percent of his $5,000 investment. For Muni-B, the 3-percent coupon bond selling for $2,310, the price of the bond will decline by 18 percent to $1,904.

The investor who plans to hold a municipal bond until maturity is not exposed to interest-rate risk. Regardless of the interest rate prevailing at the time the municipal bond matures, the issuer will redeem the issue at the maturity value. For an investor who may have to sell a municipal bond before maturity, the investor should consider current coupon bonds. By a current coupon bond we mean a bond whose coupon interest rate is close to the prevailing interest rate in the market.

If interest rates are expected to be lower when a municipal bond is scheduled to be sold by the investor, then lower coupon bonds offer greater price appreciation potential. To illustrate this, suppose that interest rates in three years are expected to drop from 10 percent to 8 percent. Muni-A with the higher coupon will increase in price by 17 percent to $5,864 whereas the lower coupon municipal bond, Muni-B, will increase in price by 23 percent from $2,310 to $2,840.

Impact on Reinvestment Risk

As we explained in Chapter 1, one source of return from holding a municipal bond is the interest-on-interest from the reinvestment of the semiannual coupon interest. This source of return becomes increasingly more important the longer the maturity of the municipal bond. For an intermediate and long-term bond, it is not unusual for the interest-on-interest source to represent more than one half of a bond's total return.

The problem with the yield-to-maturity as a measure of a bond's return is that it assumes that the semiannual coupon interest payments can be reinvested at the yield-to-maturity. For example, in January of 1982 when yields on long-term, triple-A municipal bonds were about 12.5 percent, an investor who purchased a municipal bond would only realize a 12.5-percent return by holding the bond to maturity if the coupon payments were reinvested to yield 12.5 percent.

The risk that the bondholder will realize a total return less than the promised yield when the bond is purchased because the coupon payments are reinvested at a yield less than the yield-to-maturity is known as *reinvestment risk.* As more coupon interest must be reinvested to generate the yield-to-maturity, the reinvestment risk becomes greater. Thus, the lower the coupon rate, the lower the reinvestment risk. Although low coupon bonds mitigate reinvestment risk, they do not eliminate it. Reinvestment risk can be eliminated by purchasing zero-coupon bonds since there are no coupon payments to reinvest.

Notice that there is a trade-off here between interest-rate risk and reinvestment risk when selecting a coupon rate. With a lower coupon, reinvestment risk decreases but interest-rate risk increases. With a higher coupon, the greater is the reinvestment risk, but the smaller is the interest-rate risk. Unlike interest-rate risk that will not be of concern to an investor who plans to hold a municipal bond to maturity, reinvestment risk will still be there.

Impact on Call Risk

As explained in Chapter 1, an investor who owns a callable municipal bond is subject to call risk. Call risk is the risk that the issuer will call the bond prior to maturity, usually to take advantage of a dramatic drop in interest rates since the bond was issued. When this occurs, the bondholder must reinvest the proceeds received from the issuer at a lower interest rate.

Generally, the key factor that will determine whether a bond is likely to be called is the coupon interest rate. Consider once again our two hypothetical municipal bonds—Muni-A and Muni-B. If two years from now, interest rates drop from 10 percent to 5 percent, it will probably be beneficial for the issuer of Muni-A to call the issue. For Muni-B, on the other hand, the issuer would not call the bond because the coupon interest cost to the issuer is only 3 percent, which is less than what the issuer would have to pay if it called the issue and sold a new issue of 5-percent bonds. Therefore, the lower the coupon, the smaller is the probability that the issue will be called.

MATURITY SELECTION

Determining the length of the maturity will also impact return and risk.

Impact on Return

One determinant of the yield on a bond is the number of years remaining to maturity. The yield curve depicts the relationship at a given point in time between yields and maturity for bonds that are identical

EXHIBIT 4 Three Hypothetical Yield Curves

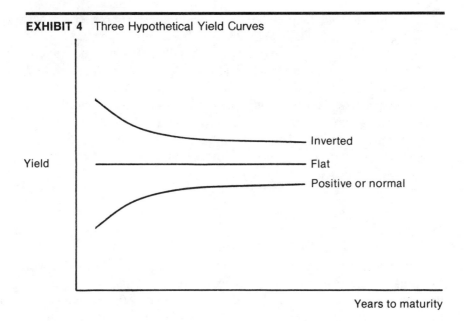

in every way except maturity. Three hypothetical yield curves are shown in Exhibit 4. When yields increase with maturity, the yield curve is said to be *normal* or have a *positive slope.* Therefore, as investors lengthen their maturity, they require a greater yield. It is also possible for the yield curve to be "inverted," meaning that long-term yields are less than short-term yields. If short, intermediate and long-term yields are roughly the same, the yield curve is said to be *flat.*

In the taxable bond market, it is not unusual to find all three shapes for the yield curve at different points in the business cycle. However, in the municipal bond market the yield curve is typically normal or upward sloping. Exhibit 5 shows a municipal yield curve for December 31, 1984. Consequently, in the municipal bond market, long-term bonds offer higher yields than short- and intermediate-term bonds.

Another characteristic of the municipal bond yield curve is that yield spreads between maturities are usually wider in the municipal bond market compared with maturity spreads in the taxable market. This is illustrated in Exhibit 6 that contrasts historical maturity spreads between bonds with 30 years and 1 year remaining to maturity for Treasuries and high-grade municipals. These historical maturity spreads were even more dramatic when viewed in terms of percentages,

EXHIBIT 5 Municipal AAA Yield Curve as of December 31, 1984

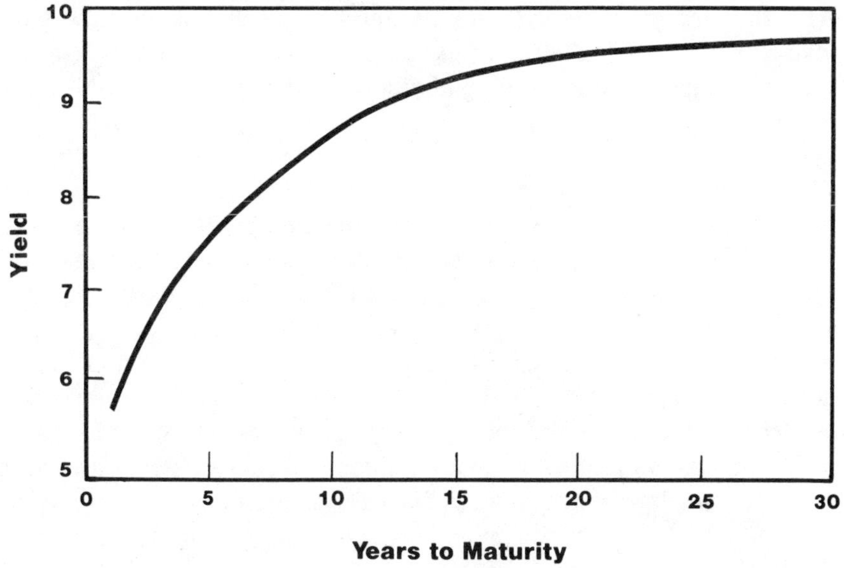

Source: Merrill Lynch Municipal Bond Research Department

as can be seen in Exhibit 7. This means that potential rewards are greater by lengthening maturity in the municipal bond market compared to the taxable bond market.

Impact on Interest-Rate Risk

An investor who does not hold a municipal bond to maturity is exposed to interest-rate risk. We stated earlier that the lower the coupon rate, the greater the interest-rate risk. Another property of a bond is that for a given coupon rate, the greater the maturity the greater is the interest-rate risk. For example, consider our hypothetical municipal bond Muni-A and another hypothetical municipal bond with the same coupon but only 5 years to maturity rather than 15 years. We'll refer to the latter municipal bond as Muni-C. Suppose for purposes of this illustration that Muni-C is also selling to yield 10 percent, so that the bond is selling at par ($5,000). If yields increase in three years from 10 percent to 12 percent, Muni-A, the original 15-year municipal bond, would decline by 13 percent to $4,373. The short-term bond, Muni-C, would only decline by slightly more than 3 percent to $4,827.

Consequently, lengthening maturity may increase return, but it also increases interest-rate risk.

SELECTING THE CREDIT QUALITY SECTOR

All other factors constant, the greater the credit risk perceived by investors, the higher the return expected by investors. Exhibit 8 shows general obligation municipal bond yields for the two weeks in November 1985, as well as 52-week highs and lows by credit quality and maturity.

The spread between municipal bonds of different credit quality is not constant over time. Reasons for the change in spreads are: (1) the outlook for the economy and its anticipated impact on issuers, (2) federal budget financing needs, and (3) municipal market supply-and-demand factors. During periods of relatively low interest rates, investors sometimes increase their holdings of issues of lower credit quality in order to obtain additional yield. This narrows the spread between high-grade and lower-grade credit issues. During periods in which investors anticipate a poor economic climate, there is often a "flight to quality" as investors pursue a more conservative credit-risk exposure. This widens the spread between high-grade and lower-grade credit issues.

Another factor that causes shifts in the spread between issues of different quality is the temporary oversupply of issues within a market sector. For example, a substantial new-issue volume of high-grade state general obligation bonds may tend to decrease the spread between high-grade and lower-grade revenue bonds. In a weak market environment it is easier for high-grade municipal bonds to come to market than for weaker credits. Therefore, it is not uncommon for high grades to flood weak markets while at the same time there is a relative scarcity of medium- and lower-grade municipal bond issues.

SELECTING BONDS WITHIN AN ASSIGNED CREDIT RATING

Bond buyers primarily use the credit ratings assigned by the commercial rating companies, Standard & Poor's and Moody's, as a starting point for pricing an issue. The final market-derived bond price is composed of the assigned credit rating by these companies and adjustments by investors to reflect their own analysis of credit worthiness and perception of marketability. For example, as we noted in Chapter 6, insured municipal bonds tend to have yields that are substantially higher than noninsured superior-investment-quality municipal bonds even though most insured bonds are given triple-A ratings by the commercial rating companies. Additionally, many investors have geo-

EXHIBIT 6 Yield Curve Spreads (30-year/1-year spreads within municipal and Treasury markets)

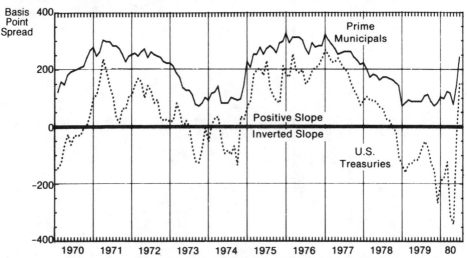

SOURCE: Martin L. Leibowitz, "The Municipal Rolling Yield: A New Approach to the Analysis of Tax-Exempt Yield Curves," in *The Municipal Bond Handbook* Vol. I, ed. Frank J. Fabozzi, Sylvan G. Feldstein, Irving M. Pollack, and Frank G. Zarb (Homewood, Ill.: Dow Jones–Irwin, 1983). © Dow Jones–Irwin, Inc.

EXHIBIT 7 Yield Curve Spreads as Percentage (30-year/1-year spreads as percentage of 1-year rate)

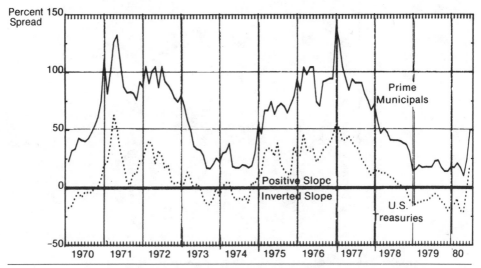

SOURCE: Martin L. Leibowitz, "The Municipal Rolling Yield: A New Approach to the Analysis of Tax-Exempt Yield Curves," Chapter 33 in *Municipal Bond Handbook* Vol. I, ed. Fabozzi et al.

EXHIBIT 8 Yields by Credit Quality and Maturity

| | Superior Investment Quality | | | | High Investment Quality | | | | Medium Investment Quality | | | | Low Investment Quality | | | |
| | November, 1985 | | 52 Week | | November, 1985 | | 52 Week | | November, 1985 | | 52 Week | | November, 1985 | | 52 Week | |
	11/21	11/14	High	Low	11/21	11/14	High	Low	11/21	11/14	High	Low	11/21	11/14	High	Low
New General Obligations																
1 Year	5.00	5.00	6.00	4.50	5.10	5.20	6.10	4.55	5.20	5.40	6.20	4.60	5.40	5.40	6.75	5.40
3 Years	5.60	5.25	7.00	5.25	5.75	5.45	7.25	5.45	5.90	5.65	7.50	5.65	6.65	6.65	7.75	6.65
5 Years	6.25	6.50	7.50	6.25	6.45	6.70	7.60	6.45	6.65	6.90	7.75	6.85	7.65	7.65	8.50	7.25
7 Years	6.75	7.00	8.10	6.75	6.90	7.10	8.75	6.90	7.10	7.35	8.40	7.10	8.15	8.15	9.25	8.15
10 Years	7.10	7.50	8.60	7.10	7.25	7.60	8.80	7.25	7.40	7.80	9.55	7.40	8.75	8.90	9.75	8.50
15 Years	7.80	8.05	9.45	7.80	8.00	8.15	9.60	8.00	8.25	8.40	9.75	8.25	9.12	9.27	10.25	8.55
20 Years	8.15	8.35	9.80	8.15	8.25	8.40	9.95	8.25	8.40	8.60	10.10	8.40	9.25	9.40	10.50	8.63
25 Years	8.20	8.40	8.85	8.20	8.35	8.50	10.00	8.35	8.50	8.75	10.15	8.50	9.37	9.52	10.75	9.37
30 Years	8.25	8.40	9.90	8.25	8.40	8.50	10.05	8.40	8.50	8.75	10.25	8.50	9.50	9.65	10.89	9.50

SOURCE: Merrill Lynch, *Bond Market Comment* 8, no. 47 (November 22, 1985).

graphical preferences among bonds, in spite of identical credit quality and otherwise comparable investment characteristics.

IN-STATE VERSUS OUT-OF-STATE ISSUES

An investor must decide whether to purchase an in-state or an out-of-state issue. The Dade County, Florida, general obligation bond, for example, is an in-state bond if the holder of the bond resides in Florida but an out-of-state bond for all holders of the bond who do not reside in Florida. An important factor in the decision to buy an in-state or out-of-state bond is state and local taxes on investment income and personal property.

The tax treatment at the state and local levels varies. There are three types of tax that can be imposed—an income tax on coupon income, a tax on realized capital gains, and a personal property tax. Only six states do not impose at least one of these taxes on individuals.

For those states that do impose at least one type of income tax, the tax treatment depends on whether the investor owns a municipal bond of an in-state issuer or an out-of-state issuer. Several states do not levy a tax on any coupon interest from municipal bonds, regardless if the issuer is in-state or out-of-state. Most states give favorable treatment to in-state issuers by exempting coupon interest paid by such issuers, but tax the coupon interest of out-of-state issuers. However, there are states that levy an income tax on coupon interest regardless of whether it is an in-state bond or an out-of-state bond.

In many states where the coupon interest is exempt if issued by an in-state issuer, the same exemption will not apply to capital gains involving municipal bonds. For example, in California, New York, and Virginia, coupon interest from in-state issuers is exempt while capital gains from the disposal of an in-state bond are subject to tax. New Jersey and Pennsylvania exempt both coupon interest and capital gains when the issuer is in-state.

The states of Alabama, Florida, Georgia, Indiana, Kansas, Kentucky, Michigan, North Carolina, Ohio, Pennsylvania, and West Virginia have a personal property tax applicable to municipal bonds. The rate varies from $1 to $5 per $1,000 of par value (or in some cases market value). There are some states, such as Ohio, in which the annual income of the municipal bond held is the basis for the property tax.

As a result of the difference in state taxes, strong investor demand for in-state issuers in states with high income taxes (for example, New

York, Massachusetts, and California) will reduce yields relative to bonds of issuers located in states where state and local taxes are not important considerations (for example, Illinois, Florida, and New Jersey). In states where there is a high individual maximum tax rate, purchasing in-state bonds may still be the most prudent investment strategy. However, a mistake is often made by some investors in certain states when buying municipal bonds of in-state issuers in order to benefit from the exemption from state and local taxes. Some investors pay too much, in terms of yield give-up, to purchase bonds of in-state issuers. Pledging requirements for local financial institutions (such as commercial banks that have state and local government deposits) sometimes create strong in-state demand for local municipal bonds. Another reason is that there are investors in some states that exhibit extreme reluctance to purchase issues from issuers outside of their state or region. In-state parochialism tends to decrease relative yields on bonds whose issuers are from states in which investors exhibit this behavior.

OPPORTUNITIES OFFERED BY ZERO, PUTTABLE, AND VARIABLE RATE BONDS

The high and volatile interest rates that prevailed in the late 1970s and through the mid-1980s made the cost of borrowing for municipal issuers of even the highest credit quality expensive. To reduce the cost of borrowing for municipal issuers, investment bankers designed bonds that were more attractive to investors than traditional offerings. Several of these new types of offerings and their investment characteristics are discussed below.

Zero-Coupon Bonds

A zero-coupon bond is a bond that is issued at a deep discount from par. The interest income is the difference between the maturity value and the purchase price. This difference is treated as interest income, not a capital gain, and therefore the income is exempt from federal income taxes.

A variation of the zero-coupon bond, known as *compound interest bond* or *municipal multiplier,* does actually have interest payments. However, the interest payments are not distributed to the holder of the bond until maturity. Rather, the issuer agrees to reinvest the undistributed interest payments at the bond's yield-to-maturity when it was issued. For example, suppose that a 10-percent, 10-year bond with a par value of $5,000 is sold at par to yield 10 percent. Every six months, the maturity value of the bond is increased by 5 percent of the maturity value of the previous six months. So at the end of 10 years, the maturity value of the bond will be equal to $13,267. In contrast, a 10-year zero-coupon bond priced to yield 10 percent would have a maturity value of $5,000 but issued for $1,884.

Zero-coupon bonds and compound interest bonds were introduced to eliminate reinvestment risk. This allows the investor to lock in the yield-to-maturity when the bond is purchased, assuming that the issuer does not default. The disadvantage for an investor who might have to sell the zero before maturity is that there is greater interest-rate risk. The greater interest-rate risk follows from the property of bonds that for a given maturity, the lower the coupon rate the greater the price volatility.

Unlike taxable zero-coupon bonds, there is no federal income tax disadvantage from buying a zero-coupon bond. For taxable zero-coupon bonds, the accrued but unpaid interest is reported annually and taxed. This results in a negative cash flow from holding a zero-coupon bond by a taxable entity. Taxable zero-coupon bonds should only be held in tax-exempt portfolios such as an IRA or Keogh Plan. Since interest income from a zero-coupon municipal bond is exempt from federal income taxes, they can be held by taxable entities with no adverse tax consequences. However, this may not be true at the state and local level where the interest on a municipal bond is taxed. Some states tax the accrued interest annually; others tax the accrued interest only when the bond is sold or redeemed. Under the former method, there will be a cash outlay for interest earned but not received. At the time of this writing, an interesting aspect of the zero-coupon municipal bond is that unlike zero taxable bonds there is no yield sacrifice by buying a zero compared to a coupon bond. In the taxable bond market, the attractive feature of zeros has resulted in lower yields on these issues compared to coupon bonds. When zero-coupon municipal bonds were first brought to the market, their yields were considerably less than current coupon bonds. A yield sacrifice of 5 percentage points was not unusual. However, as the supply of zero-coupon municipal bonds surged, yields on them increased. By mid-1986, yields on many zero-coupon municipal bonds were substantially higher than on comparable current coupon bonds.

Usually zero-coupon municipal bonds are callable in 15 years. Unlike a coupon municipal, the call price cannot be stated as a percent of the par value. Instead, the call price is based on the "compounded accreted value" (CAV) of the issue at each possible call date. The

CAV is the value of the bond at the call date if the bond grew by its yield-to-maturity when issued. To the CAV is added a premium for each possible call date that is determined by the issuer when the bond is first issued.[1]

If a zero-coupon municipal bond is called, the impact on the investor's return over the holding period depends on the price at which the issue was purchased. For an investor who purchases an issue when it is issued, the minimum return that will be realized is the stated yield-to-maturity at issuance. For an investor who purchases an issue in the secondary market at a price that is less than or equal to its CAV at the time of purchase,[2] the minimum return will be the yield-to-maturity at issuance. A capital loss may result when an issue is purchased in the secondary market for a price greater than its CAV at the time. There are special credit risks with zero-coupon bonds. These were discussed in Chapter 10.

Puttable Bonds

A puttable bond, also known as a *tender offer bond,* allows the holder of the bond to sell the bond back to the issuer at par at designated dates. The advantage of puttable bonds is that they are long maturity bonds but have the characteristics of short-term bonds. In particular, there is little interest-rate risk. Since the municipal yield curve generally has a positive slope, a puttable bond will offer the higher yield of a long-term bond but exhibit the characteristics of a short-term bond.

---

[1] The general formula for the call premium is:

$$CAV \times [1 + (M - Y) \times R]$$

where

M is the maturity date
Y is the year the bond may be called, and
R is the redemption factor.

For example, suppose that a zero-coupon municipal bond that matures on July 1, 2000, can be called on July 1, 1990, and that the redemption factor set forth for this call date by the issuer when the bond was issued is .01. Then the call price will be:

$$CAV \times [1 + (2000 - 1990) \times .01]$$
$$= CAV \times 1.10.$$

Therefore, the call price is 110 percent of the CAV.

[2] This means that the investor purchases the issue at a yield that is greater than or equal to the yield-to-maturity at issuance.

Variable Rate Notes and Variable Rate Demand Obligations

An investor who purchases zero-coupon bonds has purchased protection against a decline in interest rates. If interest rates over the life of the bond are higher, the investor would have been better off purchasing a variable rate note. For these debt obligations, the coupon rate is adjusted periodically based on some predetermined interest-rate index. For example, a variable rate note may be based on 65 percent of the 90-day Treasury bill rate, 55 percent of the prime rate, or 110 percent of the J. J. Kenny Municipal Index. The coupon rate may be adjusted as often as daily or weekly.

A variable rate note may also have a put feature. When a variable rate note has this feature, it is called a *variable rate demand obligation.* The advantages of a put feature were described above. Variable rate demand obligations are usually backed by a bank-credit facility that of course can vary widely in terms of credit quality. Because of the attractiveness of the put feature, the yield on variable rate demand obligations is less than that of variable rate notes without the put feature.

INVESTING VIA TAX–EXEMPT MUTUAL FUNDS AND UNIT TRUSTS

For investors who do not have the time nor the inclination to do the necessary analysis required to select and manage a portfolio of municipal bonds, tax-exempt mutual funds and unit trusts could be used as investment vehicles.

Mutual Funds

A mutual fund or open-end bond fund combines the monies of a number of different investors and reinvests the proceeds in a large number of municipal obligations that attempt to meet a certain set of investment objectives. Mutual funds continuously offer new shares for sale to the public and stand ready to redeem their shares at a price that is computed daily at the close of the market, which is based on the current market value of the municipal obligations in the portfolio. The major role of mutual funds is to reduce risk through diversification and to provide investors with professional selection, timing, and monitoring investments.

The structure of a mutual fund consists of a board of directors (or trustees), an adviser responsible for making the investment decisions, and a distributing and selling organization. A typical mutual fund enters into a contract with a management or advisory company to engage in research and meet the investment objectives of the fund. In addition to management fees, mutual funds incur other expenses that are included in the cost of services offered to investors. For example, they act as custodians of the assets in their portfolio and provide record-keeping services. They make certain that securities are properly transferred and registered. Officer salaries, rent, and other operating and selling costs of the mutual fund must be paid. Mutual funds also incur transaction costs in buying and selling securities for the portfolio. However, because mutual funds are institutional buyers, transactions costs are less than what an individual investor would pay if he purchased or sold securities. Information about these costs of managing and operating a particular mutual fund are contained in the prospectus. The prospectus is the publication that describes the mutual fund and offers the sale of its shares.

Mutual funds that impose a sales commission are known as *load funds.* These funds add the sales commission to the price of the share. The sales commission typically ranges from 8.5 percent on small amounts invested down to 1 percent on purchases in the amount of $500,000 and over. The load charge works as follows. On an investment of $10,000, for example, the mutual fund may deduct $800 and purchase $9,200 worth of shares for the investor. This increases the effective rate to 8.7 percent ($800/$9,200).

A mutual fund that does not impose a sales commission is called a *no-load fund.* No-load funds compete head-on with load funds and appeal to many investors who object to paying the high initial fee charged by load funds.

The price of a mutual fund share is determined by its net asset value per share. The difference between the market value of the mutual fund's portfolio of assets and liabilities divided by the number of mutual fund shares outstanding determines the net asset value per share of a mutual fund. For example, suppose that the market value of the fund's bonds is $10 million, its liabilities are $1 million and there are 1 million shares outstanding. The net asset value per share is $9.

The price of a mutual fund share is quoted on a bid-ask basis. The bid price, which is the price that the mutual fund will redeem the shares for, is the net asset value per share of the fund. The ask or offer price is the price that the mutual fund will sell the shares for. It is equal to the net asset value per share plus the sales commission.

Market quotations for mutual funds appear in the financial or business section of most daily newspapers.

Mutual funds offer an investor many services in addition to management of a portfolio and diversification. Rather than having to take physical possession of the bonds and face the danger of loss or theft, mutual funds provide an open account record that credits the buyer with interest and shows the change in the value of the account. A periodic statement is issued to investors for their record keeping. It is an efficient way of dealing with the problems of transferring and registering bonds.

Some investors can take the option to receive a steady income from mutual funds. Others may request to have their interest and other returns automatically reinvested in more shares of a fund, regardless of how small the reinvestment dollars may be. This relieves the investor of the necessity of searching for where to reinvest any return distributions paid by the mutual fund.

Although minimum initial investment varies from $1,000 to $3,500 for most mutual funds, additional amounts can be added to a fund for as little as $100. An investor can purchase fractional shares. This is a great convenience for investors, particularly those who make periodic investments that are not large enough to purchase a round lot of municipal bonds.

A wide range of mutual funds that invest exclusively in municipal bonds is available. There are mutual funds that have no restriction on the length of maturity of the bonds that they purchase but limit the investments to municipal issues that are of, at least, investment quality. There are mutual funds that invest in only intermediate-term municipal bonds—usually 10 to 15 years. And, there are high-yield municipal bond mutual funds whose objective is to achieve maximum yields. Such funds usually invest in lower-quality municipal issues and those of long maturity. Some mutual funds specialize in municipal bonds of issuers within a given state so that investors can take advantage of the exemption of interest income from in-state issuers.

There are mutual funds that invest only in the commercially insured municipal bonds and mutual funds in which the portfolio is insured even though individual issues may not be insured. The acquisition of a mutual fund that purchases only insured municipal bonds or whose portfolio is insured does not mean that an investor will eliminate interest-rate risk.[3] Also, in the case of an insured portfolio,

---

[3] Insured municipal bonds are discussed in Chapter 6.

the bonds in the portfolio are only insured as long as they are in the portfolio. Consequently, if the bonds of issuers that are having financial difficulties are sold and the price of these issues has declined, this is not covered by the insurance.

Unit Trusts

In addition to mutual funds that specialize in municipal bonds and are "buy and trade" in nature, there are unit trusts that are "buy and hold" in nature. Unit trusts are usually sponsored by a brokerage firm or underwriter of municipal bonds. A portfolio of municipal bonds is assembled by the sponsor and turned over to a trustee. The municipal bonds in the portfolio are held until redemption by the issuer. The minimum initial investment varies from $750 to $5,000.

A unit trust differs from a mutual fund in the following ways. First, unlike mutual funds, there is no active trading of municipal bonds in a unit trust. Usually, the only time that the trustee can sell an issue in the portfolio is if there is a dramatic decline in the issuer's credit quality. This means that the cost of operating the trust will be considerably less than for a mutual fund. Second, unit trusts have a fixed termination date while mutual funds do not. Third, unlike a mutual fund, the investor knows that the portfolio consists of a known collection of municipal bonds, and there is no concern that the trustee will alter the portfolio.

All unit trusts charge a sales commission. The initial sales charge for a unit trust usually is 3.5 percent to 5.5%. There is oftentimes a commission of up to 3 percent to sell units; however, trusts sponsored by some organizations do not charge a commission when the units are sold. For an investor who intends to hold a unit trust for at least five years, the effective annual cost of acquiring a unit trust is reduced.

There are unit trusts whose portfolio consists of long-term, intermediate-term and short-term municipal bonds. There is even a unit trust with variable rate municipal bonds. For investors in states with high income taxes, there are unit trusts that purchase issues which are exempt within the state.

Since the WPPSS default, insured unit trusts have been a very popular vehicle used by investors for participating in the municipal bond market. A drawback of insured unit trusts has been the lower yield on these portfolios compared to uninsured unit trusts. As indicated earlier for mutual funds with insured portfolios, the investor is still subject to interest-rate risk, and the issues in the portfolio are only insured so long as they remain in the portfolio.

TAX SWAPS

A bond swap is a transaction in which one bond is sold and a similar but not identical bond is purchased in order to meet a certain objective. Bond swaps are undertaken for a variety of reasons such as postponing taxes, improving credit quality, extending or shortening maturity or capitalizing on perceived market inefficiencies.

When the objective of a bond swap is to postpone taxes from one tax year to a future tax year, it is known as a *tax swap*. In a tax swap, a bond issue that has declined in value is sold and a similar but not identical one is purchased. The loss realized from the sale of one bond issue can be used to offset a capital gain from the sale of another security during the taxable year.

Bonds are an ideal candidate for a tax swap. The reason is that in order for the IRS to recognize the loss, an investor may not purchase "substantially identical securities" within 30 days before or after the sale of securities at a loss. If substantially identical securities are purchased within this period, the IRS treats the transaction as a "wash sale." If the security sold to generate the capital loss is common stock, an investor may not purchase the same stock within 30 days before and after the sale without voiding the capital loss. If he purchased some other stock, the composition of his portfolio will change. The new stock acquired will not have the same investment characteristics as the stock sold because no two stocks of different issuers are identical. On the other hand, bonds with similar characteristics in terms of maturity, coupon, and credit rating can be found even though they may be of different issuers. They will have the same investment characteristics since they will be influenced by changes in interest rates. The IRS will not treat a bond swap involving two different issuers as a wash sale.

FORECASTING MUNICIPAL BOND YIELDS BY MONITORING TRENDS IN OTHER MARKETS

Since the 1970s, the municipal bond market has reacted more slowly than other fixed-income markets to economic information and other information that exert influence on interest rates. Consequently, some market observers believe that tracking money market conditions and certain interest rates can be useful in forecasting the direction of future municipal bond yields and thereby timing municipal bond transactions.

One study, for example, has documented the relationship between municipal bond yields and both the federal-funds rate and discount rate.[4] The federal-funds rate is the interest rate at which federal funds are traded by commercial banks. It is pegged by the Federal Reserve through open-market operations. The discount rate is the interest rate charged by the Federal Reserve to member banks for borrowing at the discount window.

The study found that since 1971 these two rates have predicted the cylical turning points in municipal bond yields. In particular, the results of the study did indicate that "[i]f historical relationships are maintained, then the behavior of funds in the most recent 15 months can aid in predicting the general movement in the BBI *(Bond Buyer Index)* over the subsequent 15-month period." Since the discount rate is almost exclusively a confirming action of Federal Reserve policy, and not a leading overt indicator of policy as is the federal-funds rate, a shorter lag between movements in the discount rate and municipal bond yields was expected. The study did, in fact, find that municipal bond yields lagged behind movements in the discount rate by 10 months compared with 15 months for the federal funds rate.

The authors of the study conclude: "The surprisingly long lags found in this study obviously may or may not be realized in the future. There are some indications, however, that participants in the municipal market already are more sensitive to conditions in other markets than previously. This alone may cause the lags to shrink, but the relationships we have analyzed could still remain an important key to the future behavior of municipal bond rates."

NONDEDUCTIBILITY OF INTEREST ON MONEY BORROWED TO PURCHASE OR CARRY MUNICIPAL BONDS

An important thing to remember when buying municipal bonds is that interest *paid or accrued* by an individual on any money borrowed to purchase or carry municipal bonds is not tax-deductible. It does not make a difference if any tax-exempt interest is actually received in the tax year. This rule also applies to interest paid to purchase shares of mutual funds that invest primarily in municipal bonds.

To understand why interest related to debt incurred to purchase or carry municipal bonds is disallowed as a deduction, consider the following situation. Suppose that an investor in the 38-percent tax bracket borrows $100,000 at 10-percent interest to purchase municipal

---

[4] Alan C. Lerner and Philip D. Nathanson, "Forecasting Municipal Rates and Spreads by Monitoring Trends in Other Markets," in *The Municipal Bond Handbook,* Vol. I., ed. Fabozzi et al.

bonds selling at par with a coupon rate of 8 percent to yield 8 percent. If the interest expense on the borrowed money, $10,000 per year ($100,000 × 10 percent), is allowed as a deduction, the after-tax cost of the interest is $6,200. The interest from holding the municipal bond is $8,000 ($100,000 × 8-percent coupon rate). This means that the investor benefits by $1,800 per year if the deduction is allowed.

The first reaction of those who own municipal bonds and also have borrowed money may be that the IRS might disallow the interest expenses incurred. This is not the case. Unless there is direct evidence that you borrowed the funds to purchase or carry the municipal bonds, the deduction will be allowed.

MUNICIPAL BOND FUTURES CONTRACTS

A futures contract is a firm legal agreement between a buyer and an established exchange or its clearing house in which the buyer agrees to take delivery of *something* at a specified price at the end of a designated time period (known as the settlement date). The seller of a futures contract agrees to make delivery of *something* at a specified price at the settlement date. Prior to 1982, the *something* that the parties agreed to take or make delivery of was either traditional agricultural commodities (such as coffee, cocoa, and sugar), or industrial commodities. Collectively, such futures contracts are known as commodity futures.

Futures contracts based on a financial instrument or a financial index are known as financial futures and referred to by some as "pork bellies in pinstripes." In 1975, the Chicago Board of Trade pioneered trading in a futures contract based on a fixed-income instrument— Government National Mortgage Association certificates. Three months later the International Monetary Market of the Chicago Mercantile Exchange began trading futures contracts based on 90-day Treasury bills. Other contracts soon followed in which the underlying instrument was a fixed-income security, commonly referred to as interest-rate futures contracts. Prior to June 1985, the only interest-rate futures contracts traded were for taxable fixed-income securities, both short-term and long-term. In June 1985, the Chicago Board of Trade began trading an interest-rate futures contract based on an index of municipal bonds.

Contract Specifications

The municipal bond index that the contract is based on is the Bond Buyers Municipal Bond Index. There are 40 long-term municipal bonds in this index, with issues eliminated when they fail to met some criteria and replaced by other issues that satisfy the criteria. The prices of the bonds in the index are based on quotes by five dealer-to-dealer municipal bond brokers—Cantor, Fitzgerald Municipal Brokers, Inc.; Chapdelaine & Company, Inc.; Clifford Drake & Company, Inc.; J. F. Hartfield & Company, Inc., and; Titus & Donnelly, Inc. For each bond, the lowest and the highest prices are dropped and the three remaining prices are averaged.

Each contract is for $100,000 of face value. The contracts are quoted as an index and the value of a contract is $1,000 times the index quoted. For example, if a contract is quoted as 92 the value of the contract is $92,000 (92 times $1,000). The minimum price change is $\frac{1}{32}$ of a point or $31.25 per contract (one point which is $1,000 divided by 32). A quote of 92–3 means 92 $\frac{3}{32}$.

The maximum daily price limit for the contract is 2 points ($2,000). The trading months are March, June, September and December, with the eighth to last business day of the expiration month being the last trading day. Because it is based on an index, the settlement procedure for the municipal bond index futures contract is different from other interest-rate futures contracts. The contract must be settled in cash on the last trading day at a value equal to the index on that day.

When a position is taken in a futures contract, an investor must deposit a minimum dollar amount per contract as specified by the exchange. This amount is called *initial margin.* For the municipal bond index futures contract the initial margin is $2,000 for speculative positions and $1,500 for a hedge position. As the price of the futures contract fluctuates, the value of the investor's equity in the position is "marked to market" so that any gain or loss from the position is reflected in the investor's equity account. *Maintenance margin* is the minimum level specified by the exchange by which an investor's equity position may fall as a result of an unfavorable price movement before-the investor is required to deposit additional margin. For the municipal bond index futures contract, maintenance margin is $1,500. A position will be closed if additional margin is not furnished by the investor.

Although there are initial and maintenance margin requirements for buying securities, the concept of margin differs for securities and futures. When securities are acquired on margin, the difference between the price of the security and the initial margin is borrowed from the broker. The security purchased serves as collateral for the loan and interest is paid by the investor. For the futures contract, the initial margin, in effect, serves as "good faith" money indicating that the investor will satisfy the obligation of the contract. No money is borrowed by the investor.

Strategies with Futures

The primary benefit of interest-rate futures contracts is that it allows fixed-income portfolio managers to attempt to hedge interest-rate risk. Suppose that a portfolio manager knows that he must sell $10 million of bonds three months from now in order to satisfy a liability that will come due. If at the end of three months interest rates are higher, the value of the bonds in the portfolio will be lower and therefore more bonds must be sold to obtain $10 million. By selling interest-rate futures contracts, a portfolio manager will be able to hedge some or all of this risk. Should interest rates rise, the value of the bonds in his portfolio will decline; however, interest-rate futures contracts will be lower than the price they were sold for. If properly constructed the loss in value of the bonds in the portfolio will be offset by the gain in the futures market. For a portfolio manager who anticipates receiving funds at some future time and wants to hedge the risk that interest-rates will decline and therefore have to invest the funds at a lower rate, interest-rate futures contracts can be purchased.

The principle of using the futures market to hedge a potential loss in the cash market for the security sounds simple. In practice it is much more difficult because the fixed-income securities that a portfolio manager wishes to hedge and the underlying instrument for the futures contract are not the same. For example, if a portfolio manager wants to hedge a portfolio of corporate bonds, she must use a futures contract on Treasury bonds since no futures contracts on corporate bonds are currently traded. This is commonly referred to as *cross hedging*. Prior to the introduction of municipal bond index futures contracts, managers of municipal bond portfolios had to use futures contracts on Treasury bonds. It is expected that the municipal bond index futures will improve the hedging ability of managers of municipal bond portfolios.

Since futures contracts are highly leveraged positions, another popular strategy is to use futures contracts to speculate on interest-rate movements. In addition, since the municipal bond index futures contract is in its infancy stage, astute investors have traded futures contracts to take advantage of what they perceive to be mispricing. Until more is known about the pricing of these contracts, we expect that there will be a great deal of activity attempting to exploit potential mispricings.

13

Judge the Bond by Those Who Are Issuing It and Trying to Sell It to You

Still another question to ask before purchasing a municipal bond is just what kind of people are the issuers? Are they conscientious public servants with clearly defined public goals? Do they have histories of successful management of public institutions? Have they demonstrated commitments to professional and fiscally stringent operations? Additionally, issuers in highly charged and partisan environments in which conflicts chronically occur between political parties and/or among factions or personalities within the governing bodies are clearly bond issuers to scrutinize closely and possibly to avoid. Such issuers should be scrutinized regardless of the strength of the surrounding economic environment.

FOR GENERAL OBLIGATION BONDS

For general obligation bond issuers the focus is on the political relationships that exist on the one hand among chief executives, such as mayors, county executives, and governors, and on the other hand their legislative counterparts. Issuers with unstable political elites are of particular concern. Of course, rivalry among political actors is not necessarily bad. What is undesirable is competition so bitter and personal that real cooperation among the warring public officials in addressing future budgetary problems may be precluded. An example of an issuer that was avoided in the past because of such dissension is the city of Cleveland. The political problems of the city in 1978 and the bitter conflicts between Mayor Kucinich and the city council resulted in a general obligation note default in December of that year.

FOR REVENUE BONDS

When investigating revenue bond issuers, it is important to determine not only the degree of political conflict, if any, that exists among the members of the bond-issuing body, but also the relationships and conflicts among those who make the appointments to the body. Additionally, the investor should determine whether the issuer of the revenue bond has to seek prior approval from another governmental jurisdiction before the user-fees or other charges can be levied. If this is the case, then the stability of the political relationships between the two units of government must be determined.

An example of the importance of this information can be seen when reviewing the credit worthiness of the water and electric utility revenue bonds and notes issued by Kansas City, Kansas. Although the revenue bonds and notes were issued by city hall, it was the six-member board of public utilities, a separately elected body, that had the power to set the water and electricity utility rates. In the spring of 1981, because of political dissension among the board members caused by a political struggle between a faction on the board of public utilities and the city commissioners (including the city's finance commissioner), the board refused to raise utility rates as required by the covenant. The situation only came under control when a new election changed the makeup of the board in favor of those supported by city hall.

In addition to the above institutional and political concerns, for revenue bond issuers in particular an assessment of the technical and managerial abilities of the staff should be made. The professional competency of the staff is a more critical factor in revenue bond analysis than it is in the analysis of general obligation bonds, which are secured in the final instance by the full faith and credit and unlimited taxing powers of the issuers. Many revenue bonds are secured by the ability of the revenue projects to be operational and financially self-supporting.

The professional staffs of authorities that issue revenue bonds for the construction of nuclear and other public power-generating facilities, apartment complexes, resource recovery systems, hospitals, water and sewer systems, and other large public works projects should be carefully reviewed. Issuers who have histories of high-management turnovers, project cost overruns, or little experience should be avoided by the conservative investor, or at least considered higher risks than their assigned credit ratings may indicate. Additionally, it is helpful for revenue bond issuers to have their accounting records annually audited by outside certified public accountants, so as to ensure the investor of a more accurate picture of the issuer's financial health.

ON THE FINANCIAL ADVISER AND UNDERWRITER

Shorthand indications of the quality of the investment are: (1) who the issuer selected as its financial adviser, if any, (2) its principal underwriter if the bond sale was negotiated, and (3) its financial adviser if the bond issue came to market competitively. Additionally, since 1975 many prudent underwriters will not bid on competitive bond issues if there are significant credit-quality concerns. Therefore, it is also useful to learn who was the underwriter for the competitive bond sales as well.

Identifying the financial advisers and underwriters is important for two reasons.

The Need for Complete, Not Just Adequate, Investment and Call Feature Risk Disclosures

The first reason relates to the quality and thoroughness of information provided to the investor by the issuer. The official statement, or private placement papers if the issue is placed privately, is usually prepared with the assistance of lawyers and a financial adviser or by the principal underwriter. There are industry-wide disclosure guidelines that are generally adhered to, but not all official statements provide the investor with complete discussions of the risk potentials that may result from either the specific economics of the project or the community settings and the operational details of the security provisions. It is usually the author of this document who decides what to either emphasize or downplay in the official statement. The more professional and established the experience of the author to provide the investor with unbiased and complete information about the issuer and call features of the bond issue, the more comfortable the investor can be with information provided by the issuer and in arriving at an investment decision.

The Importance of Firm Reputation for Thoroughness and Integrity

By itself, the reputation of the issuer's financial adviser and/or underwriter should not be the determinant credit-quality factor, but it is a factor the investor should consider. This is particularly the case for marginally feasible bond issues that have complex flow-of-funds and security structures. The securities industry is different from other industries, such as real estate, in that trading and investment commitments are usually made verbally over the phone with a paper trail following days later. Many institutional investors, such as banks, bond funds, and casualty insurance companies, have learned to judge issuers by the "company" they keep. Institutions tend to be conservative, and they are more comfortable with financial information provided by established financial advisers and underwriters who have recognized reputations for honesty. Individual investors would do well to adopt this approach as well.

APPENDIX A

The 1986 Tax Reform Law: The Impact for Tax-Exempt Municipal Bond Investors, Issuers, and the Market*

INTRODUCTION

On October 22, 1986, the president of the United States signed into law the Tax Reform Act of 1986. This law revised many provisions of the Internal Revenue Code of 1954 and establishes the Internal Revenue Code of 1986. This new law resulted from two years of legislative activity that began in November 1984. In this appendix, we discuss the sweeping changes brought about by this tax law for municipal bond investors, the issuers, and the market. Of course, future federal regulations and clarifications could change some of our initial assessments of the new tax law.

Demand by Individual Investors

Under the 1986 tax law, individual demand for municipal bonds should remain strong, largely because municipals are one of the few remaining tax-free investments. As investors become familiar with the tax law, they will realize that (1) the highest marginal tax rate for individuals can exceed 28 percent in 1988 and later, (2) the alternative minimum tax may not affect most individuals, and (3) high income tax rates in some states will make bonds issued by those states extremely attractive. As individuals define their tax status, demand for tax-exempt municipal bonds should increase.

The top marginal tax rate for individuals drops from 50 percent to 38.5 percent in 1987 and to 28 percent in 1988. Due to additional surtaxes, however, the top marginal tax rate for many investors will be 33 percent in 1988. To phase out the benefits of the lower 15 percent tax bracket, a 5 percent surtax will be applied for joint filers with income exceeding $71,900 and for single filers with income of more than $43,150. To phase out some of the benefits of personal exemptions, an additional 5 percent surtax is enacted on income between $149,250 and $192,930 for joint filers with four exemptions and on income between $89,560 and $100,480 for single filers. Conse-

---

*Written with James L. Kochan and John G. Talty, Merrill Lynch, Pierce, Fenner & Smith, Inc.

216

quently, tax-exempt municipals will remain attractive investments as long as municipal yields remain above 0.67 percent of yields on taxable securities for households in those income brackets. Historically, almost all municipal bonds offer yields well above that threshold ratio.

When state taxes are included, tax liabilities could be even higher. In New York State, for example, the highest marginal tax rate in 1986 is 13.5 percent, which works out to a 9 percent effective state tax rate in 1988. The effective rate would be more than 11 percent for New York City residents. Accordingly, New York State tax-exempt bonds appear to be attractive investments for New York City residents in the highest marginal tax brackets when yield ratios exceed 0.56. Therefore, demand remains strong for municipal bonds, especially for bonds issued by states with high individual income taxes.

Table A–1 shows the taxable yield equivalents for different tax-exempt yields, given the 1988 marginal tax rates.

TABLE A–1 Individual Tax-Exempt/Taxable Yield Equivalents for 1988 under the 1986 Tax Law

	Income Levels			
Single return	$ 0	$17,851	$ 43,151	$100,481
(One exemption)	17,850	43,150	100,480	—
Joint return	$ 0	$28,751	$ 71,901	$192,931
(Four exemptions)	29,750	71,900	192,930	—
Marginal tax bracket	15%	28%	33%	28%
Tax-Exempt Yields (percent)	Taxable Equivalent Yields (percent)			
5.0%	5.9%	6.9%	7.5%	6.9%
5.5%	6.5	7.6	8.2	7.6
6.0	7.1	8.3	9.0	8.3
6.5	7.6	9.0	9.7	9.0
7.0	8.2	9.7	10.4	9.7
7.5	8.8	10.4	11.2	10.4
8.0	9.4	11.1	11.9	11.1
8.5	10.0	11.8	12.7	11.8
9.0	10.6	12.5	13.4	12.5
9.5	11.2	13.2	14.2	13.2
10.5	12.4	14.6	15.7	14.6
11.0	12.9	15.3	16.4	15.3
11.5	13.5	16.0	17.2	16.0
12.0	14.1	16.7	17.9	16.7

The Alternative Minimum Tax (AMT)

Individuals and corporations must include certain tax-exempt municipal bond interest as tax preference items when they calculate their alternative minimum tax (AMT). This reduces the attractiveness of tax-exempt bonds for certain taxpayers.

Both individuals and corporations must include tax-exempt income earned on all "private" activity bonds issued after August 7, 1986, except for bonds issued by 501(c)(3) organizations and for the refunding of certain bonds. Interest on "governmental" or nonprivate activity municipal bonds is not included as a separate preference item for individuals.

For Individuals. The alternative minimum tax (AMT) requires individuals to calculate their tax liability both on a conventional basis and on the basis of a 21 percent AMT. The AMT is computed by first adding certain tax preference and add-back items to their taxable income. Taxpayers then deduct an exemption of $40,000 for joint filers and $30,000 for single filers from that figure to arrive at their alternative minimum taxable income (AMTI). The exemption would drop by $0.25 for every dollar by which AMTI (before the effect of the exemption) exceeded $150,000 for joint filers, or $112,500 for single filers. A 21 percent tax rate would then be applied to the AMTI to determine the AMT liability. Tax-exempt income from all private activity bonds [except 501(c)(3)] issued after August 7, 1986, would be included as tax preference income. Refundings occurring after August 7, 1986, would still be exempt from the AMT if the original bonds were issued before that date.

Table A–2 shows the amount of tax preference and add-back income that an individual may have before being subject to an AMT. The Taxable Income column is the amount of taxable income an individual has after accounting for tax preference items and add-backs, such as state and local taxes. For example, a couple with two children and with $150,000 in annual taxable income (after accounting for tax preference items and state and local taxes) can have up to $73,000 in tax preference and add-back items before paying any additional tax under the AMT. Since the amount of state taxes and tax preference income will vary for different individuals, the exact amount of "tainted" municipal income allowed will vary. As an example, assume the couple discussed above paid $26,470 in state and local taxes ($176,470 − 15 percent = $150,000) and had no other tax preference income. This couple could purchase approximately $665,000 of private activity municipal bonds with a 7 percent coupon without paying any additional

TABLE A–2 Breakeven Tax Preference Income Levels before a
Taxpayer Becomes Subject to the AMT*

Taxable Income	Single Filer		Joint Filer (four exemptions)	
	1987	1988	1987	1988
$ 50,000	$ 43,000	$ 37,000	$ 40,000	$ 39,000
100,000	69,000	55,000	70,000	60,000
150,000	95,000	58,000	93,000	73,000
200,000	137,000	69,000	118,000	84,000
250,000	179,000	85,000	160,000	94,000
300,000	220,000	102,000	202,000	111,000
400,000	304,000	135,000	285,000	144,000
500,000	387,000	169,000	368,000	178,000
750,000	595,000	252,000	577,000	261,000
1,000,000	804,000	335,000	785,000	344,000

* It should be noted that tax-preference income can include tax-exempt
municipal interest income as well as add-backs, such as state and local
taxes and accelerated depreciation on property, among others.

tax. This par amount of 7 percent bonds would produce $46,550 of
tax-preference income, which would be added to the $26,470 of state
income taxes to equal the $73,000 of allowable tax-preference and
add-back income. Because the AMT applies only to private activity
bonds issued after August 7, 1986, individuals can continue to purchase
governmental activity bonds as well as any bonds issued before August
8, 1986, without increasing their tax preference income.

For Corporations. Corporations are required to calculate their
minimum tax liability using two methods. The first method is similar
to the calculation used by individuals but uses a 20 percent alternative
minimum tax rate instead of 21 percent. However, an additional AMT
calculation would require corporations to add to their alternative minimum taxable income (AMTI) one half of the amount by which their
"book income" exceeded their AMTI. Book income is the corporation's
income reported in financial statements filed with the Securities and
Exchange Commission or reported to shareholders, owners, or creditors (as opposed to income reported to the IRS for tax purposes).
Beginning in 1990, corporations will be required to replace the "excess
book income" calculation with an "adjusted earnings and profits"
calculation.

Since tax-exempt interest generally appears as book income, a corporation may have to pay some tax on all of its municipal holdings.
Interest income from private activity municipal bonds [except

501(c)(3)] issued after August 7, 1986, are subject to a 20 percent AMT. In addition, interest income from all other tax-exempt municipal bonds (regardless of type, issue date, or purchase date) are considered book income and are subject to a 10 percent AMT. Corporations will also be required to pay the federal "superfund" tax of 12 basis points on all untaxed book income that exceeds $2 million per year.

Property and Casualty Insurance Company Demand

Under the 1986 tax law, property and casualty insurance companies are required to decrease their deduction for losses incurred but not paid by 15 percent of the company's tax-exempt interest income. Bonds acquired prior to August 8, 1986, are exempt from this calculation. Therefore, if the loan-loss deduction for a company equals at least 15 percent of its interest income from tax-exempt securities acquired after August 7, 1986, the company should pay—beginning in 1988—an effective tax of 5.1 percent (34 percent tax rate *times* 15 percent of interest) on its municipal bond income.

If the property and casualty company is subject to an AMT, the determination of the effective tax rate is more complicated. Up to 15 percent of the income from all municipals purchased after August 7, 1986, is considered taxable income and taxed at the 20 percent AMT rate. The remaining 85 percent of the municipal interest income would then be taxed either at 10 percent as book income (if the municipal bond is a governmental use bond or a bond issued prior to August 8, 1986) or at 20 percent as tax preference income (if the municipal bond is a private activity bond issued after August 7, 1986). If the income were taxed as book income, the total effective tax would be 11.5 percent [(0.85 *times* 0.1) + (0.15 *times* 0.2)]. If the interest were taxed as tax preference income, the total effective tax would be 20 percent.

The 1986 tax law reduces property and casualty insurance company demand for tax-exempt municipal bonds, but it does not eliminate it. As their underwriting profits increase, their need to purchase tax-exempt municipals increases. Furthermore, other provisions in the 1986 tax law relating to the accounting treatment of premiums and expenses should increase their reported taxable income and thereby increase their appetite for purchasing tax-exempt municipals.

Commercial Bank Demand

Commercial banks have traditionally owned between 30 and 50 percent of the outstanding municipal debt. Over the past several years, however, the percent of outstanding tax-exempt debt held by banks has been declining. As the new issue supply of municipal debt expanded from $45 billion in 1980 to over $200 billion in 1985, individuals purchased the majority of these bonds either directly or through bond funds. Furthermore, in recent years, the deduction for interest expenses incurred to purchase tax-exempt securities by banks was reduced to 85 percent and then to 80 percent, curtailing bank demand somewhat. Although the percent of new issue volume purchased by banks during the past several years has decreased to between 5 and 20 percent, this still represented a significant source of demand.

Except for the $10 million exception noted below, the 1986 tax law repeals the ability of banks and other financial institutions, including thrifts, to deduct 80 percent of the interest expense incurred to carry tax-exempt municipal bonds acquired after August 7, 1986.

The tax law does provide an exception to the nondeductibility of interest. This is for certain governmental purpose bonds and qualified 501(c)(3) obligations purchased before January 1, 1989, if:

1. The bond is designated by the issuer for purposes of the exception.
2. The bond is issued in either 1986, 1987, or 1988.
3. The issuer or its subordinate entities expects to issue not more than $10 million of such bonds.

The following calculation can be used to determine the municipal yield required by the commercial bank to provide the same after-tax return as a taxable security, given the cost of funds, the corporate tax rate, the deductibility ratio, and the yield on taxable debt.

Municipal yield = [Taxable yield *times* (1 − Tax rate)] − [Cost of funds *times* (1 − Tax rate)] + [(Cost of funds *times* Deductible percent) × (1 − Tax rate)] + [Cost of funds *times* (1 − Deductible percent)].

The required yield ratio will vary depending on each variable. The loss of deductibility would preclude banks from buying municipals whenever taxable yields are equal to or lower than the cost of funds and municipal market yields are also low relative to a bank's cost of funds. As the market yield on taxable securities rises above the cost of funds, the required yield ratio for tax-exempt municipal bonds decreases. The explanation for these results is that as the spread between the cost of funds and tax-exempt municipal market yields becomes wider, the loss of deductibility becomes less important.

Table A–3 shows the yield ratios required to make after-tax spreads on tax-exempt municipals equal to after-tax spreads on taxable securities when a bank's cost of funds is considered. Column (3) shows the required yield ratios under the pre-1986 tax law. Columns (4) through (6) show the required yield ratios under the 1986 tax law. Column (4) is for a commercial bank which is subject to a minimum tax. Column (5) is for a bank not subject to a 20 percent minimum tax and only owns municipal private activity bonds issued after August 7, 1986. Column (6) is for a bank subject to an additional 10 percent minimum tax on excess book income (all tax-exempt interest from bonds other than private use bonds issued after August 7, 1986). For example, assume a financial institution has a 5 percent cost of funds, 5 percent available taxable yields, and is subject to a minimum tax on both tax preference income and book income. This hypothetical bank would require a yield ratio of 1.25 on private activity municipal bonds issued after August 7, 1986, and a yield ratio of 1.111 on all other municipal bonds in order to profit from purchasing them.

The loss of the deduction for interest costs incurred in carrying most tax-exempt debt acquired after August 7, 1986, would eliminate most bank demand for tax-exempt municipal bonds. A bank not subject to any minimum tax could still conceivably purchase tax-exempt municipals if the available yield ratios were above 0.9 and if the spread between the cost of funds and taxable yields were relatively wide.

TABLE A–3   The Ratio of Municipal Yields to Taxable Yields Required by Banks to Make After-Tax Spread on Municipals Equal to After-Tax Spread on Taxable Debt

		Old Law		1986 Tax Law	
(1) Cost of Funds	*(2)* Taxable Yield	*(3)* 80 Percent Deductibility, 46 Percent Tax Rate	*(4)* 0 Percent Deductiblity, 34 Percent Tax Rate	*(5)* 0 Percent Deductibility, 20 Percent Tax Rate	*(6)* 0 Percent Deductibility 20/10 Percent Tax Rate
5%	5%	0.632	1.000	1.250	1.111
	6	0.616	.943	1.208	1.074
	7	0.606	.903	1.179	1.048
	8	0.598	.873	1.156	1.028
6%	6%	0.632	1.000	1.250	1.111
	7	0.619	.951	1.214	1.079
	8	0.609	.915	1.188	1.055
	9	0.601	.887	1.167	1.037
7%	7%	0.632	1.000	1.250	1.111
	8	0.621	.958	1.219	1.083
	9	0.612	.924	1.194	1.062
	10	0.604	.898	1.175	1.044

However, most banks only purchase tax-exempt debt with maturities under 10 years. This sector of the municipal market may not offer yield ratios high enough to attract bank purchases. Furthermore, any bank subject to a minimum tax on its book income may sell its tax-exempt municipal bonds in order to decrease book income to a level where it would not be subject to a minimum tax.

THE REDUCED *SUPPLY* OF TAX-EXEMPT MUNICIPAL BONDS

Perhaps the most visible aspects of the 1986 tax law for municipal bond investors are those provisions restricting borrowers' access to the tax-exempt market. The law restricts the issuance of tax-exempt municipals by:

- Narrowly defining the legally allowable uses for tax-exempt bond proceeds, thus eliminating several types of project financing from the tax-exempt market.
- Limiting by state the annual volume of certain types of bonds.
- Specifying tight restrictions and guidelines for the remaining tax-exempt issues.

The New Definitions

The 1986 tax law reclassified the tax-exempt municipal bond market of *general obligation* and *revenue bonds* into *governmental use* and *private activity* bonds. Governmental use bonds are issued to finance traditional state and local government functions and operations or to finance facilities owned and operated by the governmental entities. A bond is a private activity bond if more than 10 percent of the bond sale proceeds are used in any private trade or business or if more than 5 percent is loaned to a private entity. However, in order to attain tax-exempt status, even private activity uses must in many cases be owned by, or used on behalf of, a governmental unit. Tax-exempt bonds whose proceeds are used to finance private activities are subject to a cap on permitted annual volume. The allowable tax-exempt private activity bonds are listed below.

- Multifamily rental housing bonds.
- Airport bonds (in which the airports are publicly owned).
- Dock and wharf-related bonds (in which the facilities are publicly owned).
- Nonvehicular mass commuting facility bonds (in which the facilities are publicly owned).
- Local furnishing of electricity or gas-related bonds.
- Local district heating or cooling-related bonds.

- Water bonds.
- Bonds for small hydroelectric facilities (on file with the Federal Electric Regulatory Commission).
- Bonds for public use hazardous waste disposal facilities.
- Sewage and solid waste disposal-related bonds.
- Certain small-issue industrial development bonds (sunset of 12/31/86 for retail and commercial facilities; 12/31/89 for manufacturing facilities).
- Certain student loan bonds.
- Certain veterans' mortgage and other mortgage revenue bonds (sunset of 12/31/88).
- Certain Section 501(c)(3) bonds.
- Certain redevelopment bonds.

Tax-exempt bond proceeds, with very few exceptions, can no longer be used to finance:

- Air and water pollution control facilities.
- Sports stadiums.
- Convention and trade show facilities.
- Parking facilities and industrial parks.

Restrictions over Governmental versus Private Activity Bonds

As noted above, tax-exempt proceeds may finance public activities only if less than 10 percent of the proceeds are used by private parties (known by investment bankers and issuers as the "trade or business test") *and* if the payments made by the private parties to the issuer in connection with the private activity are less than 10 percent of the debt service on the bonds. Use by a 501(c)(3) organization is considered trade or business use. In addition, under the 1986 tax law, an absolute limit of $15 million can be used by private parties for financing the construction, rehabilitation, or operation of certain output facilities (such as electric generating facilities) regardless of whether this figure is less than 10 percent of the proceeds.

Loan of Bond Proceeds to Private Entities Is Restricted. Further provisions of the 1986 tax law restrict the amount that can be loaned to private entities to finance nongovernmental activities. Loans to private entities are limited to the lesser of either $5 million or 5 percent of the bond proceeds, if an issue is to retain tax-exempt status as a governmental issue. (In the case of public power issuers, take-or-pay and output contracts may be regarded as loans.)

"Use" Is More Strictly Defined. *Use* generally includes leasing or otherwise using a municipal bond-financed facility, purchasing output from a facility under certain types of issuer contracts (e.g., public power take-or-pay contracts), and certain managerial arrangements. Private activities must generally be related to the governmental purpose of the bond, and under no circumstances can more than 5 percent of the proceeds be used for unrelated private activities.

The Volume Cap Restrictions

Under the 1986 tax law, annual volume caps by state are set for the private activity tax-exempt bonds. A single unified cap on the bonds issued by any state replaces the separate volume limits on certain tax-exempt bonds, such as industrial development bonds and mortgage bonds. The annual respective state cap is the greater of $75 per capita or $250 million until 1988, when the cap declines to $50 and $150 million, respectively.

This cap applies to all private activity bonds, except bonds for:

- 501(c)(3) organizations.
- Publicly owned airports, docks, and wharves.
- Publicly owned solid waste facilities.
- Qualified veterans' mortgages.

The cap also applies to certain governmental use bonds, including:

- New issues in excess of $150 million: the amount earmarked for private activities in excess of $15 million must be included in the volume cap allocation.
- Advance refundings: any private portion of the original bonds in excess of $15 million must be included in the volume cap allocation.

Table A–4 lists the estimated state cap allocations under the 1986 tax law.

The 1986 tax law does not specify how the cap will be allocated among different types of bonds. The annual allocation decisions are left to the individual states. In addition, the volume caps significantly curtail issuance for some of the larger states. For example, California issued over $4 billion of private use bonds in 1984 that would be subject to the new volume caps. The current population of approximately 25 million would allow California, as noted in Table A–4 to issue only $1.9 billion of these bonds in 1987 and $1.2 billion in 1988.

TABLE A–4 State Cap Allocations

State	1986 and 1987, $75 Cap per Resident ($ millions)	1988 and after, $50 Cap per Resident ($ millions)	Actual 1984, Total Issuance of Affected Bonds ($ millions)
Alabama	$ 299.3	$ 199.5	$ 382.5
Alaska	250.0	150.0	878.5
Arizona	250.0	152.7	360.0
Arkansas	250.0	150.0	155.0
California	1,921.7	1,281.1	4,188.5
Colorado	250.0	158.9	526.0
Connecticut	250.0	157.7	441.5
Delaware	250.0	150.0	417.0
Florida	823.3	548.8	1,616.5
Georgia	437.8	291.9	698.9
Hawaii	250.0	150.0	111.0
Idaho	250.0	150.0	102.0
Illinois	863.3	575.8	1,011.3
Indiana	412.4	274.9	390.7
Iowa	250.0	150.0	358.0
Kansas	250.0	150.0	300.0
Kentucky	279.2	186.2	357.0
Louisiana	334.7	223.1	714.0
Maine	250.0	150.0	138.0
Maryland	326.2	217.5	966.5
Massachusetts	434.9	289.9	694.9
Michigan	680.6	453.8	530.9
Minnesota	312.2	208.1	1,018.1
Mississippi	250.0	150.0	265.9
Missouri	375.6	250.4	611.0
Montana	250.0	150.0	178.1
Nebraska	250.0	150.0	354.0
Nevada	250.0	150.0	287.5
New Hampshire	250.0	150.0	122.0
New Jersey	563.6	375.8	897.5
New Mexico	250.0	150.0	147.8
New York	1,330.1	886.8	1,432.5
North Carolina	462.4	308.3	316.5
North Dakota	250.0	150.0	213.0
Ohio	806.4	537.6	756.4
Oklahoma	250.0	164.9	358.7
Oregon	250.0	150.0	207.0
Pennsylvania	892.5	595.1	1,367.0
Rhode Island	300.0	150.0	262.0
South Carolina	250.0	165.0	246.5
South Dakota	250.0	150.0	270.0
Tennessee	353.8	235.9	703.6
Texas	1,199.2	799.5	2,274.5
Utah	250.0	150.0	326.5
Vermont	250.0	150.0	88.0
Virginia	422.7	281.8	1,303.2
Washington	322.7	215.1	386.0
West Virginia	250.0	150.0	241.0
Wisconsin	357.5	238.3	371.5
Wyoming	250.0	150.0	107.5
Total	$21.01 billion	$13.57 billion	$30.45 billion

Arbitrage and Advance Refunding Restrictions

In addition to strictly defining the purposes for which tax-exempt bonds can be issued and establishing volume caps for private activity tax-exempt bonds, the 1986 tax law sets forth a comprehensive array of restrictions and guidelines affecting the issuance and use of all tax-exempt bonds. The following changes effect all tax-exempt bonds.

Restricted Arbitrage Profits. Arbitrage, or the ability of the municipal issuer to profit from the issuance of tax-exempt bonds, is essentially eliminated. In fact, only credit enhancement fees (letter of credit fees and bond insurance premiums) are considered recoverable costs when calculating the yield on bonds. *All* arbitrage profits from the investment of construction funds, debt service reserve funds, and capitalized interest accounts must be rebated to the U.S. Treasury Department.

Minor Portion Amount. A "minor portion," which can be invested at an unrestricted yield, is defined as the lesser of either 5 percent of the issue or $100,000. The debt service reserve fund is restricted to the lesser of 10 percent of the issue size or the maximum annual principal and interest requirement. It can be invested at an unrestricted yield; however, all arbitrage profits must be rebated to the U.S. Treasury Department. Furthermore, the amount invested at an unrestricted yield, except during the temporary period, cannot exceed 150 percent of the scheduled debt service for that bond year.

The three-year temporary period for investing unexpended bond proceeds is generally allowed in the 1986 tax law, although special rules apply to pooled financings. (The temporary period is the period of time, usually during construction, when bond proceeds are invested at an unrestricted yield.) Federal administrative and reporting requirements require, among other things, that issuers file periodic information reports with them.

Advance Refundings Strictly Curtailed. The 1986 tax law permits only governmental use bonds and 501(c)(3) bonds to be advance refunded and places a limit of, at most, two advance refundings for any issue. Bonds issued before January 1, 1986, can be advance refunded twice. However, the tax law permits at least one more advance refunding after March 14, 1986, even if the issue has already been refunded two or more times. If advance refunded, these bonds must be called on the first call date when the premium is 3 percent or less, and there may be debt service savings. Bonds issued after December 31, 1985, can only be advance refunded once. Other changes affecting advance refundings include the following:

- The advance refunding of an issue will end any temporary period (unrestricted yield period) for the refunded issue.
- "Abusive transactions," such as construction fund "flip-flops," are prohibited.

Other Restrictions and the 2 Percent Cost Rule

Rules that had only applied to industrial development bonds (IDBs) will now (after passage of the 1986 tax law) apply to all private activity bonds. These federal rules include:

- The average weighted maturity of a private activity bond cannot exceed 120 percent of the average useful life of the financed property. (This rule does not apply to student loan or mortgage revenue bonds.)
- No more than 25 percent of the proceeds of a private activity bond can be utilized to acquire land, and used property cannot be acquired with bond proceeds. (This rule may not apply to 501(c)(3), student loan, or mortgage revenue bonds.)
- All private activity bonds must be "publicly approved."
- Any group of related nonhospital 501(c)(3) organizations (e.g., a private university) is limited to $150 million in outstanding bonds.

Limitation on Costs of Issuance. The costs of issuance paid from the proceeds of private activity bonds cannot exceed 2 percent of the amount of the bonds, except for certain mortgage revenue bond issues of $20 million or less, in which case the limit is 3.5 percent. Issuance costs include such items as bond counsel fees, printing costs, commercial rating company fees, underwriters' spread, and accountant fees, among others.

MARKET IMPLICATIONS

The market implications of the new tax code may be grouped into three categories: (1) the differentiation between private and governmental activity bonds, (2) the prospect of less new-issue supply, and (3) the effect of lower marginal tax rates on the demand for tax-exempt interest income.

Tiering Due to AMT. The most visible effect of the tax bill may be the emergence of a tiered market for municipal bonds. So-called private activity bonds will very likely offer higher yields than governmental activity issues with similar characteristics because interest income from the private activity bonds would be subject to the alternative minimum tax. An individual investor subject to the AMT would pay a 21 percent rate on interest from private-activity bonds issued after August 7, 1986, and 0 percent on all other municipal bond interest. Therefore, an individual would currently need to receive over 150 basis points in additional yield to induce him to purchase the private-activity bonds. However, a corporation subject to the AMT would pay a 20 percent rate on interest from private-activity bonds issued after August 7, 1986, and a 10 percent rate on all other municipal interest (20 percent $\times$ one half of excess book income). Consequently, corporations would currently need over 75 basis points in additional yield for private-activity bonds issued after August 7, 1986.

The calculation used to determine the yield differential for individuals is:

$$\frac{\text{Required yield on private activity}}{\text{bonds issued after } 8/7/86} = \frac{\text{Yield on all other municipals}}{.8}$$

The calculation for corporations is:

$$\frac{\text{Required yield on private activity bonds issued after } 8/7/86}{} = \frac{(\text{Yield on all other municipals}) \times .9}{.8}$$

Since the majority of investors in municipals may not be subject to the AMT, the tiering effect will be far less severe than this calculation implies. Estimates of the yield spread required between governmental and private-activity bonds range between 25 and 50 basis points.

State income taxes will also contribute to yield differentials between otherwise comparable issues. The lower federal income tax rates contained in the 1986 law will raise the effective state income tax rates because the deduction for federal taxes is of less consequence when calculating state taxes. Under the tax law, bonds issued by borrowing authorities in states with relatively high income tax rates should attract even greater in-state demand than before, and yield differentials between bonds from high-tax and low-tax states should increase.

Cyclical Factors. In our view, the supply/demand equation implied by the new tax code should, on balance, be favorable for the market, with supply expected to shrink more than demand. However, cyclical forces will remain the dominant influence on market yields in the months ahead, and those forces are also expected to be favorable.

- This reduction in new-issue value would more than offset the reduction in demand from banks.

- The potential negative effect on individual demand of the diminished value of tax-exempt income at lower marginal tax rates is likely to be countered by the positive effect of a shift in investment funds away from tax shelters toward municipals.
- The continuation of the 1986 recovery in profits at insurance companies should push many of them into the 34 percent tax bracket.

TAXABLE MUNICIPAL BONDS

Because of the 1986 tax law, a substantial volume of borrowing will be shifted from the tax-exempt to the taxable bond market. More than 25 taxable municipal issues came to market during the first three quarters of 1986, raising over $2 billion.

Taxable municipal bonds were fairly rare prior to 1986 and were occasionally issued by large municipal bond issuers, such as the Alaska Housing Finance Agency and Los Angeles County. Alaska Housing conducted 20 taxable financings in the early 1980s. However, the 1986 tax law will push many more tax-exempt borrowers into the taxable markets.

Among the private activity bonds that would become taxable are bonds for pollution control, sports facilities, convention and trade show facilities, parking facilities, and industrial parks. Also, tougher restrictions regarding housing financing, volume caps, advance refundings, and arbitrage profits, as well as reporting requirements and associated expenses, could force issuers into the taxable market despite the retention of their tax-exempt status.

New Municipal Issuers in the Taxable Markets. Table A–5 highlights some of the larger taxable municipal bonds that came to market by late 1986. The yield spread to U.S. governments at the time of sale is also shown.

The largest percentage of taxable municipal bonds will probably be in support of state and local economic development. States always find it in their interest to encourage industrial development by subsidizing local business, and the funds for this may come from the taxable markets. States also may use the taxable markets to raise funds for other purposes, such as eliminating unfunded pension liabilities and generating arbitrage profits.

A significant number of solid waste disposal facilities may also raise capital in the taxable markets. Although many of these facilities are granted tax-exempt status in the 1986 tax law, their financing

TABLE A-5 Taxable Municipal Bond Sales in 1986

Issuer	S&P Rating	Amount ($ millions)	Maturity	Spread to U.S. Governments at Time of Sale (basis points)
Southeast Texas Housing Finance Corporation	AAA*	$300	1996	135
Louisiana Agricultural Finance Authority	AAA*	$150	1996	150
Memphis, Tennessee	AAA*	$400	1996	135
Community College District No. 508 (Cook County) Illinois	AAA†	$ 30	1987–93	30–50

* Involving a guaranteed investment contract (GIC) with an insurance company.
† Insured by AMBAC.

needs may account for too large a proportion of a state's volume caps. Furthermore, many states may prefer their waste disposal facilities to be administered on a private basis, and thus the bonds issued may not qualify for tax-exempt status.

Power authorities that sell electricity to investor-owned utilities will either finance in both the tax-exempt and taxable markets or let the investor-owned utility raise capital in the corporate markets. Pollution control facilities will be financed through the corporate market by the corporate issuer requiring the funds.

Outlook for the Taxable Municipal Market. Investor acceptance for this new investment vehicle will ultimately depend on the depth and efficiency of its secondary market. The strength of the secondary market will provide the liquidity necessary for these issues to successfully compete with corporate bonds in attracting broad-based institutional demand.

After the 1986 tax law was passed and taxable municipals began to be issued, institutional demand came primarily from banks and property/casualty companies, which have been active purchasers of tax-exempt bonds. Their interest in this market has been the result of their familiarity with the credit and structure of municipal issues. In addition, with attractive offering spreads relative to both corporate and Treasury notes, these securities appeared to be priced generously. Another factor that boosted demand for several of these issues was their noncallability, which protects the investor from unwanted early redemptions.

A potential limitation to greater institutional acceptance of the taxable municipal market will be the structure of the issues. Unlike the corporate market, which has basically been a market of single-term issues, the serial issue has been a common feature of the tax-exempt municipal market. Taxable municipals with multiple maturities may tend to reduce the market's liquidity due to the relatively small size of each maturity class. This will be of particular importance to investors who have minimum outstanding requirements of $100 million or more, which is a common restriction for pension fund managers. Problems may be avoided by selling the serial portion in the medium-term note market and the term portion in the corporate market. The relatively small size of each staggered maturity in the medium-term market would accommodate the issuer, while a purchaser (such as a bank) would be able to effectively "match fund" its liabilities. However, the term portion of the issue would still need to be large enough to ensure the traditional corporate purchaser of adequate liquidity.

A final concern for the traditional corporate buyer lies in credit analysis and name recognition. Investment firms that regularly purchase tax-exempt municipal bonds have personnel capable of analyzing the creditworthiness of these issuers. However, pension funds and many investment firms do not have the staff needed to properly analyze and value a municipal issue. Therefore, these buyers may need a period of education before they feel comfortable purchasing taxable municipals as an alternative to corporate bonds.

One factor that should help the demand for taxable municipals is that in many states, the interest income will remain exempt from state and local income taxes. This should benefit issuers in states with high tax rates, such as California and New York.

Conclusion

In summary, as a result of the 1986 tax law, both investors and issuers must become familiar with a new market. Corporate bond buyers must become familiar with the structure and credit quality of traditional municipal bonds, while the state and local government issuers must adopt some of the characteristics found in the corporate bond market in order to compete for funds. Additional issuance in the years following the passage of the 1986 tax law will provide the depth necessary to facilitate the growth of an active secondary market for taxable municipal bonds, which may foster a wider acceptance of this new financing vehicle.

DATA SOURCES

HAWKINS, DELAFIELD AND WOOD. "Analysis of Provisions of the Tax Reform Act of 1986 Affecting Tax-Exempt Obligations." New York: September 30, 1986.

MERRILL LYNCH PUBLIC FINANCE GROUP. "The 1986 Tax Bill Emerges from Conference." September 1986.

ORRICK, HERRINGTON, SUTCLIFFE. "Municipal Finance Report." San Francisco: August 29, 1986.

SQUIRE, SANDERS AND DEMPSEY. "Report on the Joint Committee Summary Dated August 16, 1986 of the Conference Agreement Affecting Tax-Exempt Obligations." New York: August 26, 1986.

APPENDIX B

Taxable Municipal Revenue Bonds Involving a GIC*

This appendix discusses municipal revenue bonds involving guaranteed investment contracts (GICs) between the issuer and an insurance company or financial institution in which bond proceeds usually are invested for a period of up to 10 years. The purpose of the issue is to provide arbitrage profits to the issuer which can be used for various public purposes. The issuer usually does not pledge any security for the bonds and does not incur any liability in the transaction. In the event that loans are made under a bond program for housing, agriculture, or other purposes, each loan generally is required to be secured with a letter of credit or by specified levels of collateral. The bonds are typically rated AAA, based on the claims-paying ability of the insurance company with whom the GIC has been placed. Also, it should be noted that each bond issue is individually secured and the credit quality varies from issue to issue.

HOW DOES THE GUARANTEED INVESTMENT CONTRACT WORK?

A GIC is a contract between an issuer and an insurance company under which the insurance company receives the bond proceeds in exchange for a fixed rate of return. The insurance company reinvests the bond proceeds at a higher yield than the rate of interest on the bonds, which finances the issuance costs and provides an arbitrage profit for the issuer. The GIC is generally structured so as not to be drawn on for the life of the issue. There are generally surrender fees that must be paid to the insurance company if the GIC is broken, which may act as a disincentive to provide loans under the various programs.

HOW SHOULD A GIC BE ANALYZED?

Since the repayment of principal and interest is secured by the GIC, one must assess the strength of the insurance company providing the

---

* Written with William E. Oliver.

GIC. How highly leveraged is the insurance company? How diversified is its risk spread through its various lines of insurance? If the bond proceeds are invested in high-risk securities, does this impair its ability to repay bondholders? Is the obligation of the insurance company under the GIC subordinate to its other debt, or does it rank on a parity with any other outstanding insurance claims? Where does the bondholder stand in the event the insurance company is placed into conservatorship by insurance regulators? Does the public entity issuing the debt retain any contingent liability for the bonds under those circumstances?

WHAT OTHER FACTORS SHOULD BE CONSIDERED?

If the issuer has the ability to make loans under the provisions of the bond issue, what is the security for the bonds to replace the GIC? If there is a requirement that the loans be secured by a letter of credit (LOC), what are the criteria for approving the LOC? Does the rating of a commercial rating company on the bank LOC have to be at the same level as that for the GIC? What other provisions have been made for credit substitution? If they are collateral requirements, do they provide the same level of protection as the original GIC?

CONCLUSION

Although these bonds are issued by public entities, the security on the bonds is derived solely from the ability of the insurance company/financial institution to meet its obligation under the terms of the GIC. Therefore, it is important to analyze the financial strength of the insurance company/financial institution, including its present leveraging ratios and its loan portfolio or insurance portfolio diversification. If loans are to be made with bond proceeds, what are the surrender fees required to be paid to the provider of the GIC and how will they be paid? Additionally, what type of credit support or collateral will be provided on loans that are made? Finally, what is the obligation on the part of the insurance company to repay the debt, and how would the bondholder fare in the case of a failure on the part of the company issuing the GIC?

APPENDIX C
Guidelines for Analyzing Certificates of Participation*

Certificates of participation (COPs) are a form of debt analogous to a lease-rental obligation, customarily used to finance the acquisition of buildings and/or equipment for a governmental entity. Although certificate financing was first used primarily in California in an attempt to circumvent the Proposition 13 restrictions, it is now being used fairly widely by other state and local governments across the country. Its increasing popularity is due to the fact that it does not require voter approval and that it is "off-balance-sheet" debt, which is not subject to statutory debt limitations. This appendix will examine the structure and legal provisions common to most COPs and will point out some of the factors analysts and investors should consider before investing in COPs.

It should be noted that COPs may be issued as either taxable or tax-exempt securities.

SECURITY

To the investor, a certificate of participation represents a proportionate interest in annual lease payments made by the lessee to the trustee during the term of the lease agreement. The certificates are secured only by these lease payments. The obligation of the lessee to make these payments constitutes neither a general obligation nor a moral obligation of the issuer. When a state acts as lessee, its obligation to make lease payments generally is subject to annual legislative appropriation, while payments by a local issuer acting as a lessee are likewise subject to annual budgetary appropriation.

In the event of nonappropriation of funds, the lease terminates and the lessee is under no obligation to make any further payments. It should also be noted that an event of nonappropriation does not generally constitute an event of default and that none of the common remedies are available to investors under this scenario.

---

* Written with Christopher Mauro and William E. Oliver.

236

SELECTIVE FACTORS TO CONSIDER

Below we describe the factors to consider in evaluating COPs.

Essential Nature of the Project

Investors should remember that COPs are subject to the risk of nonappropriation. It is important to determine whether the project has or will have a genuinely useful public purpose, such as a jail or city hall, or is for a nonessential governmental use, such as a convention center. The possibility of increasing political pressure under a worst-case scenario is an important consideration. One should question the willingness of a state legislature or city government to appropriate funds for lease payments on a nonessential facility that has become a "white elephant" during periods of budgetary stress.

Useful Life of the Assets

COPs also carry a risk of technological obsolescence. Many COPs are issued to finance the acquisition of telecommunication or other high-tech equipment. A city or state which sells long-term COPs to finance equipment that could become obsolete within five years could be exposing itself to the political pressures that may arise when paying for a white elephant. If the equipment must be replaced, it is unlikely that any legislative body would appropriate funds twice for the same project. As with any lease-rental financing, the lease term should match, in a reasonably accurate manner, the useful life of the project being financed.

Ability to Relet the Project

If the lease agreement is terminated, the trustee takes possession of the assets and attempts to relet or sell these assets. In many cases the trustee may be unable to do this because the project is too specific in nature to its original purpose or may be prohibited from doing so by the indenture. For example, a state office building may have several alternate uses if vacated, while a prison may not.

Beneficial Security Provisions

While most COPs are similarly structured, certain provisions can add strength to an issue's credit quality. Some of the questions to be asked are: Is there prohibition against substitution of assets in the event of nonappropriation? (Under some agreements, the lessee is prohibited from allocating funds to acquire any functionally similar assets for 30 to 60 days following termination of the lease.) Is there a grace period following the lease payment date which would allow the lessee to make its overdue payment and avoid termination of the lease agreement? Has interest been capitalized beyond the estimated date of completion for project construction? Has a debt service reserve fund been established? Is the lessee required to maintain an adequate level of casualty insurance or self-insurance on the assets? Such insurance should equal the principal amount of the outstanding certificates or the replacement cost of the assets, whichever is greater.

Call Features

In most cases, COPs are subject to extraordinary redemption at par on any lease payment date. Generally, an extraordinary call may result from any of the following events: the receipt of the net proceeds of an insurance claim or condemnation award, prepayment by the lessee, or termination of the lease agreement.

History of Timely Appropriation

A credit consideration in any COP issue is the lessee's demonstrated willingness to make the necessary appropriations to meet debt service. Investors can take some comfort in the COP structure if the issuer has a track record of meeting all lease-rental obligations and any other payments involving "off-balance-sheet debt" in a timely manner.

Credit Quality of the Underlying Issuer

After examining the structure and security of the COP, it is important for the investor to analyze the credit quality of the lessee to determine the ultimate ability and willingness of this issuer to meet its lease payments. Using traditional indicators of credit quality, the investor must be cognizant of the underlying economic, financial, and political trends specific to the issuer and how these trends could affect the issuer's ability to meet its COP obligations in the future. It is useful to determine the percentage of operating expenditures that will be used to pay debt service on all outstanding certificates and general obligation bonds. The stronger the economy and budgetary operations of the issuer, the stronger should be the credit quality of the COP.

APPENDIX D
Eliminating the Deductibility of State and Local Taxes: Important Credit Issues to Be Considered by Bondholders

In this appendix, we identify the potential credit problems and elements of uncertainty arising for certain municipal bonds if the deductibility of state and local individual incomes as well as property taxes on federal tax returns were ever to be repealed. Such a proposal was put forth by the U.S. Treasury Department in 1984, adopted by President Reagan in his tax change proposal to Congress in 1985, and has been under consideration by Congress.

Essentially, eliminating deductibility would reverse a tradition long embedded in intergovernmental relations whereby the federal government helps finance state and local governments through the use of tax credits. By allowing for the deductibility of state and local income and property taxes paid by individuals from their federal taxable incomes, the federal government has made it easier for the development and stabilizing of local taxing structures for thousands of general obligation bond issuers across the country. The political flexibility of state and local governments to raise general tax revenues during recessionary periods with temporary income, sales, and property tax increases has always been viewed by investors as a strong credit feature of general obligation bond security. While it is far from certain that President Reagan's deductibility proposal will be enacted into law during his term of office, the proposal does enjoy substantial political support and, if enacted at some point in the future would pose new vulnerabilities for the credit quality of certain municipal bonds. This appendix identifies some of the more important investor concerns that this potential change presents.

WHAT IS THE TAX CHANGE PROPOSAL?

Under current U.S. tax law, individuals can deduct the following state and local taxes from their taxable incomes.

- State and local real property taxes.
- State and local income taxes.

239

- State and local personal property taxes.[1]
- State and local general sales taxes.

In effect, the elimination of deductibility would for the first time treat most income and property taxes paid by individuals to state and local governments (i.e., those not incurred in business-related activity) as taxable income for federal tax purposes.

POTENTIAL CREDIT IMPACTS

From the standpoint of credit quality, there are several major types of municipal bonds that could be negatively affected if these deductibilities are eliminated. Of course, it should be noted that comprehensive federal legislation that eliminated deductibility could also diminish tax preferences and restrict the issuance of new municipal bonds. This could even impact the scarcity value of outstanding bonds, increase demand, and act to lessen the yields of municipal bonds. The potential credit factors which is our focus follow.

State General Obligation Bonds

Over the years, most states have become increasingly dependent on individual income taxes as major revenue sources. The elimination of deductibility would create political pressure on states not to rely on general taxes. However, the ability of states to raise general taxes is the basis of their "full faith and credit" pledge and for the high degree of bondholder confidence in their bonds. Clearly, eliminating deductibility could weaken the credit quality of all state general obligation bonds. It could limit the options for those few states that have no income taxes at all, and could adversely affect states with existing individual income tax rates by restricting their ability either to increase or maintain them.

Table D–1 shows the percentage of general revenues by state from individual income taxes. The data are from the most recent years available.

In general, income tax revenues flow into the general funds of the respective states and are used to pay general obligation debt service. Consequently, the dependency on income tax revenues for general obligation bond security is even greater than shown in Table D–1. If state individual income taxes were to be significantly reduced, it

---

[1] In some states, payments for registration and licensing of an automobile are wholly or partially deductible as a personal property tax.

TABLE D-1 State Individual Income Tax Revenues

State	1982 Individual Income Taxes as a Percent of Total General Revenue*	1982 Individual Income Taxes ($000)	1984 Individual Income		
			Rate	Range	Percent
New York	30.3%	$8,034,066	2.0	—	14.0%
Massachusetts	29.5	2,324,052		5.375	
Oregon	28.8	968,264	4.2	—	10.7
Delaware	26.8	288,069	1.4	—	13.5
Wisconsin	26.7	1,680,372	3.4	—	10.0
Minnesota	25.4	1,549,121	1.6	—	16.0
Virginia	25.0	1,446,187	2.0	—	5.75
Maryland	24.2	1,354,613	2.0	—	5.0
North Carolina	23.7	1,449,370	3.0	—	7.0
Georgia	22.0	1,182,783	1.0	—	6.0
Iowa	22.0	720,883	0.5	—	13.0
Idaho	21.8	220,073	2.0	—	7.5
California	21.6	7,467,709	1.0	—	11.0
South Carolina	19.2	641,838	2.0	—	7.0
Missouri	19.0	760,711	1.5	—	6.0
Kansas	18.9	459,822	2.0	—	9.0
Illinois	18.7	2,222,143		3.0	
Michigan	18.6	2,126,630		6.1	
Utah	17.8	331,145	2.75	—	7.75
Colorado	17.3	548,944	3.0	—	8.0
Arkansas	15.8	353,733	1.0	—	7.0
Hawaii	15.4	283,000	2.25	—	11.0
Maine	15.4	209,585	1.0	—	10.0
Pennsylvania	15.3	1,985,270		2.45	
Arizona	15.2	438,985	2.0	—	8.0
Vermont	15.2	112,520		†	
Oklahoma	15.1	641,428	0.5	—	6.0
Rhode Island	15.1	215,156		†	
Indiana	14.7	748,769		3.0	
Nebraska	14.5	226,560		‡	
Kentucky	14.1	600,823	2.0	—	6.0
New Jersey	14.1	1,305,567	2.0	—	3.5
Montana	13.2	143,804	2.0	—	11.0
West Virginia	12.4	305,964	2.1	—	13.0
Ohio	12.2	1,243,618	0.95	—	9.5
Alabama	11.6	480,969	2.0	—	5.0
Mississippi	6.2	168,471	3.0	—	5.0
Louisiana	3.8	220,134	2.0	—	6.0
North Dakota	3.1	35,342	2.0	—	9.0
New Mexico	0.5	14,263	0.7	—	7.8

* General revenues include intergovernmental revenue, taxes, charges, and miscellaneous general revenue.

† 26% of U.S. rate.

‡ 20% of U.S. rate.

SOURCE: *State Government Finances in 1982,* U.S. Department of Commerce, Bureau of the Census, pp. 23–35; *The Book of the States 1984–1985,* Vol. 25, The Council of State Governments, pp. 334–35.

would be reasonable to expect, for at least some issuers, a sizable reduction in general fund revenues and resulting budgetary problems as well. It should be noted that during the last recession several states, though well managed, temporarily had to increase income taxes in order to address budgetary shortfalls caused by the economy. These states included Pennsylvania, Minnesota, Wisconsin, Ohio, Michigan, and Illinois, among others. Losing deductibility may provide a significant constraint on their abilities to do so in the future, which, of course, would be of concern to bondholders.

Lastly, it should be noted that most proposals would totally eliminate deductions of all state and local tax revenues, whether they are individual income, general sales, or property taxes. Therefore, a state with income taxes may not be able to increase sales taxes to compensate for the loss of the income tax deductibility. Or a state, like Washington, that does not have an individual income tax, but does rely heavily on a sales tax, would be restrained from adopting an income tax in the future.

School District and Other Local General Obligation Bonds

Many cities and counties, and most school districts rely entirely on property taxes as the general local taxing source. Table D–2 shows local general obligation bond issuers across the country who have come to market over the past 18 months. As can be seen, property taxes represent a major portion of their respective locally raised general fund revenues. Property taxes in general funds are typically used to finance operating budget expenditures such as salaries as well as to pay the general obligation bondholders.

While not all general obligation issuers have the same high degree of dependency on property taxes as those in Table D–2, most school districts and smaller issuers do. Additionally, while large general obligation issuers such as cities have less dependency on property taxes, they usually have other general tax revenues, such as individual income and sales taxes, which combined with property taxes are significant. An example would be New York City, where approximately 23 percent of the general fund revenues in fiscal 1984 came from property taxes, 17 percent from income taxes, and 12 percent from sales taxes. All of these taxes would be affected by the elimination of deductibility.

Of course, most general obligation bonds on the local level are legally secured by the pledge of the issuer to raise property taxes to whatever rate necessary to pay bondholders. This is known as the "unlimited property tax" pledge, and was long considered the pillar

TABLE D-2 Recent School District and Other Local Government General Obligation Bond Issuers

Issuer	Property Taxes as Percent of General Fund	Property Taxes as Percent of Locally Raised General Taxes
Powell Hospital District, Wyoming	95%	100%
Lawrence Twp. Bd. of Ed., New Jersey	80	100
Salem, New Hampshire	76	100
Honolulu, Hawaii	76	96
Norwalk, Connecticut	76	100
Des Moines, Iowa	75	100
White Plains S/D, New York	74	88
Bayonne, New Jersey	69	100
Hawaii County, Hawaii	68	100
Twp. of Hamilton, New Jersey	67	100
Waterloo, Iowa	66	99
Meriden, Connecticut	64	100
Clarkstown C.S.D., New York	62	100
Miami, Florida	58	94
Charlotte, North Carolina	56	81
Ankeny, Iowa	55	100
Anson County, North Carolina	55	85
Raleigh, North Carolina	55	81
Albany, Oregon	54	100
Babylon, New York	54	99
Dallas Ind. S/D, Texas	54	89
Anchorage, Alaska	54	91
Manatee County, Florida	49	100
Eagan, Minnesota	49	100
Robeson County, North Carolina	48	76
Cochise County, Arizona	48	100
Milwaukee County, Wisconsin	43	100
Grand Forks Pub. S/D #1, North Dakota	25	100
Chandler U.S.D. #80, Arizona	24	100
Tamarac, Florida	23	100
Minneapolis, Minnesota	23	100

SOURCE: Annual Financial Reports and Official Statements of the respective general obligation bonds for 1983–84.

of security for bondholders. However, New York City's billion-dollar financial crisis in 1975 provided a new concern for holders of such unlimited property tax general obligation bonds. The crisis showed that regardless of supposedly ironclad legal protections for bond- and noteholders, when issuers have severe budget-balancing difficulties, the political stakes and financial interests of public employee unions, vendors, and community groups may be dominant forces in the decision-making process.

This reality was further reinforced by the federal bankruptcy law which took effect on October 1, 1979, and which makes it easier for municipal bond issuers to seek protection from bondholders by filing for bankruptcy.

Given the high degree of dependency on property taxes by local general obligation bond issuers, the elimination of deductibility could weaken the credit quality of such bonds. Middle-class communities with a high proportion of taxpayers who itemize deductions could be the most vulnerable. Ironically, because of the high wealth indexes of such issuers, they have been viewed historically as being of stronger credit quality.

It should also be noted that many local governments, and particularly school districts, receive substantial annual aid appropriations from their state governments. If the deductibility of state individual income taxes were ever to be repealed by Congress, state aid payments may be reduced at the same time the school districts are under local political pressure to reduce their property taxes.

Lease Rental, Certificate of Participation, and Hybrid Revenue Bonds

Lease rental and certificate of participation bonds issued by states, counties, cities, and school districts would have the same vulnerabilities as the general obligation bonds of these issuers. Bondholders usually are paid from annual appropriations from the issuers' general funds. With no unlimited property tax pledges involved, such bonds are entirely dependent on the annual budgetary soundness of the issuers. Tax revolts and dramatic general fund revenue shortfalls triggered by the elimination of deductibility could severely affect the credit quality of such bonds. Hybrid revenue bonds that are dependent on general tax revenues in the form of per capita state aid payments and grants are also vulnerable for the same reason.

THE NEED FOR CONTINUING BUDGET ANALYSIS

For states, counties, cities, and school districts, totally eliminating deductibility could initially result in pressure for compensating cuts in local general taxes. School budgets, many of which are subject to annual direct votes, would appear to be the most vulnerable. This could be particularly the case if property taxes cannot be deducted from taxable incomes. Conversely, if property taxes were excluded from being eliminated, one would expect those issuers that have more diversified general taxing sources, such as income taxes, to be under the most pressure. Of course, local political attitudes and traditions toward taxes and the provision of services could determine the intensity of pressure for specific tax reductions. In any event, if taxpayers were ever not to be allowed to deduct state and local taxes from their federal taxable incomes, there will be a great deal of uncertainty for bondholders as issuers adjust to it.

Some of these potential problems could be eased if the U.S. economy undergoes strong growth. Such growth could increase tax revenues for states and local governments. Of course, if this does not occur we would expect a period of uncertainty for many credits.

APPENDIX E
The Commercial Rating Companies and Their Differences

In this appendix the ratings of and differences between the two major commercial rating companies, Moody's and Standard & Poor's, are explained. A third and smaller rating company, Fitch, is not included. The major rating companies are part of large, growth-oriented conglomerates and typically charge fees to issuers, bond insurers, and underwriters for their ratings. Moody's is an operating unit of Dun & Bradstreet Companies, and Standard & Poor's is part of McGraw-Hill Inc. As of 1986 Moody's charged fees as high as $55,000 per bond sale and Standard & Poor's generally charged up to $25,000.

MOODY'S

The municipal bond rating system used by Moody's grades the investment quality of municipal bonds in a nine-symbol system that ranges from the highest investment quality, which is Aaa, to the lowest credit rating, which is C. The respective nine alphabetical ratings and their definitions are the following:

Moody's Municipal Bond Ratings

Rating	Definition
Aaa	Best quality; carry the smallest degree of investment risk.
Aa	High quality; margins of protection not quite as large as the Aaa bonds.
A	Upper medium grade; security adequate but could be susceptible to impairment.
Baa	Medium grade; neither highly protected nor poorly secured—lack outstanding investment characteristics and sensitive to changes in economic circumstances.
Ba	Speculative; protection is very moderate.
B	Not desirable investment; sensitive to day-to-day economic circumstances.
Caa	Poor standing; may be in default but with a workout plan.
Ca	Highly speculative; may be in default with nominal workout plan.
C	Hopelessly in default.

Municipal bonds in the top four categories (Aaa, Aa, and A, and Baa) are considered to be of investment-grade quality. Additionally, bonds in the Aa through B categories that Moody's concludes have the strongest investment features within the respective categories are designated by the symbols Aa1, A1, Baa1, Ba1, and B1, respectively. Moody's also may use the prefix *Con.* before a credit rating to indicate that the bond security is dependent on (1) the completion of a construction project, (2) earnings of a project with little operating experience, (3) rentals being paid once the facility is constructed, or (4) some other limiting condition. It should also be noted that, as of 1986, Moody's applies numerical modifiers 1, 2, and 3 in each generic rating classification from Aa through B to municipal bonds that are issued for industrial development and pollution control. The modifier 1 indicates that the security ranks in the higher end of its generic rating category; the modifier 2 indicates a midrange ranking, and the modifier 3 indicates that the bond ranks in the lower end of its generic rating category.

The municipal note rating system used by Moody's is designated by four investment-grade categories of Moody's Investment Grade (MIG):

Moody's Municipal Note Ratings

Rating	Definition
MIG 1	Best quality
MIG 2	High quality
MIG 3	Favorable quality
MIG 4	Adequate quality

A short-term issue having a "demand" feature (i.e., payment relying on external liquidity and usually payable upon demand rather than fixed maturity dates) is differentiated by Moody's with the use of the symbols VMIG1 through VMIG4.

Moody's also provides credit ratings for tax-exempt commercial paper. These are promissory obligations (1) not having an original maturity in excess of nine months and (2) backed by commercial banks. Moody's uses three designations, all considered to be of investment grade, for indicating the relative repayment capacity of the rated issues:

Moody's Tax-Exempt Commercial Paper Ratings

Rating	Definition
Prime 1 (P–1)	Superior capacity for repayment
Prime 2 (P–2)	Strong capacity for repayment
Prime 3 (P–3)	Acceptable capacity for repayment

STANDARD & POOR'S

The municipal bond rating system used by Standard & Poor's grades the investment quality of municipal bonds in a 10-symbol system that ranges from the highest investment quality, which is AAA, to the lowest credit rating, which is D. Bonds within the top four categories (AAA, AA, A, and BBB) are considered by Standard & Poor's to be of investment-grade quality. The respective 10 alphabetical ratings and definitions are the following:

Standard & Poor's Municipal Bond Ratings

Rating	Definition
AAA	Highest rating; extremely strong security.
AA	Very strong security; differs from AAA in only a small degree.
A	Strong capacity but more susceptible to adverse economic effects than two above categories.
BBB	Adequate capacity but adverse economic conditions more likely to weaken capacity.
BB	Lowest degree of speculation; risk exposure.
B	Speculative; risk exposure.
CCC	Speculative; major risk exposure.
CC	Highest degree of speculation; major risk exposure.
C	No interest is being paid.
D	Bonds in default with interest and/or repayment of principal in arrears.

Standard & Poor's also uses a plus (+) or minus (−) sign to show relative standing within the rating categories ranging from AA to BB. Additionally, Standard & Poor's uses the letter p to indicate a provisional rating that is intended to be removed upon the successful and timely completion of the construction project. A double dagger (‡) on a mortgage-backed revenue bond rating indicates that the rating is contingent upon receipt by Standard & Poor's of closing documentation confirming investments and cash flows. An asterisk (*) following a credit rating indicates that the continuation of the rating is contingent upon receipt of an executed copy of the escrow agreement.

The municipal note-rating system used by Standard & Poor's grades the investment quality of municipal notes in a four-symbol system that ranges from highest investment quality, SP–1+, to the lowest credit rating, SP–3. Notes within the top-three categories (i.e., SP–1+, SP–1, and SP–2) are considered by Standard & Poor's as being of investment-grade quality. The respective ratings and summarized definitions are:

Standard & Poor's Municipal Note Ratings

Rating	Definition
SP–1	Very strong or strong capacity to pay principal and interest. Those issues determined to possess overwhelming safety characteristics will be given a plus (+) designation.
SP–2	Satisfactory capacity to pay principal and interest.
SP–3	Speculative capacity to pay principal and interest.

Standard & Poor's also rates tax-exempt commercial paper in the same four categories as taxable commercial paper. The four tax-exempt commercial paper rating categories are:

Standard & Poor's Tax-Exempt Commercial Paper Ratings

Rating	Definition
A–1+	Highest degree of safety.
A–1	Very strong degree of safety.
A–2	Strong degree of safety.
A–3	Satisfactory degree of safety.

HOW THE RATING COMPANIES DIFFER

Although there are many similarities in how Moody's and Standard & Poor's approach credit ratings, there are certain differences in their respective approaches as well. As examples we shall present below some of the differences in approach between Moody's and Standard & Poor's when they assign credit ratings to general obligation bonds.

The credit analysis of general obligation bonds issued by states, counties, school districts, and municipalities initially requires the collection and assessment of information in four basic categories. The first category includes obtaining information on the issuer's debt structure so that the overall debt burden can be determined. The debt burden usually is composed of (1) the respective direct and overlapping debts per capita as well as (2) the respective direct and overlapping debts as percentages of real estate valuations and personal incomes. The second category of needed information relates to the issuer's ability and political discipline for maintaining sound budgetary operations. The focus of attention here is usually on the issuer's general operating funds and whether or not it has maintained at least balanced budgets over the previous three to five years. The third category involves determining the specific local taxes and intergovernmental revenues available to the issuer, as well as obtaining historical information on both tax-collection rates, which are important when looking at property tax levies, and on the dependency of local budgets on specific revenue sources, which is important when looking at the impact of federal revenue sharing monies. The fourth and last general category of information necessary to the credit analysis is an assessment of the issuer's overall socioeconomic environment. Questions that have to be answered here include determining the local employment distribution and composition, population growth, and real estate property valuation and personal income trends, among other economic indexes.

Although Moody's and Standard & Poor's rely on these same four informational categories in arriving at their respective credit ratings of general obligation bonds, what they emphasize among the categories can result at times in dramatically different credit ratings for the same issuer's bonds.

There are major differences between Moody's and Standard & Poor's in their respective approaches toward these four categories, and there are other differences in conceptual factors the two rating companies bring to bear before assigning their respective general obligation credit ratings. There are very important differences between the rating companies, and although while there are some zigs and zags in their respective rating policies, there are also clear patterns of analysis that exist and that have resulted in split credit ratings for a given issuer. The objective here is to outline what these differences between Moody's and Standard & Poor's actually are. Furthermore, although the rating companies have stated in their publications what criteria guide their respective credit-rating approaches, the conclusions here about how they go about rating general obligation bonds are not only derived from these sources, but also from reviewing their credit reports and rating decisions on individual bond issues.

How do Moody's and Standard & Poor's differ in evaluating the four basic informational categories? Simply stated, Moody's tends to focus on the debt burden and budgetary operations of the issuer, and Standard & Poor's considers the issuer's economic environment as the most important element in its analysis. Although in most instances these differences of emphasis do not result in dramatically split credit ratings for a given issuer, there are at least two recent instances in which major differences in ratings on general obligation bonds have occurred.

The general obligation bonds of the Chicago School Finance Authority are rated only Baa1 by Moody's, but Standard & Poor's rates the same bonds AA—. In assigning the credit rating of Baa1, Moody's bases its rating on the following debt- and budget-related factors: (1) The deficit funding bonds are to be retired over a 30-year period, an unusually long time for such an obligation; (2) the overall debt burden is high; and (3) the school board faces long-term difficulties in balancing its operating budget because of reduced operating taxes, desegregation program requirements, and uncertain public employee union relations.

Standard & Poor's credit rating of AA— appears to be based primarily upon the following two factors: (1) Although Chicago's economy has been sluggish, it is still well diversified and fundamentally sound; and (2) the unique security provisions for the bonds in the opinion of the bond counsel insulate the pledged property taxes from the school board's creditors in the event of a school-system bankruptcy.

Another general obligation bond wherein split ratings have occurred is the bond issue of Allegheny County, Pennsylvania. Moody's rates the bonds A, whereas the Standard & Poor's rating is AA.

Moody's A credit rating is based primarily upon four budget-related factors: (1) above-average debt load with more bonds expected to be issued for transportation related projects and for the building of a new hospital, (2) continued unfunded pension liabilities, (3) past unorthodox budgetary practices of shifting tax revenues from the county tax levy to the county institution district levy, and (4) an archaic real estate property assessment system, which is in the process of being corrected.

Standard & Poor's higher credit rating of AA also appears to be based upon four factors: (1) an affluent, diverse, and stable economy with wealth variables above the national medians, (2) a good industrial mix with decreasing dependence on steel production, (3) improved budget operations having accounting procedures developed to conform to generally accepted accounting principles, and (4) a rapid debt retirement schedule that essentially matches anticipated future bond sales.

Are state general obligation bonds fundamentally different from local government general obligation bonds? There is also another difference between the commercial rating companies in how they apply their analytical tools to the rating of state general obligation bonds and local government general obligation bonds. Moody's basically believes that the state and local bonds are not fundamentally different. Moody's applies the same debt and budget-related concerns to state general obligation bonds as they do to general obligation bonds issued by counties, school districts, towns, and cities. Moody's has even assigned ratings below A to state general obligation bonds. When the state of Delaware was having serious budgetary problems in the period beginning in 1975 and extending through 1978, Moody's gradually downgraded its general obligation bonds from Aa to Baa1. It should be noted that when Moody's downgraded Delaware general obligation bonds to Baa1 and highlighted its budgetary problems, the state government promptly began to address its budgetary problems. By 1986 the bond rating was up to Aa. In May of 1982 Moody's downgraded the state of Michigan's general obligation bonds from A to Baa1 on the basis of weak local economy and the state's budgetary problems. By 1986 the rating was back up to A–1. Another example of Moody's maintaining a state credit rating below A was in Alaska, where until 1974 the state general obligation bonds were rated Baa1. Here, Moody's cited the heavy debt load as a major reason for the rating.

Unlike Moody's, Standard & Poor's seems to make a distinction between state and local government general obligation bonds. Because states have broader legal powers in the areas of taxation and policy making that do not require home-rule approvals, broader revenue bases, and more diversified economies, Standard & Poor's seems to view state general obligation bonds as being significantly stronger than those of their respective underlying jurisdictions. Standard & Poor's has never given ratings below A to a state. Additionally, of the 38 state general obligation bonds that both Moody's and Standard & Poor's rated in mid-1986, the latter agency had given ratings of AA or better to 34 states and ratings of A to only four states. On the other hand, Moody's had given ratings of Aa or better to only 30 states, and ratings in the A range to eight states. On the whole for reasons just outlined, it seems that Standard & Poor's tends to have a higher credit assessment of state general obligation bonds than does Moody's. Furthermore, it should be noted that Moody's views these broader revenue resources as making states more vulnerable in difficult economic times to demands by local governments for increased financial aid.

How do the commercial rating companies differ in assessing the moral obligation bonds? In more than 20 states, state agencies have issued housing revenue bonds that carry a potential state liability for making up deficiencies in their one-year debt service reserve funds (backup funds), should any occur. In most cases if a drawdown of the debt reserve occurs, the state agency must report the amount used to its governor and the state budget director. The state legislature, in turn, may appropriate the requested amount, though there is no legally enforceable obligation to do so. Bonds with this makeup provision are the so-called moral obligation bonds.

Below is an example of the legal language in the bond indenture that explains this procedure.

> In order to further assure the maintenance of each such debt service reserve fund, there shall be annually apportioned and paid to the agency for deposit in each debt service reserve fund such sum, if any, as shall be certified by the chairman of the agency to the governor and director of the budget as necessary to restore such fund to an amount equal to the fund requirement. The chairman of the agency shall annually, on or before December first, make and deliver to the governor and director of the budget his certificate stating the sum or sums, if any, required to restore each such debt service reserve fund to the amount aforesaid, and the sum so certified, if any, shall be apportioned and paid to the agency during the then current state fiscal year.

Moody's views the moral obligation feature as being more literary than legal when applied to legislatively permissive debt service reserve makeup provisions. Therefore, it does not consider this procedure a credit strength. Standard & Poor's, to the contrary, does. It views moral obligation bonds as being no lower than one rating category below a state's own general obligation bonds. Its rationale is based upon the implied state support for the bonds and the market implications for that state's own general obligation bonds should it ever fail to honor its moral obligation.

As for the result of these two different opinions of the moral obligation, there are several municipal bonds that have split ratings. As examples, in mid-1986 the Nonprofit Housing Project Bonds of the New York State Housing Finance Agency, the General Purpose Bonds of the New York State Urban Development Corporation, and the Series A Bonds of the Battery Park City Authority have the Moody's credit rating of Ba, which is a speculative investment category. Standard & Poor's, because of the moral obligation pledge of the state of New York, gives the same bonds a credit rating of BBB+, which is an investment-grade category.

How do the commercial rating companies differ in assessing the importance of withholding state aid to pay debt service? Still another difference between Moody's and Standard & Poor's involves their respective attitudes toward state-aid security-related mechanisms. Since 1974 it has been the policy of Standard & Poor's to view as a very positive credit feature the automatic withholding and use of state aid to pay defaulted debt service on local government general obligation bonds. Usually the mechanism requires the respective state treasurer to pay debt service directly to the bondholder from monies due the local issuer from the state. Seven states have enacted security mechanisms that in one way or another allow certain local government general obligation bondholders to be paid debt service from the state-aid appropriations, if necessary. In most instances the state-aid withholding provisions apply to general obligation bonds issued by school districts.[1]

Although Standard & Poor's does review the budgetary operations of the local government issuer to be sure there are no serious budgetary problems, the assigned rating reflects the general obligation credit rating of the state involved, the legal base of the withholding mechanism, the historical background and long-term state legislative support for the pledged state aid program, and the specified coverage of the state aid monies available to maximum debt-service requirements on the local general obligation bonds. Normally, Standard & Poor's applies a blanket rating to all local general obligation bonds covered by the specific state-aid withholding mechanism. The rating is one or two notches below the rating of that particular state's general obligation bonds. Whether the rating is either one notch below or two notches below depends on the coverage figures, the legal security, and the legislative history and political durability of the pledged state-aid monies involved. It should also be noted that, although Standard & Poor's stated policy is to give blanket ratings, a specified rating is only granted when an issuer or bondholder applies for it.

Although Moody's recognizes the state-aid withholding mechanisms in its credit reviews, it believes that its assigned rating must in the first instance reflect the underlying ability of the issuer to make timely debt-service payments. Standard & Poor's, to the contrary, considers a state-aid withholding mechanism that provides for the

---

[1] The states involved are Indiana, Kentucky, New Jersey, New York, Pennsylvania, South Carolina, and West Virginia.

payment of debt service equally as important a credit factor as the underlying budget, economic, and debt-related characteristics of the bond issuer.

What is the difference in attitudes toward accounting records? Another area of difference between Moody's and Standard & Poor's concerns their respective attitudes toward the accounting records kept by general obligation bond issuers. In 1980 Standard & Poor's stated that if the bond issuer's financial reports are not prepared in accordance with generally accepted accounting principles (GAAP) it will consider this a "negative factor" in its rating process. Standard & Poor's has not indicated how negative a factor it is in terms of credit rating changes but has indicated that issuers will not be rated at all if either the financial report is not timely (i.e., available no later than six months after the fiscal year-end) or is substantially deficient in terms of reporting. Moody's policy here is quite different. Because Moody's reviews the historical performance of an issuer over a three- to five-year period, requiring GAAP reporting is not necessary from Moody's point of view, although the timeliness of financial reports is of importance.

Glossary

Accrued Interest. Coupon interest accumulated on a bond or note since the last interest payment or, for a new issue, from the dated date to the date of delivery.

Additional-Bonds Test. A legal requirement that additional bonds that will have a claim to revenues already pledged to outstanding revenue bonds can only be issued if certain financial or other requirements are met first.

Ad Valorem Tax. A state or local government tax based on the value of real property.

Advanced Refunded Bonds. Bonds for which monies have been already placed in escrow to be used for paying debt service.

Amortization of Debt. The annual reduction of debt through the use of serial bonds or term bonds with a sinking fund.

Arbitrage. The interest rate differential between the rate on a municipal bond and the yield on the investments made with the bond proceeds.

Assessed Valuation. The worth in dollars placed on real estate and/or other property for the purpose of taxation.

Authority or Agency. A state or local unit of government created to perform a single activity or a limited group of functions.

Authorizing Ordinance. A law that when enacted allows the unit of government to sell a specific bond issue or finance a specific project.

Average Life. The average length of time an issue of serial bonds and/or term bonds with mandatory sinking funds and/or estimated prepayments is expected to be outstanding.

Balloon Maturity. An inordinately large amount of bond principal maturing in any single year.

Basis Point. 0.01 percent.

Bearer Bond. A bond that is payable to the holder; such bond does not carry the owner's name.

Bid. An offer to buy.

Bond or Note. A security whereby an issuer agrees, by written contract, to pay a fixed principal sum on a specified date (maturity date) and at a specified rate of interest.

"Bond Buyer." A daily trade paper of general interest to participants in the municipal bond industry since 1891.

Bond Counsel. A lawyer who writes an opinion on the security, tax-exempt status and issuance authority of a bond or note.

Bond Fund (Tax-Exempt). A portfolio of municipal bonds that offers shares to investors either through (1) closed-end funds or unit trusts, which offer shares of a fixed portfolio of municipal bonds; or (2) open-end or

256

managed funds, which offer shares in a managed portfolio of municipal bonds whose size will vary as shares are purchased or redeemed.

Bond Insurance. Insurance purchased by an issuer for either an entire issue or specific maturities that is supposed to provide for payment of principal and/or interest by a private insurance company. This will provide a higher credit rating and thus a lower borrowing cost for the issuer.

Bond Premium. The amount at which a bond or note is bought or sold above its par value without including accrued interest.

Bonded Debt. That portion of an issuer's debt structure represented by outstanding bonds.

Book Entry. A system of security ownership in which the ownership is held as a computer entry on the records of a central company for its owner.

Callable Bond. A bond or note that is subject to redemption at the option of the issuer prior to its stated maturity.

Chinese Coverage. A rate covenant that specifies that rates charged are to provide cover only to the extent necessary to pay for debt-service operations and *required improvements* with excess monies being credited against the succeeding year's revenue requirements. The term *Chinese coverage* is also used to describe the liberal approach to the calculation of coverage for a second-lien revenue bond. This is usually done by subtracting the debt service on the first-lien bonds from the available revenues and then calculating the coverage figure. A more conservative approach is to combine the debt service of both liens and then derive the coverage figure.

Coupon. The detachable part of a bond that evidences interest due. Coupons are detached from the bonds and presented to the paying agent for payment on the interest due date.

Coupon Rate. The specified annual interest rate payable to the bond or noteholder.

Covenant. A legally binding commitment by the issuer of municipal bonds to the bondholder.

Coverage. This is the margin of safety for payment of debt service on a revenue bond that reflects the number of times the actual and/or estimated project earnings or income for a 12-month period of time exceed debt service that is payable.

Current Yield. The ratio of the coupon rate on a bond to the dollar purchase price; expressed as a percentage.

Dated Date. The date carried on the face of a bond or note from which interest normally begins to accrue.

Dealer. A corporation or partnership that buys and sells and maintains an ongoing position in bonds and/or notes.

Debt Limit. The maximum statutory or constitutional amount of debt that the general obligation bond issuer can either issue or have outstanding at any time.

Debt Ratio. The ratio of the issuer's general obligation debt to a measure of value, such as real property valuations and personal income.

Debt Service. Required payments for principal and interest.

Debt-Service Reserve Fund. An account established as a backup security for an issuer's bonds.

Default. Failure to pay in a timely manner principal and/or interest when due, or the occurrence of an event as stipulated in the Indenture of Trust resulting in an abrogation of that agreement.

Defeased Bonds. Bonds for which the payment of principal and interest has been assured through the structuring of a portfolio of government securities, the principal and interest on which will be sufficient to pay debt service on the refunded, outstanding bonds. When a bond issue is defeased, the claim on the revenues of the issuer is usually eliminated.

Delinquent Taxes. Property taxes that have been levied but remain unpaid on and after the due date.

Delivery. The time when payment is made to, and the executed bonds and notes are received from, the issuer. New-issue delivery takes place several weeks after the sale to allow the bonds and notes to be printed and signed.

Denomination. The face or par amount that the issuer promises to pay at a specific bond or note maturity.

Direct Debt. In general obligation bond analysis, the amount of debt that a particular local unit of government has incurred in its own name or assumed through annexation.

Discount. The amount in dollars by which market value is less than par value.

Discount Bonds. Bonds which sell at a dollar price below par in which case the yield would exceed the coupon rate.

Discount Note. Noninterest-bearing note sold at a discount and maturing at par.

Dollar Bond. Generally a term bond that is quoted and traded in dollars rather than in yield-to-maturity.

Double-Barreled Bond. A bond with two distinct pledged sources of revenue such as earmarked monies from a specific enterprise or aid payments as well as the general obligation taxing powers of the issuer.

Effective Interest Cost. The rate at which the debt service on the bonds would be discounted to provide a present value equal to the bid amount on the bonds.

Escrow Fund. A fund that contains monies that only can be used to pay debt service.

Ex-Legal. Bonds that are without an attached legal opinion.

Feasibility Study. A financial study provided by the issuer of a revenue bond that estimates service needs, construction schedules, future project revenues, and expenses.

Financial Adviser. Generally a bank or investment-banking company that will advise the issuer on all financial matters pertaining to a proposed issue and is not part of the underwriting syndicate.

Fiscal Agent. The bank, designated by the issuer, to pay interest and principal to the bondholder.

Fiscal Year. A 12-month time horizon by which state and local governments annually budget their respective revenues and expenditures.

Flow of Funds. The annual legal sequence by which enterprise revenues are paid out for operating and maintenance costs, debt service, sinking fund payments, and so on.

Full Faith and Credit. A phrase used primarily in conjunction with state general obligation bonds to convey the pledge of utilizing all taxing powers and resources, if necessary, to pay the bondholders.

Funded Debt. Total debt that is issued and outstanding. Does not include other debt such as short-term loans and notes.

General Obligation Bond. A bond secured by a pledge of the issuer's taxing powers (limited or unlimited). More commonly the general obligation bonds of local governments are paid from ad valorem property taxes and other general revenues.

General Property Tax. A tax levied on real estate and personal property.

Gross Debt. The sum total of a state or local government's debt obligations.

Gross Revenues. Generally, all annual receipts of a revenue bond issuer prior to the payment of all expenses.

Indenture of Trust. A legal document describing in specific detail the terms and conditions of a bond offering, the rights of the bondholder, and the obligations of the issuer to the bondholder; such document is alternatively referred to as a bond resolution.

Industrial Development Bonds. Bonds used to finance facilities for private enterprises, water and air pollution control, ports, airports, resource-recovery plants, and housing, among others.

Interim Borrowing. (1) Short-term loans to be repaid from general revenues or tax collections during the current fiscal year; (2) short-term loans in anticipation of bond issuance or grant receipts.

Intermediate Range. Bonds maturing in 5 to 15 years.

Investment Banker. A firm engaged in raising capital for an issuer. Participates as the middleman in purchasing securities from the issuer and in selling the same securities to investors.

Issuer. A state or local unit of government that borrows money through the sale of bonds and/or notes.

Joint and Several Obligation. A form of contract in which each of the signers is obligated for the full contract amount if other signers should default.

Lease-Rental Bond. Bonds whose principal and interest are payable exclusively from rental payments from a lessee. Rental payments are often derived from earnings of an enterprise that may be operated by the lessee or the lessor. Rental payments may also be derived from taxes levied by the lessee.

Legal Opinion. A written opinion from bond counsel that an issue of bonds was duly authorized and issued. The opinion usually includes the statement if interest received thereon is exempt from federal taxes and, in certain circumstances, from state and local taxes.

Letter of Credit. A form of supplemental or, in some cases, direct security for a municipal bond under which a commercial bank or private corporation guarantees payments on the bond issue under certain specified conditions.

Level Debt Service. Principal and interest payments that together represent equal annual payments over the life of a loan. Principal may be serial maturities or sinking fund installments.

Lien. A claim on revenues made for a specific issue of bonds.

Limited-Tax Bond. A bond secured by the pledge of a tax that is limited as to rate or amount.

Maximum Annual Debt Service. The maximum amount of principal and interest due by a revenue bond issuer on its outstanding bonds in any future fiscal year.

Merrill Lynch "500." A municipal bond index that represents yields on about 500 of the largest bond issues. It is published weekly in the *Wall Street Journal.*

Mortgage Bond. A bond backed by a lien on a specific property.

Municipal Bond. Bonds issued by any of the 50 states, the territories and their subdivisions, counties, cities, towns, villages, and school districts, agencies, such as authorities and special districts created by the states, and certain federally sponsored agencies such as local housing authorities. Historically, the interest paid on these bonds has been exempt from federal income taxes and is generally exempt from state and local taxes in the state of issuance.

Municipal Futures. A municipal index futures contract that has been traded at the Chicago Board of Trade since June 11, 1985. The index, known as the Bond Buyer Municipal Bond Index, is composed of 40 bonds.

Municipal Notes. Short-term municipal obligations, generally maturing in three years or less. The most common types are (1) bond anticipation notes, (2) revenue anticipation notes, (3) tax anticipation notes, (4) grant anticipation notes, (5) project notes, and (6) construction loan notes.

Negative Pledge Covenant. This term is usually used in conjunction with a hospital revenue bond in which the bondholders do not have a mortgage interest in the facility. Instead, the issuer covenants that the revenue-generating facilities will not otherwise be pledged or mortgaged.

Net Bonded Debt. Gross general obligation debt less self-supporting general obligation debt.

Net Interest Cost. Net Interest Cost (NIC) represents the average coupon rate weighted to reflect the time until repayment of principal and adjusted for the premium or discount.

Net Revenue Available for Debt Service. Usually, gross operating revenues of an enterprise less operating and maintenance expenses but exclusive of depreciation and bond principal and interest. Net revenue as thus defined is used to determine coverage on revenue bond issues.

Official Statement. A document (prospectus) circulated for an issuing body prior to a bond sale with salient facts regarding the proposed financing.

Original Issue Discount. A bond issued at an offering price substantially below par; the appreciation from the original price to par over the life of the bonds is treated as tax-exempt income.

Overlapping Debt. The proportionate share of the general obligation bonds of local governments located wholly or in part within the limits of the reporting unit of government that must be borne by property owners within the unit.

Par Value. The face value of a bond, usually $5,000 due the holder at maturity. It has no relation to the market value.

Parity Bonds. Revenue bonds that have an equal lien or claim on the revenues of the issuer.

Pay As You Go. A phrase that means that capital projects are being permanently financed from current operating revenues or taxes rather than by borrowing.

Paying Agent. Generally a bank that performs the function of paying interest for the issuing body.

Premium. The amount, if any, by which the price exceeds the principal amount (par value) of a bond.

Price to Call. The yield of a bond priced to the first call date rather than maturity.

Primary Market. The new issue market.

Principal. The face value of a bond, exclusive of interest.

Put Bond. A bond that can be redeemed on a date or dates prior to the stated maturity date by the bondholder. Also known as an *option tender* bond.

Qualified Legal Opinion. Conditional affirmation of the legal basis for the bond or note issue.

Rate Covenant. A legal commitment by a revenue bond issuer to maintain rates at levels to generate a specified debt-service coverage.

Ratings. Various alphabetical and numerical designations used by institutional investors, Wall Street underwriters, and commercial rating companies to give relative indications of bond and note credit worthiness.

Red Herring. A preliminary offering statement, subject to change upon completion of a sale of bonds.

Redemption. Process of retiring existing bonds prior to maturity from excess earnings or proceeds of refunding bonds.

Refunding Bond. The issuance of a new bond for the purpose of retiring an already outstanding bond issue.

Registered Bond. A nonnegotiable instrument in the name of the holder either registered as to principal or as to principal and interest.

Reinvestment Rate. Interest rate assumed to be earned on the reinvestment of the coupon payments.

Repo. A financial transaction in which one party "purchases" securities (primarily U.S. government bonds) for cash and simultaneously the other agrees to "buy" them back at some future time according to specified terms. Municipal bond and note issuers have used repos to manage cash on a short-term basis.

Revenue Bond. A municipal bond whose debt service is payable solely from the revenues derived from operating the facilities acquired or constructed with the proceeds of the bonds.

Secondary Market. The trading market for outstanding bonds and notes.

Security. The legally available revenues and assets from which are derived the monies to pay the bondholders.

Self-Supporting Bonds. Bonds payable from the earnings of a municipal utility enterprise.

Serial Bond. A bond of an issue that has maturities annually or semiannually over a period of years.

Several Obligation. A form of contract in which each signer is obligated only to the amount of his designated participation.

Short Term. Bonds or notes sold on an interim basis with tax-exempt securities for a period of from one to five years.

Sinking Fund. Money set aside on a periodic basis to retire term bonds at or prior to maturity.

Sinking Fund Schedule. A schedule of payments required under the original revenue bond resolution to be placed each year into a special fund, called the sinking fund, and to be used for retiring a specified portion of a term bond issue prior to maturity.

Special Assessment Bond. A bond secured by a compulsory levy made by a local unit of government on certain properties to defray the cost of local improvements and/or services.

Swap. The exchange of one bond for another. Generally, the act of selling a bond to establish an income tax loss and replacing the bond with a new item of comparable value.

Tax Base. The total resources of the community that is legally available for taxation.

Taxable Equivalent Yield. The yield an investor would have to obtain on a taxable corporate or U.S. government bond to match the same aftertax yield on a municipal bond.

Tax-Exempt Bond. Bonds exempt from federal income, state income, or state and local personal property taxes.

Technical Default Bond. Failure by the issuer to meet the requirements of a bond covenant.

Tender. The act of offering bonds to a sinking fund.

Term Bond. A bond of an issue that has a single maturity and is subject to a sinking fund.

Thin Market. A scarcity of secondary market supply or few bid or offer quotes for a particular security.

Tombstone. An advertisement placed for information purposes, after bonds or notes are sold, that describes certain details of the issue and lists the managing underwriters and the members of the underwriting syndicate.

Trading Position. The holding of bonds for purposes of buying or selling.

Trustee. A bank designated as the custodian of funds and official representative of bondholders and who is to see that the bond covenants are not neglected.

Underlying Debt. The general obligation bonds of smaller units of local government within a given issuer's jurisdiction.

Underwrite. An agreement to purchase an issuer's unsold securities at a set price, thereby guaranteeing the issuer proceeds and a fixed borrowing cost.

Variable-Rate Bond. A bond whose yield is not fixed but is adjusted periodically according to a prescribed formula.

Variable-Rate Demand Obligation (VRDO). A hybrid instrument that combines long-term and short-term financing techniques. Usually, while carrying a nominal maturity ranging from 1 to 40 years, the demand or "put" feature permits investors to request repayment of the principal amount, with accrued interest, within a predetermined notice period. Usually, a VRDO can be, at any time during the life of the obligation, converted to a fixed-rate, long-term security.

Yield Curve. Graph depicting the relationship between yields and current maturity for securities with identical default risk.

Yield-to-Call. Return available to call date taking into consideration the current value of the call premium, if any.

Yield-to-Maturity. Return available taking into account the interest rate, length of time to maturity, and price paid. It is assumed that the coupon reinvestment rate for the life of the bonds will be the same as the yield-to-maturity.

Zero-Coupon Bond. A municipal bond in which no current interest is paid, but instead at bond maturity the investor receives compounded interest at a specified rate.

INDEX

265